Half Title Page

Full Title Page

REDEMPTION✦PRESS

Printed in the United States of America

Published by Redemption Press, PO Box 427, Enumclaw, WA 98022

Unless otherwise noted, all Scripture references are taken from the New American Standard Bible, © 1960, 1963, 1968, 1971, 1972, 1973, 1975, 1977 by The Lockman Foundation. Used by permission.

Scripture references marked KJV are taken from the King James Version of the Bible.

ISBN 978-1-63232-262-3 - Print
ISBN 978-1-63232-263-0 - ePub
Library of Congress Catalog Card Number: 2003115320

Table of Contents

Acknowledgments

To God be the Glory!

About the Author

I have been a born-again Christian for more than thirty years. I am not affiliated with any organization, or denomination. I, like Paul in Philippians 3:7–8, "Counted all things lost in order that I may gain Christ." The church I attended for fifteen of those years was chosen for the man behind the pulpit and not the denomination in which the church belonged. I looked for a man who loved God with all his heart and had a love for the truth at any cost. The past thirty plus years were used to know God and *not* for the study of religion. I truly counted all things as rubbish to gain the knowledge of Christ. My passion was single in focus; I wanted to know Christ Jesus my Lord and Savior, and the God who sent Him. This has given me a love for all who love God and the truth, regardless of their affiliation. Therefore, I endeavor to minister to anyone who is willing to listen. My purpose with this book is to benefit people of all affiliations in the knowledge of God, and help every called-out-one safely into the Kingdom of God.

God's Call on My Life as a Watchman

A watchman is just a very ordinary man who is placed in an advantageous position where he has an unobstructed view to see an enemy or trouble coming from afar. A watchman's sole objective is to sound a warning whenever he sees trouble coming so everyone has ample opportunity to get prepared and thereby ultimately be saved. Spiritually speaking, I'm just a *very* ordinary man who God has supernaturally placed in a position to have eyes to see the enemy or trouble coming from afar, contemporaneous to our times. And then motivated by a supernatural love placed within my heart for God's Church, *I sound the warning.* Inasmuch as it was God who placed this love in my heart for His Church and then placed me in a position to see, I have nothing to boast in, nor am I better than anyone else. *To God be the glory!*

In order to fulfill my call as a watchman to God's Church, God has given me a heartfelt desire to see every *called-out-one* safely into God's heavenly kingdom. Therefore, when God allows me to see trouble, or our enemy (Satan) encroaching upon His Church, I *must* cry out a warning with everything that is within me. Knowing well, with tears, there will be some who will be offended, and some who will just completely ignore the warning. But I also know, with tears of joy that some will hear the warning, respond, and therefore be saved.

I have always known my calling would never make me popular with the masses, but I must tell you that I would *literally* not trade places with anyone for all the riches and/or the popularity this old world has to offer. How exceedingly rich and truly blessed I am to be called as a watchman to God's *precious* saints. To spy out and then expose the enemy and/or trouble coming from afar, in order to give God's saints *ample* time to take cover under God's wings by prayer; to avoid our enemy's *deceptive* snares; to avoid our enemy's *cunning* subversions. And finally, so we're not caught sleeping, but awake, fully equipped, and prepared to resist the evil one's onslaught in the might and power of God. Yes, I have the best job in the world! *To God be the glory!*

Preface

2 Corinthians 13:5: "Test yourselves to see if you are in the *faith*; examine yourselves! Or do you not recognize this about yourselves, that Jesus Christ is in you—unless indeed you fail the test?"

If there was ever a time in the entirety of mankind's history to take the above verse of Scripture seriously, it is today. In the above portion of Scripture, the Apostle Paul was *not* speaking to the unbeliever, but he was directly addressing his admonishment (warning) to those who identify themselves as Christians. This is very significant as Paul seemed to be *very* concerned about the *very* real possibility that everyone in Corinth who identified himself as a Christian may in fact *not* be a genuine born-again Christian at all.

So the Apostle Paul urged the Corinthian Christians to examine themselves to see if Jesus Christ was indeed dwelling within them, i.e., to see if they were actually born-again with His Spirit. And now if we were to combine the Apostle Paul's admonishment to the Corinthian Christians with his prophetic warning in

2 Thessalonians 2:3 of a last-days apostasy (falling away) from the *faith* within God's Church, the above verse about testing ourselves to see if we are in the *faith*, becomes a bone-chilling warning that *cannot* be ignored.

When I first became a Christian and started to study God's Word, there was one thing that profoundly stood out to me. *How could the Pharisees of that time* not *recognize Jesus as their Messiah?* After all, they knew the Holy Scriptures better than our most brilliant contemporary theologians; their words and even their behavior seemed to be in order. *Yet they did* not *recognize Jesus!* Jesus put it this way: They were religious (God-fearing) on the outside, but dead within. Their apparent spiritual blindness presents to us a profound problem as it exposes to us the real possibility of being spiritually blind ourselves; even though, as with the Pharisees, we have knowledge and appear clean on the outside.

Therefore, we must *be honest with ourselves in these last days that there is at least the possibility that we, too, could be spiritually blind.* Yet, if we are to examine ourselves to see if Jesus lives within us, we must also have the ability (the spiritual eyes) to recognize Him. Obviously, by looking at the Pharisees, we know that an overwhelming head knowledge of Scripture, the ability to quote it, and doing righteous works will not insure us the spiritual eyesight to allow us to recognize Jesus. So how can we attain this spiritual eyesight, which is so essential to our self-examination? How can we attain this spiritual eyesight to see if we recognize the Spirit of Jesus Christ within us?

As I pondered this dilemma, it became clear to me that the only way anyone could recognize Jesus was by the Spirit of Jesus; or you could also say, by the Spirit of God, inasmuch as the Father, the Son, and the Holy Spirit are one. I then began to ask the Holy

Spirit to reveal to me the Spirit behind God's Word, since Jesus was the Word made flesh (John 1:14). It became my heartfelt desire to use, or allow, God's Word to reveal His nature (Spirit) to me. No longer was I content to just memorize God's Word so I could recite it by rote, I wanted to be able to recognize His Word by the Spirit behind it.

Nevertheless, it remained an imperative to me to know His written Word as it was the only way I had to know God intimately, i.e., to know His very nature or spirit. So I proceeded to spend a lot of time reading and listening to God's Word; but then I went a step further, I also spent much time with God in prayer. No longer was I interested in a religious study of Scripture; I wanted to know the Spirit behind the words in the Bible. Over the years, as my intimacy with God grew, I found something truly remarkable; although several people wrote the Bible, I began to recognize that God's awesome unchanging Spirit was truly behind every word from Genesis to Revelation.

But now my heart began to break. As my spiritual eyesight became clearer and clearer so I could begin to recognize the Spirit of Jesus Christ, to my horror, it also became harder and harder for me to recognize the Spirit of Jesus Christ within "God's" Church at large. Oh, I indeed saw many within God's Church saying the right words (even quoting Holy Scripture better than I could), and everything on the outside seemed to be reasonably righteous, but something was missing. I did not recognize the Spirit of Jesus Christ.

My heart sank within me. *Something was very wrong!* My heart profoundly sank into my innermost being. It was then I knew in my heart of hearts that this insight was *not* given to me to judge anyone, but to *help* every called-out-one safely into the Kingdom of God. I wanted to somehow spiritually paint *"the portrait of a*

Christian" in order that all who professed to be Christians would then be able to examine themselves to see if they could recognize the Spirit of Jesus Christ within themselves. And, God forbid, if they failed the test, just maybe, if they had ears to hear, they could then turn their mere Christian profession into a truly born-again experience.

With this in mind, the title I have given to the following thirty-one stand-alone commentaries is: *The Portrait of a Christian*. The title comes from the knowledge that the best way to warn (admonish) of a fault is to expose the genuine—to expose the Spirit behind the Holy Scriptures so you can examine yourself to see if you recognize the Spirit of Jesus Christ (The Word) in you. *This is one examination that all professing Christians must pass; to fail this examination has eternal infernal consequences.*

As a Watchman, it is my heart's desire to lovingly warn and/or admonish the professing Christian by profiling a portrait of the Spirit of God—by profiling the portrait of a Christian from the perspective of the Spirit, and not by what we see through our physical eyes. From the vantage point of our physical eyes, the Pharisees had everyone fooled (even themselves); but from the Spirit's vantage point, Jesus could see nothing but darkness within. Matthew 23:27: "Woe to you, scribes and Pharisees, hypocrites! For you are like whitewashed tombs which on the outside appear beautiful, but inside they are full of dead men's bones and all uncleanness."

So as a Watchman who wishes none to perish, and who is filled with a love that can only come from God *(to God be the glory)*, I place before you thirty-one commentaries—warnings—admonishments, in order for you to see if you recognize the Spirit of Jesus Christ in yourself. This is something that is between you and God, as only God can truly expose the state of your heart to you. Therefore, may God forbid anyone in using my commentaries to judge another. For not even I, who wrote the following admonishments (warnings), would even dare to judge my brother or sister as far as his/her salvation is concerned.

So as you begin to read, I pray that those who *do* recognize the Spirit of Christ Jesus within themselves will also find comfort and security in these most troubling times. And for you who *cannot*, may you know that God loves you enough to expose it to you now so you can reevaluate the profession of your faith before it's too late and you become condemned with the rest of the world. Matthew 25:7–13: "Then all those virgins (notice that they all identified themselves as virgins of the bridegroom, i.e., Christians) rose, and trimmed their lamps. And the foolish said to the prudent, 'Give us some of your oil, for our lamps are going out.' But the prudent answered, saying, 'No, there will not be enough for us and you too; go instead to the dealers and buy some for yourselves.' And while they were going away to make the purchase, the bridegroom came, and those who were ready went in with him to the wedding feast; and the door was shut. And later the other virgins also came, saying, 'Lord, lord, open up for us.' But he answered and said, *'Truly I say to you, I do not know you.'* Be on the alert then, for you do not know the day nor the hour."

2 Corinthians 6:1–2: "And working together with Him, we also *urge* you not to receive the grace of God in vain, for He says: *'At the acceptable time I listened to you, and on the day of salvation I helped you; behold,* now *is the acceptable time, behold,* now *is the day of salvation.'"*

CHAPTER ONE

Jesus Instructed Them to Tell No One

Luke 8:52–56: "Now they were all weeping and lamenting for her; but He said, 'Stop weeping, for she has not died, but is asleep.' And they began laughing at Him, knowing that she had died. He, however, took her by the hand and called, saying, 'Child, arise!' And her spirit returned, and she rose immediately; and He gave orders for something to be given her to eat. And her parents were amazed; *but He (Jesus) instructed them to tell no one what had happened.*" Luke 5:12–14: "And it came about that while He was in one of the cities, behold, there was a man full of leprosy; and when he saw Jesus, he fell on his face and implored Him, saying, 'Lord, if You are willing, You can make me clean.' And He stretched out His hand, and touched him, saying, 'I am willing; be cleansed.' And immediately the leprosy left him. *And He (Jesus) ordered him to tell no one,* 'But go and show yourself to the priest, and make an offering for your cleansing, just as Moses commanded, for a testimony to them.'" Matthew 9:28–30: "And after He had come into the house, the blind men came up to Him, and Jesus said to them, 'Do you believe that I am able to do this?' They said to Him, 'Yes, Lord.' Then He touched their eyes, saying,

'Be it done to you according to your faith.' And their eyes were opened. *And Jesus sternly warned them, saying, 'See here, let no one know about this!'"*

Isn't it amazing that Jesus would perform such awesome miracles and then instruct them to tell no one? Apparently, Jesus did not know how to build a large successful ministry. Surely, Jesus should have proclaimed His miracles from the mountain tops, placed full-page ads worldwide to herald His miracles, and then immediately begun a worldwide miracle crusade. After all, these miracles would assure that millions would come to Jesus the Christ. Oh, if only we were there to advise our Lord on the effective and proper way to build His Church, because now we have the tools and knowledge to successfully bring millions to Jesus. All you have to do is appeal to the creature comforts and desires of this world, and then just stand back and marvel at your success. And what better way to appeal to mankind's creature comforts than through miracles. The whole world would show up for health and wealth, which extrapolates to the whole world coming to Jesus. Right? After all, why else would Jesus do miracles if it was not to attract the whole world to Him? *So why would Jesus instruct them to tell no one?* Well, let's try to answer that question.

Matthew 11:2–6: "Now when John in prison heard of the works of Christ, he sent word by his disciples, and said to Him, 'Are You the Expected One, or shall we look for someone else?' And Jesus answered and said to them, 'Go and report to John what you hear and see: the blind receive sight and the lame walk, the lepers are cleansed and the deaf hear, and the dead are raised up, and the poor have the gospel preached to them. And blessed is he who keeps from stumbling over Me.'" *There was only one reason for Jesus to do miracles, He needed to fulfill the Old Testament Scriptures written about Him in order to identify Himself as the Expected One—the*

Deliverer—to those who were already seeking God's Deliverer. Jesus never wanted the miracles to become the object the multitudes sought after. The miracles were meant only to be an attesting sign that He was indeed God's Deliverer, God's sacrificial Lamb, who was spoken of in the Old Testament Scriptures. Hence, Jesus' miracles were only meant to identify God's Deliverer to those who were seeking to be delivered, one who would emancipate them from this present world of Satan's (Egypt). Jesus passionately wanted to identify Himself to those who were seeking salvation, but at the same time, conceal Himself from those who were only seeking His miracles.

Jesus was being very careful not to allow the miracles to become the desired object; hence, *He instructed them to tell no one.* Which is why, even today, we will see many more miracles in areas where there is an ignorance of the identity of God's Deliverer. But once identified to those who are seeking to be delivered, the miracles will decline so that the miracles will not become the object of our affection, and thereby, become sought after instead of God's Deliverer, which is our greatest need. Even the awesome miracle of raising one from the dead is still at best a temporary life, but those who seek God's Deliverer will find eternal life. *God will still do miracles, but they will always be used to further the gospel. The miracles themselves must never become the gospel.* Therefore, Jesus (God in the flesh), being aware of our weakness—our tendency to make the miracles themselves the gospel (the good news)—*instructed them to tell no one.*

So then, if creature comforts and miracles cannot build God's Church, inasmuch as they are not the gospel, what can? Luke 1:15–17: "For he (John the Baptist) will be great in the sight of the Lord, and he will drink no wine or liquor; and he will be *filled with the Holy Spirit*, while yet in his mother's womb. And he will turn back many of the sons of Israel to the Lord their God. And it is he who will go as a forerunner before Him in the spirit and power of Elijah, *to turn the hearts of the fathers back to the children, and the disobedient to the attitude of the righteous; so as to make ready a people prepared for the Lord."*

The only way God's Church can be built is by the Holy Spirit, as He is the only one who can turn our hearts away from seeking miracles and the things of this world, to seeking after God's righteousness. In other words, only He, the Holy Spirit, can cause us to genuinely seek after God's Deliverer, the One who can rescue us from the corruption of our old nature, which is infatuated with this world of Satan's. Whereas, if we try to increase the size of God's Church by appealing to mankind's flesh, it will only increase one's infatuation and love affair to Satan's world and become a real hindrance to the gospel of God's Deliverer. The gospel of God's Deliverer is, deliverance from our corrupt worldly-minded heart (spirit), to His own righteous heart (spirit), i.e., to become born-again. Therefore, a miracle has the potential to become a real hindrance if it becomes more than just an identifier, and becomes more important than being born-again. *And Jesus instructed them to tell no one.*

So then, it's the Holy Spirit's job to prepare our hearts to seek after God's Deliverer by convicting us of sin, righteousness, and judgment. Our hearts (spirit) must first be brought to a place where we are seeking to be delivered, in other words, to a place of repentance. We need a repentant, contrite heart, which is not infatuated with the temporal (Satan's) world, otherwise, our hearts will be found seeking miracles, instead of God's Deliverer. The awesome miracle of being delivered within our hearts from the desires of our old nature, which is in love with Satan's fallen world, to that of God's, is truly a miracle that only God's Holy Spirit can do. *Only the Holy Spirit can convince our hearts that what we once thought to be good is actually evil, and what we once thought to be evil is actually good.* If you do not believe that, just try to get someone who is committing adultery to admit from their heart that adultery is a sin by means of a miracle, a persuasive argument, or an eloquent sermon—it cannot be done. At best, these earthly things can only produce a temporary sorrow or regret, which is not enough to cause someone to seek a Deliverer. There is no power on earth, except for the Holy Spirit, that can turn our hearts around so completely as to cause us to desire and value God's Deliverer much more than the miracles, which at best, are only temporal.

Now we are beginning to understand why Jesus said in Mark 3:28–30, "Truly I say to you, all sins shall be forgiven the sons of men, and whatever blasphemies they utter; but whoever blasphemes against the Holy Spirit never has forgiveness, but is guilty of an eternal sin, because they were saying, 'He has an unclean (evil) spirit.'" It is *impossible* for you to begin seeking after God's Deliverer if you are at the same time calling evil, good and good, evil. After all, if you believe this world (Egypt) and its ways to be good, why would you need a Deliverer? And why would you seek a Deliverer if you perceive Him as evil? To you, the statement, "He who wishes to be the greatest, should seek to be a servant to all," is just moronic and absurd. After all, we know that in this world, the greatest is the one who dominates over all. Everything, and I mean everything, of value in God's Kingdom is the antithesis of what this world considers of value. You may indeed seek miracles as they will appeal to your old worldly nature, inasmuch as the miracles will make you more comfortable in this world; but to crucify this world so that Christ may live in you, well, that's just moronic to our old worldly nature or spirit. *Therefore, there is no other way (path) to Christ (the Deliverer), but by the Holy Spirit.* So if you close your ears (heart) to the Holy Spirit, who or what is left to convince you that you need to seek out God's Deliverer? Why would you want to be delivered (saved) from a world that you love? Although, your worldly-minded sin nature would be more than willing to accept any miracles from God's Deliverer if the miracle would make this worldly life you love more comfortable and/or last longer.

This brings us to Matthew 8:19–20, "And a certain scribe came and said to Him, 'Teacher, I will follow You wherever You go. And Jesus said to him, 'The foxes have holes, and the birds of the air have nests; but the Son of Man has nowhere to lay His head.'" Over and over again Jesus made it crystal clear that this world of Satan's, with its ways, was *not* His home. So if we want to follow after and embrace Jesus, we must also acknowledge from our heart that this world of Satan's is not our home; only then can we embrace Jesus as God's Deliverer (Savior) from this world (Egypt). *On the other hand, if we still love and embrace this world, and its ways, Jesus can never become our Deliverer, because we would not be seeking one.* And if we do not embrace Jesus as the Deliverer, but we do embrace His miracles and favors, we are embracing another gospel, which is *no* gospel at all. We must be very careful not to accept signs, wonders, and miracles, or even creature comforts as the gospel (good news), since God's true gospel is salvation out of Satan's world—not salvation within Satan's world. *Hence, Jesus instructed them to tell no one.*

John 8:37–38: "I know that you are Abraham's offspring; yet you seek to kill Me, because My word has no place in you. I speak the things which I have seen with My Father; therefore you also do the things which you heard from your father." *There are only two Kingdoms, and it is absolutely impossible for anyone to embrace both.* The two Kingdoms are such an antithesis to one another, it is impossible for them to coexist. Therefore, we who are born into this world of Satan's will naturally find the things that Jesus said as completely absurd and moronic, such as: "Salvation is found in the cross, and whoever wishes to follow Me must deny himself and take up his/her cross." What kind of foolish, moronic nonsense this must be to the natural man; no wonder so many rejected Jesus, and some even sought to kill Him. The only way Jesus' words (God's Word) can find a place within our hearts is by the power of the Holy Spirit. To embrace such words that Jesus spoke as wisdom is truly a miracle in itself. So I ask the question, "Can we build God's Church on a foundation built by appealing to our flesh through signs, wonders, and miracles, or must we rely totally on the power of the Holy Spirit to make a place within our hearts for God's Word?" John 6:43–44: "Jesus answered and said to them, 'Do not grumble (over My words) among yourselves. No one can come to Me, unless the Father who sent Me draws him; and I will raise him up on the last day.'"

You cannot read the four Gospels in the New Testament without coming away with the understanding that Jesus strongly disapproved of those who sought after signs, wonders, and miracles; yet He did not hesitate to identify Himself as the Deliverer (Savior) through miracles to those who were seeking a Deliverer—to those who reject this earthly Kingdom to seek after God's Kingdom where righteousness dwells. But once again, only the Holy Spirit can prepare a place within someone's heart for God's Kingdom. He, the Holy Spirit, must always be the forerunner to prepare a way, a path for the Deliverer. John 10:40–42: "And He (Jesus, the Deliverer) went away again beyond the Jordan to the place where John was first baptizing, and He was staying there. And many came to Him and were saying, 'While John (the Baptist) performed no sign, yet everything John said about this man was true.' And many believed in Him (Jesus) there." John, in the power of the Holy Spirit, preached a baptism of repentance—opening up hearts to acknowledge a need to change Kingdoms, which paved the way for God's Deliverer, Jesus.

Trying to build God's Church on the gospel of creature comforts and miracles is simply a futile effort, because it's a false gospel. Why? Because one day everything we now embrace and seek after on this earth will be destroyed by fire. 2 Peter 3:10–13: "But the day of the Lord will come like a thief, in which the heavens will pass away with a roar and the elements will be destroyed with intense heat, and the earth and its works will be burned up. Since all these things are to be destroyed in this way, what sort of people ought you to be in holy conduct and godliness, looking for and hastening the coming of the day of God, on account of which the heavens will be destroyed by burning, and the elements will melt with intense heat! But according to His promise we are looking for new heavens and a new earth, in which righteousness dwells." That being the case, the only gospel which is good news indeed is the good news of God's Deliverer (Savior), since He (Jesus) is the *only* door available to us to enter into the new heavens and new earth. Everything else is temporal, and therefore, cannot be the good news. *Hence, Jesus instructed them to tell no one.*

Why am I saying all this? Luke 3:7–8: "He (John) therefore began saying to the multitudes who were going out to be baptized by him, 'You brood of vipers, who warned you to flee from the wrath to come? *Therefore bring forth fruits in keeping with repentance,* and do not begin to say to yourselves, 'We have Abraham for our father,' for I say to you that God is able from these stones to raise up children to Abraham.'" Calling yourself Abraham's child, a Christian, or even being baptized will not save you. The road to salvation *must* be paved by repentance. God's Holy Spirit must first convict you of sin, righteousness, and judgment, because before you can accept God's Deliverer, you *must* see a need for a Deliverer.

My heart breaks when I read about the church at Laodicea (Revelation 3:14–22), which was filled with all the things this world of Satan's values, yet they were actually poor, blind, and naked. Why? Because, it was not built on a foundation of repentance. God was still on the outside knocking to come in, but no one answered, because they rejected the Holy Spirit's message of repentance so they were not looking for a Deliverer (Savior) to show up at their door. Tragically, they were spiritually deaf to the sound of the knocking upon their hearts.

Before I end this commentary, I need to make sure I'm not misunderstood. I strongly believe that God still does miracles, and there is nothing wrong with modest creature comforts; but they must not become the focus of our desires. About a year before I came to Jesus, the Holy Spirit had already prepared my heart by convicting me of sin, righteousness, and judgment, so I was already desperately looking for a Deliverer (Savior). I never even heard about signs, wonders, or miracles; I just needed a Deliverer. I was not worried about creature comforts, because I did not care if I lived or died; I just needed a Deliverer. *Miracles and creature comforts meant absolutely nothing to me, so how could they be good news (gospel) to me?* The only good news I was looking for was the good news about God's Savior. Nevertheless, once saved, I'll now pray for finances for this ministry, and when I'm sick, I'll pray for healing. I'll even pray the same for others. And I've seen God do awesome miracles. But because I came to Jesus through the convicting power of the Holy Spirit, my desire—my passion—my focus remains on God's holiness and righteousness, which was, and still is, my greatest need.

There is no greater gift God can give me than His Holy Spirit so I can reflect His holiness, righteousness, and love to this world. *There is no miracle I desire more than for people to see more and more of God's nature reflected in my everyday life.* If God never used me to perform another temporal miracle, I would be more than satisfied with being filled with the Holy Spirit like John the Baptist, preaching nothing but repentance, even if it meant I would be scorned and hated by this world. Why? Because the convicting power of God's Holy Spirit is the *only* road to God's Deliverer (Savior), i.e., salvation. If I was on my deathbed, and my Lord withheld His healing from me, I would be more than satisfied if with my last breath I could show the awesome miracle of God's nature within me, just as Stephen did when he was being stoned to death. Stephen did not use his last breath to pray for temporal deliverance from his death, but he used his last breath to glorify and reflect God's nature to those who were stoning him: Acts 7:60, "And falling on his knees, he cried out with a loud voice, *'Lord, do not hold this sin against them!'* And having said this, he fell asleep."

The gospel (good news) was never about making Satan's world a better place for us to live in through signs, wonders, and miracles, because it's going to be destroyed by fire and made completely new; therefore, *Jesus instructed them to tell no one.* However, the gospel is all about God's Deliverer. And no one can comprehend this mystery without the Holy Spirit first preparing his/her heart. We must never try to build God's Church by using this world's techniques (tools), or any other kind of church programs, because such things cannot save anyone, and would only end up profaning God's work. Exodus 20:25: "And if you make an altar of stone for Me, you shall not build it of cut stones, *for if you wield your tool (techniques) on it,* you will profane it."

Chapter Two

Satan, Disguised as an Angel of Light

2 Corinthians 11:12–15: "But what I am doing, I will continue to do, that I may cut off opportunity from those who desire an opportunity to be regarded just as we are in the matter about which they are boasting. For such men are false apostles, deceitful workers, disguising themselves as apostles of Christ. *And no wonder, for even Satan disguises himself as an angel of light.* Therefore it is not surprising if his servants also disguise themselves as servants of righteousness; whose end shall be according to their deeds."

When you mention the name Satan, it immediately conjures up an image of evil, depravity, sorcery, and so on; but that is just a diversion to keep us from discovering Satan's most effective infernal scheme of disguising himself, and his servants, as Anti-Christs. *Satan and his servants will not appear to the majority of the world or "Church" as angels of darkness, but they will appear as angels of light, inasmuch as they will tell the people what they want to hear.* Satan and his servants will go as far as imitating our Anointed One (Christ) by means of counterfeit signs and wonders so they can effectively set themselves up as an attractive anti—an attractive alternative—to Christ. Or you could say it this way: So they can become an attractive, but false alternative to God Himself. As angels of light, Satan and his servants can go into the world, and "Church," and effectively deaden the voice of God within the hearts of those who have hardened their hearts toward the truth and accepted Satan's attractive alternative, but they do so to their own destruction.

To help us better understand this most effective infernal scheme let's first look at Exodus 7:20–23, "So Moses and Aaron did even as the Lord had commanded. And he lifted up the staff and struck the water that was in the Nile, in the sight of Pharaoh and in the sight of his servants, and all the water that was in the Nile was turned to blood. And the fish that were in the Nile died, and the Nile became foul, so that the Egyptians could not drink water from the Nile. And the blood was through all the land of Egypt. *But the magicians of Egypt did the same with their secret arts*; and Pharaoh's heart was hardened, *and he did not listen to them, as the Lord had said.* Then Pharaoh turned and went into his house with no concern even for this."

In the above portion of Scripture, we clearly see Satan using his Anti-Christ deception to the utmost. God, by producing signs and wonders through Moses, was trying to get the Pharaoh of Egypt to soften his heart toward His demand to allow Israel to leave Egypt. And God's display of power was actually beginning to persuade Pharaoh's heart through the fear of self-preservation, until Satan moved in with his servants, the magicians of Egypt. *Their effective imitation of God's power allowed Pharaoh to ignore God for a more attractive alternative which accommodated his own desires instead of God's.* The magicians' alternative made no demands on Pharaoh, hence, his heart could remain comfortably unchanged. From the beginning, Pharaoh's heart was hard against God's demand to let Israel go because it would cost him something. Yet he did fear God's power for a time, because he feared it would cost him more if he did not obey God than the cost associated with losing his slaves. Although Pharaoh appeared to waver favorably toward God, his heart really remained fixed upon his own welfare. *The Egyptian magicians, by their display of counterfeit signs and wonders, became Pharaoh's Anti-Christ (Anti-God) and replaced the fear of God in Pharaoh's heart with a false sense of security.* Therefore, Pharaoh could once again ignore God's word, and his heart could remain fixed upon his own welfare and follow the desires of his own heart, which is the very essence of Satanism.

In the same way, many have the common sense to fear God for self-preservation, yet tragically not enough to deny themselves, take up their cross, and follow God. Therefore, those who love themselves more than God, just as the Pharaoh of Egypt did, will look for a church where a servant of the Anti-Christ abides with all the paraphernalia of Christianity, especially signs and wonders, so they can comfortably ignore God's Word (unabridged Word) with a false sense of security and continue in their secular self-indulgent lifestyle. 2 Timothy 4:3–4: "For the time will come when they will not endure sound doctrine; *but wanting to have their ears tickled, they will accumulate for themselves teachers in accordance to their own desires; and will turn away their ears from the truth, and will turn aside to myths.*" You must come to God with a contrite heart, desiring His ways over your own, not simply because you fear the personal cost of hell; that will only prove your fear of God, like Pharaoh's fear, is only based on self-preservation and profit. And if that's the case, then the Anti-Christ will be lurking at the door of your heart with an attractive alternative.

You cannot blame your infernal end on Satan's deception, be-cause as with Pharaoh, you chose to wholeheartedly pursue Satan's deception because your love of self and self-indulgence was much greater than your love of God and His righteousness. Deuteronomy 13:1–3: "If a prophet or a dreamer of dreams arises among you and gives you a sign or a wonder, and the sign or the wonder comes true, concerning which he spoke to you, saying, 'Let us go after other gods (whom you have not known) and let us serve them,' you shall not listen to the words of that prophet or that dreamer of dreams; *for the Lord your God is testing you to find out if you love the Lord your God with all your heart and with all your soul."* And 2 Thessalonians 2:11–12: "And for this reason God will send upon them a deluding influence so that they might believe what is false, in order that they all may be judged who did not believe the truth, but took pleasure in wickedness."

Does it sound unfair for God to allow a deluding influence to deceive the hardhearted into believing a lie so they would reject the Lamb of God? Exodus 12:43: "And the Lord said to Moses and Aaron, 'This is the ordinance of the Passover: no foreigner is to eat of it.'" Verse 48: "But if a stranger sojourns with you, and celebrates the Passover to the Lord, let all his males be circumcised, and then let him come near to celebrate it; and he shall be like a native of the land. *But no uncircumcised person may eat of it (the Passover lamb)."* And Deuteronomy 30:6: "Moreover the Lord your God will *circumcise your heart* and the heart of your descendants, to love the Lord your God with all your heart and with all your soul, in order that you may live." *God makes it crystal clear that He will not allow anyone to partake of the Passover lamb (Jesus) who is un-circumcised of heart!* It is written, God is the same yesterday, today, and forever; therefore, if you do not love the Lord your God with all your heart and with all your soul, He will allow you, by means of your own hardheartedness, to be deluded into believing a lie and allow you to perish with the rest of Egypt, i.e., the world. That's right, if you miss partaking of the Passover lamb (Jesus), it's not God's fault; you were led astray by your own hard, uncircumcised heart, just as a proud narcissistic bull is easily led away to slaughter by the ring in its nose.

The deeds of those with an uncircumcised heart are obvious to all as their love and desires remain identical to the love and desires established in this world, a world in which Satan remains as god. The uncircumcised of heart may have a desire for God, but that desire can only be motivated by their lust for power, for secular wealth, and/or for a sanctuary of personal comfort without contrition. Since their love is solely focused on themselves, they will follow after God only as long as there is a perceived personal benefit. The uncircumcised of heart deceive themselves into thinking that to love God is synonymous with loving themselves to the exclusion of God's desires. In contrast, the Word of God tells us how the circumcised of heart demonstrate their love for God in 1 John 5:3–4, "For this is the love of God, that we keep His commandments; *and His commandments are not burdensome.* For whatever is born of God *overcomes the world;* and this is the victory that has overcome the world—our faith." God's commandments are not burdensome to the circumcised of heart, because God has placed His own heart (spirit) within us so His desires become our desires. The circumcised of heart overcomes the world, and the god of this world, Satan, by becoming holy, i.e., distinct and separate from the world by their God-inspired deeds of righteousness. Having fully embraced God's Holy Spirit as their own, they now can be nothing like the world in their actions, desires, or priorities.

Matthew 7:20–23: *"So then, you will know them by their fruits.* Not everyone who says to Me, 'Lord, Lord,' will enter the kingdom of heaven; but he who does the will of My Father who is in heaven.

Many will say to Me on that day, 'Lord, Lord, did we not prophesy in Your name, and in Your name cast out demons, and in Your name perform many miracles?' And then I will declare to them, 'I *never* knew you; depart from Me, you who practice lawlessness.'" And 2 Thessalonians 2:3: "*Let no one in any way deceive you, for it (the day of the Lord) will not come unless the apostasy (falling away from God) comes first.*" Contemporary "prophets" are telling us that we're moving into a time of abundant signs and wonders; and along with the signs and wonders, there will be a great harvest of souls. However, if this great harvest is occurring in the last days, as I believe it is, according to the Holy Scriptures it will be a harvest of the hardhearted to a very attractive alternative, i.e., an Anti-Christ. On that day (the day of the Lord) *many* will indeed be saying "Lord, Lord," yet God tells us in His Word, He *never* knew them. These contemporary "prophets" seem to be rejoicing over signs, wonders, and numbers; but as for me, I'll be looking at the fruit. And so far, the overall fruit seems to confirm lawless apostasy, and *not* righteousness and holiness, which is the fruit of the circumcised of heart.

To gain even more insight, let's look at Matthew 16:22–23: "And Peter took Him aside and began to rebuke Him, saying, 'God forbid it, Lord! This shall never happen to You.' But He (Jesus) turned and said to Peter, '*Get behind Me, Satan! You are a stumbling block to Me; for you are not setting your mind on God's interests, but man's.*'" In this verse of Scripture there are three points we must understand and never forget. First, Jesus confronted Peter with the words, "Get behind Me, Satan! You are a stumbling block to me." *Wow!* Those were some very offensive words Jesus spoke to Peter, yet Peter did *not* get offended, inasmuch as he continued to walk with Jesus. In contrast, if your proud ego can be easily offended, Satan has already won; if Satan can get you offended by the truth, i.e., offended at God's Word, he will be more than happy to dress-up for you in his best Sunday Anti-Christ suit and give you a pampering alternative which will not offend you, a more attentive and attractive god, one your ego can easily embrace.

The second point ties into the first, an attractive alternative. Let's review the very words which caused Jesus to react with such impassioned opposition: "God forbid it, Lord! This shall never happen to You." *What an awesome, beautiful alternative to Jesus' cross!* Jesus, you do not have to go to the cross, because God is a merciful God; surely He will not allow His only Son to endure the agonizing torture of crucifixion. Peter's words were not only beautiful to Jesus' ears, but at the same time, it made God look cruel if He made His Son Jesus go to the cross. And how do we know that Peter's (Satan's) words were beautiful to Jesus' ears? Matthew 26:38–39: "Then He said to them, 'My soul is deeply grieved, to the point of death; remain here and keep watch with Me.' And He went a little beyond them, and fell on His face and prayed, saying, *'My Father, if it is possible, let this cup pass from Me;* yet not as I will, but as Thou wilt.'" And in Luke 22:44, we are told that Jesus' flesh reacted so passionately against God's will that His flesh actually sweated blood. Therefore, Jesus had to react passionately against Peter's (Satan's) words. Yet, Jesus remained without sin, because within His heart He strongly desired God's will over and above His own; and with His Father's help, He overcame His flesh. *Truly, by His actions, Jesus defined the biblical definition of being an overcomer.*

And the third point we need to take from Matthew 16:22–23, is the biblical definition of Satanism. In Jesus' own words He made it *very* clear why He attributed Peter's words as being from Satan himself: "Get behind Me, Satan! You are a stumbling block to Me; *for you are not setting your mind on God's interests, but man's."* Satan doesn't care if you call yourself a Christian, as long as you place your own interests (desires) over and above God's. If you keep your eyes focused on yourself, and on your own desires, you are Satan's sons and daughters by default, even if you call yourself a Christian. Satanism is all about you, whereas biblical Christianity is all about self-denial and the cross. *Satanism can be compared to a black hole that sucks everything in, even light, and then consumes it so nothing of benefit can return.* Whereas, Christianity can be compared to the sun, which consumes itself in order to benefit others with light; only unlike our sun, we cannot be exhausted, because our heavenly supply—our God—is infinite. Is it any wonder that the Bible describes hell as eternal, utter darkness, whereas heaven has the inexhaustible eternal light of God that exists to benefit all. Daniel 12:3: *"And those who have insight will shine brightly like the brightness of the expanse of heaven, and those who lead the many to righteousness, like the stars forever and ever."*

Matthew 19:21–22: "Jesus said to him, 'If you wish to be complete (perfect), go and sell your possessions and give to the poor, and you shall have treasure in heaven; and come, follow Me.' But when the young man heard this statement, he went away grieved; for he was one who owned much property." It is amazing to me that so many Christians still stumble over these verses. Yes, to the world it would be foolishness, but to the Christian it should be understood as the wisdom of God. Jesus understood it, that's why He allowed Himself to be completely consumed for our benefit. And what personal benefit did He receive in return? Absolutely nothing! Jesus only returned to His former position with God the Father. And yet, He did benefit much in heaven's economy, an economy where personal treasure is measured by selflessness, and our personal satisfaction is derived by seeing others benefit from our sacrifice. In this world's economy Jesus was completely consumed, yet we find that in heaven He is rich beyond measure, inasmuch as He sits at the right hand of God the Father.

John 6:26–27: "Jesus answered them and said, 'Truly, truly, I say to you, you seek Me, not because you saw signs, but because you ate of the loaves, and were filled. Do not work for the food which perishes, but for the food which endures to eternal life, which the Son of Man shall give to you, for on Him the Father, even God, has set His seal.'" *Even today we can fill our churches by using Satan's very attractive alternative of self-consumption, but if we do, that would necessitate the exclusion of the cross and self-denial, which are the essence of Christianity.* Today we seem to have lost the essence of Christianity proportionately to our belief that church size and worldly wealth equates with being blessed by God. On the other hand, Jesus never equated church size or worldly wealth as being blessed by God. Instead, He gave life to this world by allowing this world to consume Him, and He spoke the truth even when all walked away. John 6:51: "I am the living bread that came down out of heaven; if anyone eats of this bread, he shall live forever; and the bread also which I shall give for the life of the world is My flesh." Verse 60: "Many therefore of His disciples, when they heard this said, 'This is a difficult statement; who can listen to it?'" And verse 66: "As a result of this many of His disciples withdrew, and were not walking with Him anymore."

If you are filling your church without the cross, your church is only an illusion. It is the heart that matters to God, not the numbers. A church, large or small, having a form of godliness, and yet its members are statistically comparable to the world in their lifestyle, it is also a church which God has *never* known. Matthew 7:22–23: "Many will say to Me on that day, 'Lord, Lord, did we not prophesy in Your name, and in Your name cast out demons, and in Your name perform many miracles?' And then I will declare to them, 'I never knew you; depart from Me, you who practice lawlessness.'" Today, it is a fact that we who call ourselves Christians are quickly becoming identical to the world in our desires, our objectives in life, the amount we donate, and the kind of entertainment we spend our money on, even hardcore pornography. *Isn't that the definition of an end-time apostate church?* Matthew 7:13–15: "Enter by the narrow gate; for the gate is wide, and the way is broad that leads to destruction, and many are those who enter by it. For the gate is small, and the way is narrow that leads to life, and few are those who find it. Beware of the false prophets, who come to you in sheep's clothing, but inwardly are ravenous wolves." *Ravenous wolves, what an appropriate description for a consummate all-consuming black hole!*

Many may find this commentary blunt and offensive, especially if it touches an area in your life that you do not wish to change or give up. But please, I beg you, do not look for a more attractive alternative that demands little or nothing from you. It's only Satan, or one of his servants, disguising himself as an angel of light to keep your heart uncircumcised so you cannot partake of the Passover Lamb of God, Jesus. So please do not be offended, but prayerfully consider the words in this commentary. Matthew 24:24–25: "For false Christs and false prophets will arise and will show great signs and wonders, so as to mislead, if possible, even the elect. *Behold, I have told you in advance.*" I have written this commentary from my heart as a safeguard to whosoever reads it; my purpose is not to judge nor condemn, I just truly, truly desire no one to perish. The deception in these last days that we are living in is exceedingly great, but God's amazing grace is immeasurably greater! *Lord, keep us from temptation, and all the lies of the evil one! Amen!*

Chapter Three

Do You Genuinely Desire Heaven?

What would happen if I went into the streets and asked a multitude of people, both the general public and professing Christians, the question: *Do you genuinely desire heaven?* Without question, I'm sure the majority answer would be a wholehearted and enthusiastic—*yes!* But do we really understand the question? Can we really know within our heart of hearts that we would genuinely desire heaven if we do not first understand God's image of heaven, the very image that makes heaven so heavenly? *After all, without that knowledge you may indeed be saying yes with your lips, but in actuality within your heart of hearts despise—even abhor—heaven.* Do you think it's impossible for anyone to despise or abhor heaven? Well, maybe after reading this commentary you'll find out it's not only possible, but probable!

None of us can truly imagine what heaven is actually like, because it is impossible to embrace infinite heaven through the eyes of our finite earthly experiences. Yet, many will try to do just that as they clutter their image of heaven with all their impulsive desires, and simultaneously, devoid it of all their vexing dislikes. Even the angelic being, Lucifer, tried to create his own image of heaven by placing himself upon the throne of heaven; but the only thing he achieved was discovering and initiating hell. Hence, God changed his name to Satan, the adversary, or you could say, one who is opposed (in rebellion) to heaven. There is only one possible image of heaven as every other image only results in hell. Yet, we do not despair, because the Holy Scriptures give us enough information to understand the image which is heaven indeed—the image that makes heaven so heavenly. Therefore, let us proceed to see if you genuinely desire the Holy Scripture's image of heaven, also known as God's image of heaven. But beware; you may be surprised at your answer.

First of all, in God's image of heaven, there must be complete unity; otherwise, heaven would cease to be heaven and end up falling into utter chaos and darkness, i.e., hell. Therefore, *all* who genuinely desire heaven *must* be of one mind and heart in their image of heaven. John 17:20–23: "I do not ask in behalf of these alone, but for those also who believe in Me through their word; that they may all be one; even as Thou, Father, art in Me, and I in Thee, that they also may be in Us; that the world may believe that Thou didst send Me. *And the glory which Thou hast given Me I have given to them; that they may be one, just as We are one; I in them, and Thou in Me, that they may be perfected in unity,* that the world may know that Thou didst send Me, and didst love them, even as Thou didst love Me." Consequently, one of the essential ingredients of God's image of heaven is complete, consummate, and undisputed unity.

Printed on the coins of the United States of America is the Latin phrase, E Pluribus Unum, which when translated means, Out Of Many, One. This Christian (heavenly) concept is one of the pillars that has made the USA a great nation. Imagine my horror when I heard an ex-vice president of the United States, in a publicized speech, misquote E Pluribus Unum as Many Out Of One. Although, I'm sure this ex-vice president did not mean to misquote E Pluribus Unum, yet he did continue on in his speech to extol the "virtues" of this concept of "many out of one" as being paradisiacal. However, in reality, it is not paradisiacal nor virtuous, but is hellish in nature, producing not only the fruit of rebellion, but the flames of chaos. This so-called paradisiacal and virtuous image of "many out of one" was originally birthed by Satan, and now it seems to be working overtime within the USA as we now have entrenched within our society the much vaunted hyphenated Americans, i.e., African-American, Mexican-American, and so on. Should not our identity just simply be Americans?

But wait, before anyone tries to condemn this ex-vice president, or anyone else, know that these same hellish forces of darkness—forces of separation—are at work (if not in speech, in action) within the best of our churches as we, the bride of Christ, also extol this hellish concept of many out of one. How? By extolling and entrenching within God's church our own concept of "many out of one" by hyphenating the name of God's bride as in Christian-Baptist, Christian-Presbyterian, and so on. Should not our identity just simply be Christians? But we did not stop there, as we now find this hellish concept within our marriages when a bride chooses to hyphenate her last name in order to maintain a sense of her individually—her separation. Should not a husband and wife become as one flesh?

All I can pray is that this is done in ignorance, and not in knowledge, because in God's eyes it is impossible to say, I genuinely desire heaven, and at the same time say, I genuinely desire many out of one. Why? Because in heaven there is complete, consummate, and undisputed unity, also known as "out of many, one." John 17:22–23:

"And the glory which Thou hast given Me I have given to them; that they may be one, just as We are one; I in them, and Thou in Me, that they may be perfected in *unity*, that the world may *know* that Thou didst send Me, and didst love them, even as Thou didst love Me." So let me now ask you another question, what does the world *know* about God, Jesus, and heaven through our hellish acts of separation?

What else makes heaven so heavenly? Many believe it's found in Revelation 21:18–21, "And the material of the wall was jasper; and the city was pure gold, like clear glass. The foundation stones of the city wall were adorned with every kind of precious stone. The first foundation stone was jasper; the second, sapphire; the third, chalcedony; the fourth, emerald; the fifth, sardonyx; the sixth, sardius; the seventh, chrysolite; the eighth, beryl; the ninth, topaz; the tenth, chrysoprase; the eleventh, jacinth; the twelfth, amethyst. And the twelve gates were twelve pearls; each one of the gates was a single pearl. And the street of the city was pure gold, like transparent glass."

Many who remain influenced by this earthly economy may look at the exoteric (external) beauty of heaven as being an essential ingredient in making heaven so heavenly, but nothing could be further from the truth. *Can a precious stone reflect its beauty in darkness? Can gold have any value in chaos? No!* But what is essential to both the beauty and value of heaven is God Himself. Revelation 21:10–11: "And he carried me away in the Spirit to a great and high mountain, and showed me the holy city, Jerusalem, coming down out of heaven from God, *having the glory of God.* Her brilliance was like a very costly stone, as a stone of crystal-clear jasper." And Revelation 21:23: *"And the city has no need of the sun or of the moon to shine upon it, for the glory of God has illumined it, and its lamp is the Lamb."* Yes, God Himself is the essential ingredient, the essential essence, who causes heaven to be so heavenly in both beauty and majesty. The gold and precious stones in heaven are only the instruments God chooses to use to reflect His glory, just as the moon has no glory within itself, but is only an instrument to reflect the glory of the sun.

So who is this God who brings the glory, which is so essential to making heaven so heavenly? 1 John 4:16: "And we have come to know and have believed the love which God has for us. *God is love*, and the one who *abides* in love *abides* in God, and God *abides* in him." Inasmuch as the essence of God is love, it is God's love that makes heaven so heavenly. Did you notice the unity in the word "abides" repeated in 1 John 4:16? Therefore, we *must* be in complete, consummate, and undisputed unity with the essence of God's love. A love we must fully embrace as our own before we can truly answer yes to the question: *Do you genuinely desire heaven?* As it is impossible to say you genuinely desire heaven without also genuinely desiring that which makes heaven so heavenly—God's love. So how is God's love manifested in our everyday lives, thereby proving our genuine desire for heaven? 1 Corinthians 13:4–7: "Love is patient, love is kind, and is not jealous; love does not brag and is not arrogant, does not act unbecomingly; it does not seek its own, is not provoked, does not take into account a wrong suffered, does not rejoice in unrighteousness, but rejoices with the truth; bears all things, believes all things, hopes all things, endures all things."

Do you genuinely desire heaven? If so, then you *must* genuinely desire the following: You *must* genuinely desire to be patient and kind. You *must* genuinely desire to rejoice with, and eagerly embrace, the truth. You *must* genuinely desire to be willing to bear and endure all things, even the qualities or nature of someone who seems unbearable. Why? Because, your innermost desire for everyone is restoration and salvation, not judgment. You must genuinely desire *not* to be one who remembers or seeks revenge for a wrong that was inflicted upon you. You must genuinely desire *not* to be braggadocios, nor arrogant. You must genuinely desire *not* to seek after your own interests over and above someone else's, nor be jealous of anyone. You must genuinely desire *not* to act in any manner that is contrary to God's view of morality. You must genuinely desire *not* to be one who would accept, rejoice, or laugh at any kind of unrighteousness. You must genuinely desire *not* to be one who can be provoked, or inflamed.

1 John 4:17: "By this, love is perfected with us, that we may have confidence in the day of judgment; *because as He is, so also are we in this world.*" The only way we can say with *confidence* that we genuinely desire heaven, is to reflect heaven in our daily lives now in this world. In other words, to be a citizen—an ambassador—of heaven while we are living in the hostile environment of this world; showing by our conduct, that our citizenship is *now* recorded in heaven. 1 John 3:1–3: "See how great a love the Father has bestowed upon us, that we should be called children of God; and such we are. For this reason the world does not know us, because it did not know Him. Beloved, *now* we are children of God, and it has not appeared as yet what we shall be. We know that, when He appears, we shall be like Him, because we shall see Him just as He is. And *everyone* who has this hope fixed on Him purifies himself, just as He is pure."

Throughout this commentary I have carefully chosen to use the word desire, inasmuch as, desire can only be produced from within; hence, desire is the essence of the real you, an essence which cannot be diluted by external forces, making it impossible for us to quit or give up, even if we encounter much external resistance. For example, if we desire heaven, we will eventually forgive a wrong done against us, even if our emotions continue to scream *no.* Why? Because it is impossible to betray who we really are within, unless we have deceived ourselves and our heavenly traits are actually only skin deep—fashioned and designed for external consumption only. The book of 1 John puts this concept very well in 1 John 3:9–10, *"No one* who is born of God practices sin, *because His seed (God's Holy Spirit) abides in him; and he cannot sin, because he is born of God.* By this the children of God and the children of the devil are obvious: anyone who does not practice righteousness is not of God, nor the one who does not *love* his brother."

Now the question becomes, can we genuinely desire heaven and still falter or stumble in our heavenly traits? Yes! But the desire, the Holy Seed within, will not allow us to remain in our transgression (sin). But now you may ask, "How could we falter if the heavenly desire is truly genuine?" Because, the heavenly desire must still battle the corruptible flesh which needs to be put to death daily, sometimes even moment by moment, by our inward heavenly desire (seed) until our redemption becomes complete when the corruptible flesh puts on the incorruptible.

The Apostle Paul brings this concept alive in the book of Romans. Romans 7:14–21: "For we know that the Law is spiritual; but I am of flesh, sold into bondage to sin. For that which I am doing, I do not understand; for I am not practicing what I would like (desire) to do, but I am doing the very thing I hate. But if I do the very thing I do not wish (desire) to do, I agree with the Law, confessing that it is good. So now, no longer am I the one doing it, but sin which indwells me. For I know that nothing good dwells in me, that is, in my flesh; for the wishing (desire) is present in me, but the doing of the good is not. For the good that I wish (desire), I do not do; but I practice the very evil that I do not wish. But if I am doing the very thing I do not wish (desire), I am no longer the one doing it, but sin which dwells in me. I find then the principle that evil is present in me, the one who wishes (desires) to do good."

Did you notice that the Apostle Paul in Romans 7:14–21 was making reference to a genuine desire which can only be birthed from within? *How absurd it would be to think that we could obtain entrance to heaven by "acting" good if the genuine desire (Holy Spirit) was not present.* If you are just "acting" heavenly you will always be looking for an excuse to act unheavenly—ungodly. Why? Because you still genuinely desire the unheavenly, although for a time you may see a self-serving benefit for "acting" heavenly. On the other hand, those who genuinely desire heaven will display heavenly traits even if there is no earthly benefit. Why? Because they are already citizens of heaven, and therefore, genuinely desire the heavenly. Do you now see that it is impossible to "act" your way into heaven? You *must* have a genuine desire for heaven!

So I ask the question again, *do you genuinely desire heaven?* Only you and God know that answer. All I'm trying to do is to make you ask yourself that question before it's too late. If through the eyes of this commentary you now know you cannot truly say, "Yes, I genuinely desire heaven," please also know that it's not too late to change your answer to a yes. *There is only one way anyone can truly answer yes to the question: Do you genuinely desire heaven?* How? By being reborn from within with God's Holy Spirit, and thereby, bringing back the unity of spirit and desire we once had in the Garden of Eden when God originally fashioned us for heaven by making us in His own image, the image we lost when Adam broke his unity with God. Adam, with the help of Satan's deception, desired to be a god too, and embraced the hellish concept of "many out of one." Hence, our desire—our nature—our essence—was now forever corrupted by inheritance.

If you cannot say I genuinely desire heaven but you want to, you have just made the first step. By you professing a desire to have within you the nature, the essence, the love, that makes heaven so heavenly, you are in fact saying, I desire God's nature, God's essence, God's love over your own, which is what God calls repentance. *Repentance is nothing more than turning away from the desires you inherited from Adam, to embrace the heavenly desires of God.* You are saying, "God I agree with You, and I now know that I have sinned (missed the mark) against You and heaven and I ask for Your forgiveness."

But now we have another problem. God would stop being God if He was not also a God of justice, so He cannot let you or me go unpunished, for it is written, "The wages of sin is death." So what can God do as we already know His heavenly nature—His innermost desire—compels Him to not only forgive, but to also bring about restoration? Well, to the praise of God's glory and wisdom, He solved this seemly unsolvable dilemma by allowing His Son Jesus to be born into this world by a virgin (and thereby, free from the corrupt inheritance of Adam) to pay the penalty for our sin by experiencing hell and death for us. And yet, hell and death had no right to hold Him as He was sinless by virtue of His virgin birth, conceived by the Holy Spirit, which was confirmed by His historically provable resurrection, thus our broken unity with God could be lawfully restored.

Now, through repentance, you are made new (clean) by accepting the death and resurrection of God's only Son Jesus for the forgiveness of your debt of sin. Now cleansed, you can ask God to replace your old corruptible spirit with His own Holy Spirit and be literally born-again. Now you can answer the question, "Do you genuinely desire heaven?" with a genuine *yes* and *amen*. Although, for a time, we must all wait for the perfect to come, the redemption of our corruptible body (flesh), you can now enthusiastically join the spiritual warfare for control of your earthly body (flesh) by means of your heavenly born-again nature or desire. A desire which may indeed lose a battle from time to time, but will never lose the war. Why? Because you are now a new creature, born-again with God's Holy Spirit—a holy fire—an innermost desire—which cannot be quenched.

Now is the time to look up and make sure your salvation is genuine. Do not harden your heart, but answer the question from your heart: *Do you genuinely desire heaven?* God's age of grace will not last forever. Even now we see the signs that this age of grace is about over. Please, I beg you, having God's Spirit within me, before it's too late, accept God's gracious offer of restored unity and heaven; as your only other alternative is hell, and then finally, for eternity, the Lake of Fire which was designed for Satan and those who despise, abhor, and reject heaven's unity, and God's kind of love. *You'll only end up in the Lake of Fire for eternity if you harden your heart and insist on your own desires even as Satan did, and thereby, you are establishing a unity with Satan's desire of "many out of one" which will lead to complete chaos, lovelessness, and hell.*

Please accept God's most gracious invitation to live in heaven with Him before it's too late. Proverbs 29:1: "A man who hardens his neck after much reproof will suddenly be broken beyond remedy." 1 Thessalonians 5:2–3: "For you yourselves know full well that the day of the Lord will come just like a thief in the night. While they are saying, 'Peace and safety!' then destruction will come upon them suddenly like birth pangs upon a woman with child; and they shall not escape."

It is my heartfelt prayer that after reading this commentary, everyone who is willing to accept God's gracious offer of redemption, His heavenly invitation, would be able to say with me, "My desire for heaven is absolutely—unequivocally—undoubtedly—indisputably genuine!"

CHAPTER FOUR

Baptized for the Dead

1 Corinthians 15:29–32: "Otherwise, what will those do who are *baptized for the dead?* If the dead are not raised at all, why then are they baptized for them? Why are we also in danger every hour? I protest, brethren, by the boasting in you, which I have in Christ Jesus our Lord, *I die daily.* If from human motives I fought with wild beasts at Ephesus, what does it profit me? If the dead are not raised, let us eat and drink, for tomorrow we die."

If we truly wish to become salt and light to this world, it is extremely important for us to understand and embrace this difficult, but extremely powerful verse of Scripture. Since we seem to be losing the battle for souls, in spite of all our grandiose evangelistic programs, perhaps we are in need of regaining this *essential fragrance of Christ in our lives.* When I say we seem to be losing the battle for souls, I'm not talking about body count, but the battle for the hearts of mankind. Yes, through manipulation we seem to be able to gather crowds, but are they born-again? Does God have their hearts? Or does the allure of this world still hold their hearts captive? That's a question on this side of heaven we will never know the answer to, but as I examine the fruit that is being produced within much of the Church, it does give me cause to tremble. So let us press on to understand this essential fragrance of Christ, being baptized for the dead, so we can at least make sure our own hearts belong to God, and as an individual, each is salt and light to this fallen world.

First of all, we know by context that the Apostle Paul was defending the reality of the resurrection of the dead unto the eternal life which awaits those who are in Christ Jesus at His second coming. And to do this, Paul does something very remarkable—he uses his own life and the lives of other godly, faithful men and women as *tangible* proof of this resurrection to a glorious eternal existence with God. One of the words the Apostle Paul chooses to use in defense of this resurrection is the word "baptized." In the Greek, this word gives us a very powerful word picture of complete immersion. Although we are accustomed to simply seeing this word applied to an immersion in water, to those in Paul's time, it could just as easily mean a complete immersion in both identification and participation with someone, or something. Paul used this concept in 1 Corinthians 10:1–4, "For I do not want you to be unaware, brethren, that our fathers were all under the cloud, and all passed through the sea; and all were *baptized* (complete immersion in identification and participation) into Moses in the cloud and in the sea; and all ate the same spiritual food; and all drank the same spiritual drink, for they were drinking from a spiritual rock which followed them; and the rock was Christ."

To help us to receive a more penetrating understanding of this concept of complete immersion in identification and participation, let's look at John 6:53–58. In this Scripture Jesus painted an extremely powerful word picture, so powerful in fact, that it literally offended everyone who heard Him. John 6:53–58: "Jesus therefore said to them, 'Truly, truly, I say to you, unless you eat the flesh of the Son of Man and drink His blood, you have *no* life in yourselves. He who eats My flesh and drinks My blood has eternal life, and I will raise him up on the last day. For My flesh is true food, and My blood is true drink. He who eats My flesh and drinks My blood *abides* in Me, and I in him. As the living Father sent Me, and I live because of the Father, so he who eats Me, he also shall live because of Me. This is the bread which came down out of heaven; not as the fathers ate, and died, he who eats this bread shall live forever.'" Now that's being completely immersed in identification and participation, i.e., being *baptized* into Christ Jesus.

With this baptism in mind, and using the Greek's grammar notations as an aid, let us revisit 1 Corinthians 15:29. In the first sentence the grammar notation for the word baptized is both passive and continuous. And in the second sentence the grammar notation for the word baptized is both passive and contemporaneous. The grammar notation passive denotes something happening to you without any personal participation on your part to make it happen. Therefore, the point the Apostle Paul was trying to make in 1 Corinthians 15:29 was: "Otherwise, what will those do who are *baptized for the dead* (passive and continuous, i.e., those who are continually subjecting (participation) themselves to the possibility of death by the hands of others)? If the dead are not raised at all, why then are they *baptized for them* (contemporaneous and passive, i.e., those who actually have succumbed (participation) to death by the hands of others)?" This exegesis is confirmed as Paul goes on to say in the very next verses, 1 Corinthians 15:30–31: "*Why are we also in danger every hour?* I protest, brethren, by the boasting in you, which I have in Christ Jesus our Lord, *I die daily.*"

Paul's life was an awesome illustration of this concept of being *"baptized for the dead."* 2 Corinthians 11:23–27: "Are they servants of Christ? (I speak as if insane) I more so; in far more labors, in far more imprisonments, beaten times without number, often in danger of death. Five times I received from the Jews thirty-nine lashes. Three times I was beaten with rods, once I was stoned, three times I was shipwrecked, a night and a day I have spent in the deep. I have been on frequent journeys, in dangers from rivers, dangers from robbers, dangers from my countrymen, dangers from the Gentiles, dangers in the city, dangers in the wilderness, dangers on the sea, dangers among false brethren; I have been in labor and hardship, through many sleepless nights, in hunger and thirst, often without food, in cold and exposure." And later Paul's life became the illustration for *"baptized for them"* as his immersion for the dead became literal, or complete. 2 Timothy 4:6–7: "For I am already being poured out as a drink offering, and the time of my departure has come. I have fought the good fight, I have finished the course, I have kept the faith." Yes, Paul's life in every way fulfilled this concept of being *"baptized for the dead,"* and he offered it up as proof of the resurrection.

With this in mind, we can completely understand the Apostle Paul's thought process in 1 Corinthians 15:19, *"If we have hoped in Christ in this life only, we are of all men most to be pitied,"* and 1 Corinthians 15:32: "If from human motives I fought with wild beasts at Ephesus, what does it profit me? *If the dead are not raised, let us eat and drink (fulfill our fleshly desires to the utmost, and make the most of this earthly life), for tomorrow we die."* The Apostle Paul's life was a living testament to the reality of the resurrection. His life was giving off a very pungent fragrance of Christ as a witness, to those who are saved the fragrance of life, and to those who are not, the fragrance of death. Even if Paul said not a word, his life would *scream*, I am *not* of this world, and I'm looking forward to a better resurrection!

So we understand that this concept of being *"baptized for the dead"* is *not* a new concept. Let's look at a few other examples before the Apostle Paul's time. Hebrews 11:8–10: "By faith Abraham, when he was called, obeyed by going out to a place which he was to receive for an inheritance; and he went out, not knowing where he was going. By faith he lived as an alien in the land of promise, as in a foreign land, dwelling in tents with Isaac and Jacob, fellow heirs of the same promise; for he was looking for the city which has foundations, whose architect and builder is God." Hebrews 11:13–16: "All these died in faith, without receiving the promises, but having seen them and having welcomed them from a distance, *and having confessed that they were strangers and exiles on the earth.* For those who say such things make it clear that they are seeking a country of their own. And indeed, if they had been thinking of that country from which they went out, they would have had opportunity to return. *But as it is, they desire a better country, that is a heavenly one. Therefore God is not ashamed to be called their God; for He has prepared a city for them."*

Abraham, by walking away from the family and land of his birth, demonstrated to all that he believed God when God promised him a better land—a heavenly land—prepared by God Himself. In doing so, he made himself as a stranger to the land (world) and the family of his birth (Adam). He allowed himself to be *"baptized for the dead,"* i.e., he moved out of his safety zone and placed himself in a difficult position amongst strangers in order to gain a better resurrection. No, it was not Abraham's lips which said, "I believe God," it was his heart which manifested itself through his actions; therefore, God was not ashamed to be called his God.

Hebrews 11:24–26: "By faith Moses, when he had grown up, refused to be called the son of Pharaoh's daughter; choosing rather to endure ill-treatment with the people of God, than to enjoy the passing pleasures of sin; *considering the reproach of Christ greater riches than the treasures of Egypt (world); for he was looking to the reward (resurrection)."* Moses turned away from everything this world had to offer and, with enthusiasm, embraced the reproach of Christ. Moses could not live by the world's philosophy of "let's eat and drink, for tomorrow we die." Why? Because he believed in God and that there was a better resurrection that awaited him. So once again, if someone wanted proof of the resurrection of the dead, all Moses had to do is point at his life.

Hebrews 11:35–38: "Women received back their dead by resurrection; and others were tortured, *not accepting their release, in order that they might obtain a better resurrection;* and others experienced mockings and scourgings, yes, also chains and imprisonment. They were stoned, they were sawn in two, they were tempted, they were put to death with the sword; they went about in sheepskins, in goatskins, being destitute, afflicted, ill-treated (men of whom the world was not worthy), wandering in deserts and mountains and caves and holes in the ground." *All these people showed themselves to be great men and women of* faith, *not by what they were able to gain in this world, but by what they were willing to give up in this world;* which is the exact opposite of what is now being taught in many of our churches today.

Therefore, we must be very careful not to fall into the same trap (sin) as described in Psalm 106:24–25: "Then they despised the pleasant land (heaven and the resurrection); (why) they did not believe in His word, (how) but grumbled in their tents; they did not listen to the voice of the Lord." And who was Psalm 106:24–25 talking about? Exodus 16:2–3: "And the whole congregation of the sons of Israel grumbled against Moses and Aaron in the wilderness. And the sons of Israel said to them, Would that we had died by the Lord's hand in the land of Egypt, when we sat by the pots of meat, when we ate bread to the full; for you have brought us out into this wilderness to kill this whole assembly with hunger." They did not long for the promised land, heaven, the resurrection, but longed for the "good old days" back in Egypt, i.e., the world. Their philosophy was let's eat and drink, for tomorrow we die.

The value we place on anything is equal to the amount we are willing to sacrifice for it. Although all these people were joined to Moses, i.e., baptized into Moses, they were in fact nothing like Moses. The true longing within their hearts could not have been for the promised land (heaven), because they were so willing to turn back to Egypt (the world) for the very small price of a dinner. In contrast, Jesus placed such a great value on mankind and heaven that He was willing to be *"baptized for them"* (immersed in death) so that we may enter the promised land—a better resurrection. Luke 12:50: "But I (Jesus) have a *baptism* to undergo, and how distressed I am until it is accomplished!"

Have we been guilty of alluring people to Christ by telling them how much of the world they could gain through Christ, instead of telling them what they must lose? James 4:3–4: "You ask and do not receive, because you ask with wrong motives, so that you may spend it on your pleasures. You adulteresses, do you not know that friendship with the world is hostility toward God? Therefore whoever wishes to be a friend of the world makes himself an enemy of God." And yet we still have preachers who boast in their worldly treasures and continue to tell others that such worldly gain is equal to God's blessing. You tell me who's right—the Holy Scriptures, or many of our present-day preachers? They both cannot be right, can they? Jesus the Son, an exact representation of God the Father, always made sure He used language as strong and as direct as possible to make absolutely sure we understood the cost of a better resurrection.

Luke 14:25–27 & 31–32: "Now great multitudes were going along with Him; and He turned and said to them, If anyone comes to Me, and does not hate his own father and mother and wife and children and brothers and sisters, yes, and even his own life, he cannot be My disciple. Whoever does not carry his own cross and come after Me cannot be My disciple. Or what king, when he sets out to meet another king in battle, will not first sit down and take counsel whether he is strong enough with *ten* thousand men to encounter the one coming against him with *twenty* thousand? Or else, while the other is still far away, he sends a delegation and asks for terms of peace." Are we willing to be *"baptized for the dead"* and become as aliens in this world? If so, then we will always be outnumbered by those who oppose us. Luke 14: 33–35: "So therefore, no one of you can be My disciple who does not give up all his own possessions. Therefore, salt is good; but if even salt has become tasteless, with what will it be seasoned? *It is useless either for the soil or for the manure pile; it is thrown out.* He who has ears to hear, let him hear." Are we losing the battle for souls because we are unwilling to be baptized for the dead, and thereby, exposing our own unbelief in a better resurrection?

2 Peter 3:10–13: "But the day of the Lord will come like a thief, in which the heavens will pass away with a roar and the elements will be destroyed with intense heat, and the earth and its works will be burned up. *Since all these things are to be destroyed in this way, what sort of people ought you to be in holy conduct and godliness, looking for and hastening the coming of the day of God,* on account of which the heavens will be destroyed by burning, and the elements will melt with intense heat! But according to His promise *we* are looking for new heavens and a new earth, in which righteousness dwells."

You tell me, what constitutes God's blessings—treasures on earth, or treasures in heaven? Or what is the measure of great faith? The amount of this world's things we are able to gain, or the things of this world we're willing to give up? Or who is the heroic Christian of faith, who becomes as salt and light to this world? The one baptized in water, or the one baptized for the dead? Have we lost our saltiness in this world, because we are unwilling to subject ourselves to being baptized for the dead? Do we despise our promised land, heaven, by quickly backing off the minute we feel any kind of deprivation? Do we quickly compromise our Christian values if our wilderness (earthly) journey becomes a bit unpleasant? *All these things are signs to both God, and this world, that we "really" do not believe in a better resurrection.* So then, the measure of our saltiness is *not* in what we say, but it is in direct proportion to what we are willing to give up.

By the mercies of God, most of us do not find ourselves in a position where our very lives are in danger for our faith; nevertheless, almost every day we are placed in a situation, or trial, to test our faith to see if it's really genuine. And every day the world watches to see through the eyes of our passion if there is really a God—if there is really a better resurrection—if there is really a heaven. Romans 5:3–5: "And not only this, but we also exult in our tribulations, knowing that tribulation brings about perseverance; and perseverance, proven character (genuineness); and proven character, hope; and hope does not disappoint, because the love (Spirit) of God has been poured out within our hearts through the Holy Spirit who was given to us." When we persevere, we are powerfully showing the world that we already have a portion of heaven (God's Spirit) within us; hence, we know with certainty that there is a better resurrection, inasmuch as God already dwells within us. *Now that's a saltiness, a passion, that neither this world, nor God can ignore.* Our lives will not only reflect being baptized for the dead, but will permeate with the fragrance of Christ for the world to *joyfully* accept, or to become *zealously* offended; and God will not be ashamed to be called our God.

Therefore, let's look at some very practical everyday expressions of being *"baptized for the dead"* in Romans 12:1–3, "I *urge you therefore, brethren, by the mercies of God, to present your bodies a living and holy sacrifice, acceptable to God,* which is your spiritual service of worship. *(How)* And do not be conformed to this world, but be transformed by the renewing of your mind, that you may prove what the will of God is, that which is good and acceptable and perfect. For through the grace given to me I say to every man among you not to think more highly of himself than he ought to think; but to think so as to have sound judgment, as God has allotted to each a measure of faith."

And again in Romans 12:6–21, "And since we have gifts that differ according to the grace given to us, let each exercise them accordingly: if prophecy, *according to the proportion of his faith;* if service, *in his serving;* or he who teaches, *in his teaching;* or he who exhorts, *in his exhortation;* he who gives, *with liberality;* he who leads, *with diligence;* he who shows mercy, *with cheerfulness.* Let love be without hypocrisy (acting). Abhor what is evil; cling to what is good. Be devoted to one another in brotherly love; give preference to one another in honor; not lagging behind in diligence, fervent in spirit, serving the Lord; rejoicing in hope, *persevering in tribulation,* devoted to prayer, contributing to the needs of the saints, practicing hospitality. Bless those who persecute you; *bless and curse not.* Rejoice with those who rejoice, and weep with those who weep. Be of the same mind toward one another; do not be haughty in mind, but associate with the lowly. Do not be wise in your own estimation. Never pay back evil for evil to anyone. Respect what is right in the sight of all men. If possible, so far as it depends on you, be at peace with all men. Never take your own revenge, beloved, but leave room for the wrath of God, for it is written, 'Vengeance is Mine, I will repay,' says the Lord. But if your enemy is hungry, feed him, and if he is thirsty, give him a drink; for in so doing you will heap burning coals upon his head. *Do not be overcome by evil, but overcome evil with good.*"

In closing, please allow me to show you a very practical application of this commentary by reading an Email I received concerning a mission trip: "While I had many conversations with various Mormon and non-Mormon individuals during our outreach, the most exciting conversation I had was with a police officer. For nearly two of the three days I served during the outreach, it rained almost constantly. Friday was the coldest day as the temperature had dropped to about 39 degrees, and even with my heavy clothes, snow boots, poncho, and umbrella I was still somewhat cold as I stood in the muddy gravel parking lot handing out the literature to the passing cars.

Right in the middle of the pouring rain, a police officer pulled up to the edge of the road, got out of the car, and walked over to me. He said, 'I'm a detective from another town who investigates double homicide cases. My job is to determine the motive behind these cases. I just came up here to help out for a few days in order to get a break from my regular job. I'm not a Mormon, or anything like that, but for the past two days I've been watching you hand this literature out and I just can't help but wonder. *Why are you doing this?* What makes your religious beliefs better than someone else's beliefs? Usually, I just drive by, but today I decided to stop and ask.'"

The moment this woman was willing to embrace the hardships of the day to reach out to people she did not know, and who most likely hated her, she began to give off the inescapable fragrance of Christ. What was her motive? She *genuinely* believed in the resurrection of the dead, and proved it by being willing to endure a trial, or hardship. This very intelligent detective was not seduced by promising the world to him, he was seduced by someone who was willing to put up with a little discomfort so a nameless stranger could obtain a better resurrection. A motive that he could neither recognize, nor understand. The world is asking, is there a God? Is there a heaven? *Our lives should be screaming yes, unless we do not really believe it ourselves.*

Acts 20:22–24: "And now, behold, bound in spirit, I am on my way to Jerusalem, not knowing what will happen to me there, except that the Holy Spirit solemnly testifies to me in every city, saying that bonds and afflictions await me. *But I do not consider my life of any account as dear to myself,* in order that I may finish my course, and the ministry which I received from the Lord Jesus, to testify solemnly of the gospel of the grace of God." All of us will be confronted by a ministry which needs to be filled, spanning from that of a prophet, to giving with liberality, to the graceful act of forgiveness; but if we count our lives as dear to ourselves in any way, that ministry call will be thwarted. Do we *really* believe in a better resurrection, or do we "eat and drink, for tomorrow we die;" hence, living our lives as if there is no resurrection at all? Our lives, our actions, will always reflect what we really believe within our hearts. The Apostle Paul endured the hardship of subjecting himself to the possibility of death (baptized for the dead), and later succumbed to death (baptized for them), because he believed in God's testimony of a better resurrection. But will we endure even the much lesser hardships of an imperfect relationship, including marriage, or the perceived indignity of overcoming evil with good, because we believe in God's testimony of a better resurrection? *Do we really believe?*

Chapter Five

Break Up Your Fallow Ground

Hosea 10:12 & 11:2: "Sow with a view to righteousness, reap in accordance with kindness; *Break up your fallow (hard, unproductive) ground, for it is time to seek the Lord until He comes to rain righteousness on you.* The more they (my Prophets) called them, the more they went from them; they kept sacrificing to the Baals and burning incense to idols."

The book of Hosea equates God's relationship and love for His creation (mankind) to that which is experienced by a husband and wife. As a husband and wife are supposed to become as one, so also was mankind created to be as one with Him (God). He created mankind (first man then woman from man) in His own image. Nevertheless, God's beloved bride (mankind) leaped into the arms of another lover (Satan) as he successfully slandered God's love and motives toward His bride, and proceeded to allure her with the illusion of self-gratification—*the illusion that somehow loving self was more precious, and had greater value and reward than being loved by another, than being the beloved of God.*

But God, still devoted and in love with His bride, devised a plan to restore her righteousness, or right standing with Him. John 17:20–21 & 23: "I do not ask in behalf of these alone, but for those also who believe in Me through their word; that they may all be one; even as Thou, Father, art in Me, and I in Thee, that they also may be in Us; that the world may believe that Thou didst send Me. I in them, and Thou in Me, that they may be perfected in unity, that the world may know that Thou didst send Me, *and didst love them, even as Thou didst love Me."* Ephesians 5:28–32: "So husbands ought also to love their own wives as their own bodies. He who loves his own wife loves himself; for no one ever hated his own flesh, but nourishes and cherishes it, just as Christ also does the church, because we are members of His body. For this cause a man shall leave his father and mother, and shall cleave to his wife; and the two shall become one flesh. *This mystery is great;* but I am speaking with reference to Christ and the church."

Tragically, as with any drug, this illusion of self-gratification (self-love) was at best nothing more than a temporary fix which left its victims in an even worse condition, wanting and empty, as a flame which would burn for eternity as all efforts to find love, contentment, and peace give way to the gashing teeth of hopelessness. *A self-perpetual hell!* An eternal, inescapable flame sustained by an inexhaustible supply of fuel—the fuel of discontentment. As with any drug, it deceived and hardened the victim's hearts into thinking if a little self-gratification brought temporary peace, an abundance would bring eternal peace; yet in reality, it brought eternal wanting and emptiness—eternal hell and death! However, God's faithful, undying, and passionate love for his bride (mankind) remained, and therefore, He was unwilling to leave His bride in such an infernal predicament. Relentlessly God cried out to her through His prophets, *"Break up your fallow ground!"* God desperately yearned to redeem His bride from such an infernal fate by replacing her adulterous heart (spirit) with His own faithful heart (spirit) through the sacrifice of His only begotten Son, Jesus.

But would the bride listen to her first and faithful husband in the face of Satan's continuing slanderous lies about God's love and motives toward His beloved? And as if his slander of God was not enough deception, he followed it up with insincere and deceitful flattery of her (the bride's) own comeliness and beauty. Tragically, God's adulterous bride continued to harden her heart against her husband; and to Satan's delight, her lover was now herself and she delighted in self-gratification at the expense of anything, or anyone. She even began to fashion gods and idols in her own image, because they would justify and not divert her passion away from self-gratification. Hence, the god she created was either a harsh god who seeks from us unimaginable horrors as penance, or duty, all for his own ghoulish self-gratification; or a mindless, oblivious god who dutifully agrees with everything we ask for, and then marvels at the wisdom of our requests. Oh, that truly is a god in our own image, but it's *not* the God of Jacob, Isaac, and Abraham, the God of the Bible, nor is it the God I serve.

It was not God's unfaithfulness, nor the lack of His love, which brought this infernal fate upon His bride; it was the fallow, adulterous heart of His bride that accepted Satan's lies and left no earth for the truth to take root. Yet, driven by a love unknown in this world, God once again through His only begotten Son, pleaded with His bride, *"Break up your fallow ground."* Jesus, using a parable, did His best to make it as clear as anyone could, that if this infernal fate of hell and death descended upon us, we had only ourselves and our own hardheartedness to blame.

The following parable identified God's love and truth (His Word) as good seed, and the soil as our heart; making it crystal clear to all that if there was a failure unto hell and death, it was caused by the hard soil of our heart, *not* God's seed—God's love—God's truth—God's word. Mark 4:14–15: "The sower sows the word. And these are the ones who are beside the road (the hard ground) where the word is sown; and when they hear, immediately Satan comes and takes away the word which has been sown in them." *I'm always amazed at the length people will go to avoid the truth and settle for a lie, hence, exposing the grotesque hardness of their heart.* These people can look at the mind-numbing complexity of just one gene and call it an accident of chance, but then look at the simplicity of a light switch and say it had to be an act of creation. It took years and a supercomputer to map the mind-numbing complexity of just one gene. A complexity that is so great, it makes no difference at all how many billions of years you add to the mathematical equation, the probability of it happening by chance remains in the realm of the impossible. These same hardhearted people will trust mathematics to send a spacecraft to the edge of our universe, but to use it to prove the existence of God—*never!* Instead, they spend all their time, and millions of dollars, looking for evidence that they came into existence from the evolution of a worm. Seeking to exchange God's glory for the glory of a worm. *If that is what this world calls wisdom, count me out!*

In the same way, we also have those who say we cannot believe in something we cannot see. But these same people will sit on a jury and listen objectively to the evidence, and based entirely on that evidence, put someone in jail for the rest of his life, or even put him/her to death. They did not *see* the crime happen, did they? Yet, when it comes to their own eternal lives, they turn their backs on the overwhelming evidence of creation and say capriciously, "We must see to believe." You would think looking at even the possibility of an eternity in hell, they would love their own lives enough to objectively look at the evidence, would you not?

God loves skeptics as long as they do not harden their hearts against the evidence. John 20:24–25 & 27–29: "But Thomas, one of the twelve, called Didymus, was not with them when Jesus came. The other disciples therefore were saying to him, 'We have seen the Lord!' But he said to them, *'Unless I shall see in His hands the imprint of the nails, and put my finger into the place of the nails, and put my hand into His side, I will not believe.'* Then He (Jesus) said to Thomas, 'Reach here your finger, and see My hands; and reach here your hand, and put it into My side; and be not unbelieving, but believing.' Thomas answered and said to Him, 'My Lord and my God!' Jesus said to him, 'Because you have seen Me, have you believed? Blessed are they who did not see, and yet believed.'" God is willing to meet you wherever you are, if your heart is right.

But seeing to believe is not the real problem, is it? Luke 16:27–31: "And he said, 'Then I beg you, Father, that you send him (Lazarus) to my father's house for I have five brothers that he may warn them, lest they also come to this place of torment.' But Abraham said, 'They have Moses and the Prophets; let them hear them.' But he said, 'No, Father Abraham, but if someone goes to them from the dead, they will repent!' But he said to him, 'If they do not listen to Moses and the Prophets, *neither will they be persuaded if someone rises from the dead.*'" There is enough historical evidence of Jesus' resurrection to convince even the worst skeptic; that is, if you're willing to seek it out. But if your heart is hard, Satan will come immediately with a lie, and the deliberation of the truth will flee from your thoughts. The lie being, you would lose your godlike status, *but in reality all you would lose is the glory of your ancestor, the worm, and exchange it for the glory and image of God.*

Mark 4:16–17: "And in a similar way these are the ones on whom seed was sown on the rocky places, who, when they hear the word, immediately receive it with joy; and they have no firm root in themselves, but are only temporary; then, when affliction or persecution arises because of the word, immediately they fall away." Here we have a people who are still hardhearted, but love themselves enough to be allured by the parts of Christianity which are attractive. These are the people who flock to the churches that prepare for them the milk and cookies of God's Word and edit out the "offensive" parts; such as the words Jesus spoke, "Anyone who wishes to come after me *must* deny himself, take up his cross, and follow me." These blind guides are indeed destined to end up in the same pit as their followers.

To show the alarming prevalence and lamentable extent of this shallowness within today's church, please allow me to once again go back to the marriage analogy God so often used in His Word. Does not the fact that divorce is as high, or higher, within the church as it is within the world also show the shallowness within our hearts? *Many are allured by someone's attractiveness, and/or someone's ability to fulfill a particular need, but when the heat of reality comes, their "love" evaporates into thin air.* Hosea 6:3–4: "So let us know, let us press on to know the Lord. His going forth is as certain as the dawn; and He will come to us like the rain, like the spring rain watering the earth. What shall I do with you, O Ephraim? What shall I do with you, O Judah? For your loyalty is like a morning cloud, and like the dew which goes away early (in the heat of the day)." Does not God's prophet Hosea describe a people whose first love is themselves—a people who will quickly discard anyone, including God, if he/she loses their perceived attractiveness, or benefit?

But you may ask, "What does divorce have to do with my Christian walk?" *There's room for only one heart within the human body; if you are shallow in your relationships with mankind, you will also be shallow in your relationship with God.* As soon as the heat comes, or God's Word steps on your toes, you will fall away, or at the very least find another church that will once again pamper and cuddle you, until a more attentive and attractive lover (church) comes along. Ask yourself, how many churches have you left, not because you prayed about it and God moved you on, nor because of doctrinal error, but just because of the heat produced by the preaching of God's Word, or some other perceived offense? Is that not evidence of a shallow, fallow heart? If so, then it's time to confess it as such, and *break up your fallow ground.*

Mark 4:18–19: "And others are the ones on whom seed was sown among the thorns; these are the ones who have heard the word, and the worries of the world, and the deceitfulness of riches, and the desires for other things enter in and choke the word, and it becomes unfruitful." Here the trouble seems to be the lack of care and cultivation, and not so much the initial hardness of the soil, or heart. Nevertheless, the outcome is no less tragic as the heart (ground) seems to be ready to receive the seed (God's Word), yet the preoccupation with the things of this world prevents any fruit production. *It's a picture of a heart (ground) that's left so uncultivated and so neglected that it allowed the thorns of this world to render the work of the seed (fruit production) ineffective.* Matthew 7:20–23: "So then, you will know them by their fruits. Not everyone who says to Me, 'Lord, Lord,' will enter the kingdom of heaven; but he who does the will of My Father who is in heaven. Many will say to Me on that day, 'Lord, Lord, did we not prophesy in Your name, and in Your name cast out demons, and in Your name perform many miracles?' And then I will declare to them, 'I never knew you; depart from Me, you who practice lawlessness.'"

I've seen so many Christians that are so preoccupied by the worries of this world, and the desire for other things that it sucked the life (God's life) right out of them. They're so focused on what they do not have, by default, they end up neglecting the one and only thing that truly matters—the things of God. They neglect the one thing which would give them abundant, eternal life to focus intensely on the temporal, which choked God right out of their heart. Habakkuk 3:17–18: "Though the fig tree should not blossom, and there be no fruit on the vines, though the yield of the olive should fail, and the fields produce no food, though the flock should be cut off from the fold, and there be no cattle in the stalls, yet I will exult in the Lord, I will rejoice in the God of my salvation." Can you tell me how the prophet Habakkuk could make such a statement? If not, I plead, no, I beg you to pull up the weeds, crucify your desire for this world, and cultivate the things of God before the implanted seed dies. Galatians 5:22–24: "But the fruit of the Spirit is love, joy, peace, patience, kindness, goodness, faithfulness, gentleness, self-control; against such things there is no law. *Now those who belong to Christ Jesus have crucified the flesh with its passions and desires.*"

Galatians 6:8: "For the one who sows to his own flesh shall from the flesh reap corruption (rot and decay), but the one who sows to the Spirit shall from the Spirit reap eternal life." *Can anyone tell me just one thing in this world which does not rot and decay?* Why then are so many of our "Christian" leaders using the rotting and decaying things of this world to motivate Christians to give? Do not our fund raisers sound just like a worldly investment seminar on how to increase our worldly wealth? These "Christian" leaders are sowing to and building up our flesh instead of sowing and building up our born-again spirit that will lead to eternal life. *Satan must love that!* When we give to ministries, should it not be out of the fruit (love) of God's Holy Spirit? The same love which motivated God to *give* that which was of most value to Him, His only Son to ransom our lives from hell and death? Do we still need to have our flesh motivated in order to give just mammon (money) toward the proclamation of the gospel to ransom other lives from hell and death? If so, then our hearts remain uncultivated and the weeds (thorns) will never allow the fruit of God's love to develop within our hearts. And if that's the case, keep your money, because you're only fooling yourselves; it does not impress God. 1 Corinthians 13:3: "And if I give all my possessions to feed the poor, and if I deliver my body to be burned, but do not have *love*, it profits me *nothing*."

The Apostle Paul gave Timothy some excellent advice, advice which we all should take to heart. 1 Timothy 6:6–12: "*But godliness actually is a means of great gain, when accompanied by contentment.* For we have brought nothing into the world, so we cannot take anything out of it either. And if we have food and covering, with these we shall be content. But those who want to get rich fall into temptation and a snare and many foolish and harmful desires that plunge men into ruin and destruction. For the love of money is a root of all sorts of evil, and some by longing for it have wandered away from the faith, and pierced themselves with many a pang. *But flee from these things, you man (woman) of God; and pursue righteousness, godliness, faith, love, perseverance, and gentleness.* Fight the good fight of faith; take hold of the eternal life to which you were called, and the good confession you made in the presence of many witnesses."

Mark 4:20: "And those are the ones on whom seed was sown on the good soil; and they hear the word and accept it (hold it dear), and bear fruit, thirty, sixty, and a hundredfold." *Why this commentary?* Because, God wants all of us to know that if we do not believe in God, or have become separated from Him, the problem exists within the soil, i.e., our heart; and therefore, we will have no excuse before the judgment seat of God. God will meet you wherever you are, if you will just *break up your fallow ground.* God cannot begin the process for us, but once we break up the fallow ground, God Himself will bring it to completion. Mark 4:26–28: "And He (Jesus) was saying, 'The kingdom of God is like a man who casts seed upon the soil; and goes to bed at night and gets up by day, and the seed sprouts up and grows. *How? He (the man) himself does not know.* The soil produces crops by itself; first the blade, then the head, then the mature grain in the head.'"

But how many times does God have to plead with us? What more can He do to show His love for us, but give His only Son as a ransom? How much evidence do you need to see before you believe that He is? As God pleads through His prophet Isaiah, "Can we not just reason together? I'm ready! Is your heart?" Isaiah 1:18: "'Come now, and let us reason together,' says the Lord, 'though your sins are as scarlet, they will be as white as snow; though they are red like crimson, they will be like wool.'"

2 Peter 3:9: "The Lord is not slow about His promise, as some count slowness, *but is patient toward you,* not wishing for any to perish but for all to come to repentance." *Nevertheless, there is an end to His patience, and He is coming again!* Luke 21:25–28: "And there will be signs in sun and moon and stars, and upon the earth dismay among nations, in perplexity at the roaring of the sea and the waves, men fainting from fear and the expectation of the things which are coming upon the world; for the powers of the heavens will be shaken. And then they will see the Son of Man (Jesus) coming in a cloud with power and great glory. But when these things begin to take place, straighten up and lift up your heads, because your redemption is drawing near" *I beg you, be ready! Before it's too late, break up your fallow ground!*

Chapter Six

We Are Not Blind
Too, Are We?

John 9:39–41: "And Jesus said, 'For judgment I came into this world, that those who do not see may see; and that those who see may become blind.' Those of the Pharisees who were with Him heard these things, and said to Him, '*We are not blind too, are we?*' Jesus said to them, 'If you were blind, you would have no sin; but since you say, '*We see,*' your sin remains.'"

Jesus, the Son of God, came to earth to give us sight, but obviously the sight Jesus was talking about was more than just physical eyesight. But tragically, this group of Pharisees had no need for Jesus, because in their heart of hearts they regarded their sight, or perception, to be without a flaw. However, they were in reality completely blind spiritually, but because they said, *"We see,"* they had no need of a physician so their malady—their sin remained. What further compounded this tragedy was the fact that these "men of God" were shepherds who were supposed to point God's people to the way, the truth, and the life, yet they themselves were blind to the pathway to God. In essence, they literally became blind guides who were appointed to guide the blind, just as Jesus said in Matthew 15:14, "Let them alone; they are blind guides of the blind. And if a blind man guides a blind man, both will fall into a pit."

Now you may be saying to yourself, *"I'm so glad I'm not like one of those blind Pharisees."* But wait, they also thought themselves to be God's chosen people and holy in God's sight. As a matter of fact, they were so proud of their self-perceived holy image, their hearts were hardened to the point that they vehemently opposed anyone, or anything that threatened to tarnish their self-perceived holy image. Besides, who does this carpenter from Nazareth think he is telling us, the holy-ones of God, that we're blind? *That's right, the Pharisees were blinded by their own comeliness and splendor.*

Or you could be saying to yourself, "But brother, I'm not a leader, or a guide; so what does this commentary have to do with me?" But you are mistaken. If you call yourself a Christian, you are a witness (guide) to the unsaved. Everything the world (unsaved) sees you do, or hears you say, becomes part of their definition of Christianity. Therefore, we do not have the luxury to look past Jesus' words to Pharisees. But instead, let us fearfully and with great regard consider the words of Jesus concerning this blindness so that we may avoid the same tragic outcome; saying, *"We see,"* but end up being nothing more than a blind guide for the blind with both of us falling into a pit.

Matthew 23:16–22: "Woe to you, blind guides, who say, *'Whoever swears by the temple, that is nothing; but whoever swears by the gold of the temple, he is obligated.'* You fools and blind men; which is more important, the gold, or the temple that sanctified the gold? And, *'Whoever swears by the altar, that is nothing, but whoever swears by the offering upon it, he is obligated.'* You blind men, which is more important, the offering, or the altar that sanctifies the offering? Therefore, he who swears by the altar, swears both by the altar and by everything on it. And he who swears by the temple, swears both by the temple and by Him who dwells within it. And he who swears by heaven, swears both by the throne of God and by Him who sits upon it."

In the above verses of Scripture, Jesus made a profound observation. By the Pharisees saying, "Whoever swears by the temple, that is nothing; but whoever swears by the gold of the temple, he is obligated," and saying, "Whoever swears by the altar, that is nothing, but whoever swears by the offering upon it, he is obligated," *were actually saying that it was the gold and offerings that constituted the glory of the temple and God was summarily vanquished to some other inferior role.* That's right! In their eyes, it was the gold and offerings which were of greatest value and thereby obligated the oath. Oh, they could look in the mirror and without hesitation call themselves servants of God, but their own words betrayed them. They were indeed worshiping a god, but the god they were worshiping was the gold and offerings. The Pharisees were in a state of self-deceit—blinded by their own hearts, and consequently, blind guides for the blind.

Tragically, the Pharisees in their hearts treasured the temple's gold and offerings so much that the gold and offerings became the temple's glory; but they should have been treasuring the things of God so that God's glory would have received the preeminent place within their hearts. And what is God's glory? Exodus 33:22 & 34:6–7: "And it will come about, while *My glory* is passing by, that I will put you in the cleft of the rock and cover you with My hand until I have passed by. Then the Lord passed by in front of him and proclaimed, 'The Lord, the Lord God, compassionate and gracious, slow to anger, and abounding in loving-kindness and truth; who keeps loving-kindness for thousands, who forgives iniquity, transgression and sin; yet He will by no means leave the guilty unpunished, visiting the iniquity of fathers on the children and on the grandchildren to the third and fourth generations." This impiety toward God, or double mindedness, was also confirmed by Jesus Himself with the very next line in Matthew, Matthew 23:23, "Woe to you, scribes and Pharisees, hypocrites! For you tithe mint and dill and cummin, and have neglected the *weightier* provisions of the law: *justice and mercy and faithfulness*; but these are the things you should have done without neglecting the others."

Jesus said in Matthew 6:19–24, "Do not lay up for yourselves treasures upon earth, where moth and rust destroy, and where thieves break in and steal. But lay up for yourselves treasures in heaven, where neither moth nor rust destroys, and where thieves do not break in or steal; for where your treasure is, there will your heart be also. The lamp of the body is the eye; if therefore your eye is clear, your whole body will be full of light. *But if your eye is bad, your whole body will be full of darkness. If therefore the light that is in you is darkness, how great is the darkness!* No one can serve two masters; for either he will hate the one and love the other, or he will hold to one and despise the other. You cannot serve God and mammon (money)." This impiety toward God, or double mindedness, caused a darkness within their hearts that was so great and so comprehensive, that the Scribes and Pharisees completely missed God's salvation—God's deliverer, and continued to insist they had need of nothing.

I don't think Jesus could have made it any clearer than He did in Matthew 6:19–24, you are either in total light, or you are in total darkness and it's all determined by what you treasure within your heart. That's why Jesus continued on and said in Matthew 6:25, *"For this reason I say to you, do not be anxious for your life, as to what you shall eat, or what you shall drink; nor for your body, as to what you shall put on. Is not life more than food, and the body than* clothing?" Which brings us to this question: What is of most importance, or of greatest value in your life, the righteousness and glory of God, or the so-called glory of this world? But let us not be too quick to answer like the Pharisees, but with humility of mind, let us take a second look to see if there is anything in our (your) heart that displaces God's glory with something in this world which actually has no glory at all, *something that would cause a veil of blindness to descend upon us (you).*

Matthew 19:16–25: "And behold, one came to Him and said, 'Teacher, what good thing shall I do that I may obtain eternal life?' And He (Jesus) said to him, 'Why are you asking Me about what is good? There is only One who is good; but if you wish to enter into life, keep the commandments.' He said to Him, 'Which ones?' And Jesus said, 'You shall not commit murder; You shall not commit adultery; You shall not steal; You shall not bear false witness; Honor your father and mother; and You shall love your neighbor as yourself.' The young man said to Him, *'All these things I have kept; what am I still lacking?'* Jesus said to him, 'If you wish to be complete, go and sell your possessions and give to the poor, and you shall have treasure in heaven; and come, follow Me.' But when the young man heard this statement, *he went away grieved; for he was one who owned much property.* And Jesus said to His disciples, 'Truly I say to you, it is hard for a rich man to enter the kingdom of heaven. And again I say to you, it is easier for a camel to go through the eye of a needle, than for a rich man to enter the kingdom of God.' *And when the disciples heard this, they were very astonished and said, 'Then who can be saved?'"*

I heard it said by a very popular TV preacher one day that the reason Jesus told the rich young ruler to sell all he had was so Jesus could multiply his wealth back to him. Wait a minute, you mean Jesus who was born into this world in a cave set aside for animals, whose first bed was nothing more than an animal's feeding trough, and finally left this world with nothing more than the clothes He had on His back was concerned about this man's wealth? *That TV preacher could not have been more wrong!* Jesus wanted to be sure that the rich young ruler's eyes remained clear (single) in focus so his heart would be and remain full of light, and free from the potential intrusion of darkness. Jesus wanted to impress upon both him and His disciples that there's room for only one God in our hearts. Jesus wanted to impress upon both him and His disciples that there was only one treasure that was truly important and that treasure was worth more than everything else in this world combined. *And that treasure was our rebirth through the death and resurrection of God's only Son Jesus unto eternal life—that treasure was the kingdom of heaven.*

Matthew 13:44–46: "The kingdom of heaven is like a treasure hidden in the field, which a man found and hid; and from joy over it he goes and sells *all* that he has, and buys that field. Again, the kingdom of heaven is like a merchant seeking fine pearls, and upon finding one pearl of great value, he went and sold *all* that he had, and bought it." And Luke 12:13–15: "And someone in the crowd said to Him, 'Teacher, tell my brother to divide the family inheritance with me.' But He said to him, 'Man, who appointed Me a judge or arbiter over you?' And He said to them, '*Beware, and be on your guard against every form of greed; for not even when one has an abundance does his life consist of his possessions.*'" And finally Matthew 16:26: "For what will a man be profited, if he gains the whole world, and forfeits his soul? Or what will a man give in exchange for his soul?"

John 6:26–27: "Jesus answered them and said, 'Truly, truly, I say to you, you seek Me, not because you saw signs, but because you ate of the loaves, and were filled. Do not work for the food which perishes, *but for the food which endures to eternal life,* which the Son of Man shall give to you, for on Him the Father, even God, has set His seal.'" Sadly, Jesus knew the crowds were coming to Him in order to fulfill their earthly hunger as they were completely blind to their greatest need, deliverance, i.e., salvation. *Jesus performed miracles in this world (Egypt) for only one reason, to make known to all that He, just like Moses, was God's deliverer to lead us out of Egypt, to lead us out of Satan's world.* Acts 7:36–37: "This man (Moses) led them out (of Egypt, i.e., this world), *performing wonders and signs in the land of Egypt* and in the Red Sea and in the wilderness for forty years. This is the Moses who said to the sons of Israel, *'God shall raise up for you a prophet like me from your brethren.'"* And God did raise up another prophet in the order of (like) Moses, His only Son, Jesus.

But as the people were with Moses in the wilderness, so were the people that came to see Jesus, they were only interested in how God was going to fulfill their earthly desires in the here and now as they wandered through this wilderness of Satan's world. Psalm 78:18, 22, 40–41: "And in their heart they put God to the test by asking for food according to their desire. Because they did not believe in God, and did not trust in His salvation. How often they rebelled against Him in the wilderness (this world), and grieved Him in the desert! And again and again they tempted (tested) God, and *pained* the *Holy One of Israel.*" And even today, it's still no different as we gather by the hundreds of thousands to receive our miracle at some miracle crusade. *As we keep our eyes and hearts intensely focused and zealous for the things we lack from this world's so-called glory, while at the same time we hardly give any notice, or attention to the things we lack of God's true glory within our hearts.*

John 6:28–29 & 32–33: "They said therefore to Him, 'What shall we do, that we may work the works of God?' Jesus answered and said to them, *'This is the work of God, that you believe in Him whom He has sent.'* Jesus therefore said to them, 'Truly, truly, I say to you, it is not Moses who has given you the bread out of heaven, but it is My Father who gives you the true bread out of heaven. For the bread of God is that which comes down out of heaven, *and gives life to the world.'"* But alas, with hearts full of greed, not only did the crowds continue to lust after miracles, they also lusted after the ability to perform the miracles themselves. *They were not interested in some far off promised land.* Psalm 106:24–25: "Then they despised the pleasant (promised) land; they did not believe in His word, but grumbled in their tents; they did not listen to the voice of the Lord." And John 6:66–69: "As a result of this many of His disciples withdrew, and were not walking with Him anymore. Jesus said therefore to the twelve, 'You do not want to go away also, do you?' Simon Peter answered Him, 'Lord, to whom shall we go? *You have words of eternal life. And we have believed and have come to know that You are the Holy One of God.'"*

Finally, Peter got it right: the miracles Jesus performed, as with Moses, were meant to only expose Jesus as the deliverer sent by God, the one who would set us free from the bondage of hell and death, and lead the way to the promised land, i.e., heaven. Luke 4:17–21: "And the book of the prophet Isaiah was handed to Him. And He (Jesus) opened the book, and found the place where it was written, *the Spirit of the Lord is upon Me, because He anointed Me to preach the gospel to the poor. He has sent Me to proclaim release to the captives, and recovery of sight to the blind, to set free those who are downtrodden, to proclaim the favorable year of the Lord.* And He closed the book, and gave it back to the attendant, and sat down; and the eyes of all in the synagogue were fixed upon Him. And He began to say to them, 'Today this Scripture has been fulfilled in your hearing.'" *Or you could say it this way, the Spirit of the Lord is upon Me to let all know that I am the deliverer sent from God to lead you out of Egypt (this world of Satan's) and into the Promised Land (heaven).*

Mark 2:3–11: "And they came, bringing to Him (Jesus) a paralytic, carried by four men. And being unable to get to Him because of the crowd, they removed the roof above Him; and when they had dug an opening, they let down the pallet on which the paralytic was lying. And Jesus seeing their faith said to the paralytic, *'My son, your sins are forgiven.'* But there were some of the scribes sitting there and reasoning in their hearts, 'Why does this man speak that way? He is blaspheming; who can forgive sins but God alone?' And immediately Jesus, aware in His spirit that they were reasoning that way within themselves, said to them, 'Why are you reasoning about these things in your hearts? Which is easier, to say to the paralytic, 'Your sins are forgiven'; or to say, 'Arise, and take up your pallet and walk'? *But in order that you may know that the Son of Man has authority on earth to forgive sins, (i.e., God's deliverer),* I say to you (the paralytic), rise, take up your pallet and go home.'"

John 16:33: "These things I have spoken to you, that in Me you may have peace. *In the world you have tribulation, but take courage; I have overcome the world."* Over and over again, Jesus tried to make us understand that our greatest need was deliverance and salvation *out* of Satan's world, not salvation *in* Satan's world. Yet, even today the words of our prayers betray the focus of our hearts as we pray for what this world calls glory, and delegate what God calls glory to some obscure spiritual concept. We zealously pray for health, wealth, and prosperity, but at the same time scarcely mention in our prayers a desire for the *weightier* provisions of faithfulness, mercy, forgiveness, and a heart like unto our Lord and God's which is the heart of a servant. Am I saying we should never pray to God for earthly provisions as we walk this wilderness journey here on earth? No! God forbid! But we all need to have our eyes considerably more focused on the *weightier* provisions and give our hearts over to trusting in God's salvation (provisions), i.e., not being fearful to end our prayers as Jesus did with the words, *"Yet not as I will, but as You will."*

If we're willing to accept it, Revelation 3:15–17 may just be a warning for us, "I know your deeds, that you are neither cold nor hot; I would that you were cold or hot. So because you are lukewarm, and neither hot nor cold, I will spit you out of My mouth. Because you say, 'I am rich, and have become wealthy, and have need of nothing,' and you do not know that you are wretched and miserable and poor and blind and naked."

So what do we need to do to keep ourselves from becoming blind too? Matthew 6:31–34: "Do not be anxious then, saying, 'What shall we eat?' or 'What shall we drink?' or 'With what shall we clothe ourselves?' For all these things the Gentiles eagerly seek; for your heavenly Father knows that you need all these things. *But seek first His kingdom and His righteousness; and all these things shall be added to you.* Therefore do not be anxious for tomorrow; for tomorrow will care for itself. Each day has enough trouble of its own." And pray at *all* times that our Lord will keep us (you) from temptation and Satan's schemes.

Chapter Seven

The Tragedy of Being *Left Behind*

Matthew 7:15–23: "Beware of the false prophets, who come to you in sheep's clothing, but inwardly are ravenous wolves. You will know them by their fruits. Grapes are not gathered from thorn bushes, nor figs from thistles, are they? Even so, every good tree bears good fruit; but the bad tree bears bad fruit. A good tree cannot produce bad fruit, nor can a bad tree produce good fruit. Every tree that does not bear good fruit is cut down and thrown into the fire. So then, you will know them by their fruits. *Not everyone who says to Me, 'Lord, Lord,' will enter the kingdom of heaven;* but he who does the *will* of My Father who is in heaven. *Many* will say to Me on that day (the day of the Lord), 'Lord, Lord, did we not prophesy in Your name, and in Your name cast out demons, and in Your name perform many miracles?' *And then I will declare to them, 'I never knew you; depart from Me, you who practice (whose lifestyle is) lawlessness.'*"

From the beginning of my Christian walk I saw the above end-time prophecy to be the most tragic, the most lamentable end-time prophecy in the Bible. Tragic, inasmuch as it's clearly understood that our Lord was speaking to those who profess themselves to be Christians when He said, "And then I will declare to them, 'I never knew you; depart from Me, you who practice lawlessness.'" They were professing Christians who were deceived into a state of complacency—deceived into maintaining an affinity with the world's moralities by false prophets, i.e., wolves in sheep's clothing. Lamentable, knowing this worldliness or lawlessness would be the attribute which would permeate the end-time "Christian" Church; inasmuch as Jesus chose to use the word *many* as He described those who say, "Lord, Lord," yet they were *left behind!*

The Apostle Paul said it this way in 2 Thessalonians 2:1–3, "Now we request you, brethren, with regard to the coming of our Lord Jesus Christ, and our gathering together to Him, that you may not be quickly shaken from your composure or be disturbed either by a spirit or a message or a letter as if from us, to the effect that the day of the Lord has come. Let no one in any way deceive you, for it will not come unless the *apostasy* comes first, and the man of lawlessness is revealed, the son of destruction."

The Greek word *apostasia*, which we translate apostasy in the above verse, is a composite word made up of *apo* (from) and *histemi* (to place or stand). *Although many think the great apostasy the Apostle Paul was talking about indicated a time of great disassociation with Christianity in general, I maintain a better understanding of the word apostasy used by Paul would be a disassociation from sound doctrine, yet maintaining the use of the word Christianity.* We can come to this conclusion as Paul goes on to say in 2 Thessalonians 2:10, "Because they did not receive the love of the truth so as to be saved." And again, Paul said in 2 Timothy 4:3–4, "For the time will come when they will not endure sound doctrine; but wanting to have their ears tickled, they will accumulate for themselves teachers in accordance to their own desires; and will turn away their ears from the truth, and will turn aside to myths."

In other words, the above verses of Scripture paint a picture of the end-time apostate Church as being filled with signs, wonders, and miracles, yet void of any evidence of the sanctifying work of the Holy Spirit unto godliness. A Church whose morals are becoming indistinguishable from the secular world. A Church wishing to have their ears tickled by having their own desires validated instead of God's. A church led by wolves in sheep's clothing who are seeking their own glory instead of God's. Loving themselves more than the sheep, they seek to maintain their fame and fortune by tickling ears and avoiding any mention of the offense of the cross. For fame and fortune, they give their flock exactly what they want to hear, which is: How to get their desires fulfilled from God through the tenacity of self-willed prayer, and at the same time, completely avoid the teaching of submissiveness—the self-denial demeanor of the cross. These self-seekers are always learning, but never coming to understand that having a heart after God's own heart, a heart passionately panting after God to fulfill His desires, is the only *true* portrayal of knowing God, or better yet, God knowing you.

Matthew 16:24–26: "Then Jesus said to His disciples, 'If anyone wishes to come after Me, let him deny himself, and take up his cross, and follow Me. For whoever wishes to save his life shall lose it; but whoever loses his life for My sake shall find it. For what will a man be profited, if he gains the whole world, and forfeits his soul?'" Satan tried to tickle Jesus' ears with the same self-indulgent, offense avoiding, cross avoiding spirit in Matthew 16:21–23, "From that time Jesus Christ began to show His disciples that He must go to Jerusalem, and *suffer* many things from the elders and chief priests and scribes, and be killed, and be raised up on the third day. And Peter took Him aside and began to rebuke Him, saying, *'God forbid it, Lord! This shall never happen to You.'* But He turned and said to Peter, *'Get behind Me, Satan! You are a stumbling block to Me; for you are not setting your mind on God's interests, but man's.'"*

Tragically as the Church becomes more and more statistically like the world in sin, wants, and desires, the Church also becomes more and more appealing to the world. As the Church becomes more and more appealing to the world, as the offense of the cross is removed, the Church will proportionally begin to increase in number. Puffed up with pride, do we then delude ourselves into thinking we are doing a great work for God, inasmuch as we think an increase in number to be synonymous with revival? *Is making God's Church more and more palatable to the world and becoming successful in marketing God's Church to the world, revival?* Ironically, rapid church growth can be nothing more than an end-time sign of an apostate Church, the very thing we would expect to see if we were indeed approaching the end-time return of our Lord. Hence, we find ourselves living in a very dangerous time, being seduced by the appearance of revival, yet in reality it's nothing more than the prophesied apostasy.

You might ask, "If the outward display of signs, wonders, miracles, and even saying, 'Lord, Lord,' will not save us from the wrath to come, what will?" The answer to that dilemma is actually quite apparent, we simply must find another way to examine ourselves to see if God abides in us, and we in Him, before we find out the truly tragic way by being *left behind*. We begin our alternative self-examination by having a good understanding of the difference between regret and repentance, works and fruit. And finally, we must understand how God's grace not only can coexist with His law, but how grace works to establish God's law. Therefore, let's first examine the difference between regret and repentance.

Regret is something the secular world understands very well. Regret is something you feel after the repercussions of your deed are revealed over time. In other words, you begin your deed believing that you are totally justified, because of the circumstances that surrounded you at the time. But afterward, a day, or perhaps years later, you discover that the repercussions of your deed left you in a worst state; ergo, you *regret* doing the said deed. Hence, you do not regret the deed itself, but you do regret the very unpleasant repercussions. Therefore, those who are restrained by regret are restrained only by the law of punishment, which is the only way the lawless can be restrained as they loathe only the punishment and not the deed itself. *Hence, if regret was the motivation which drove you to Jesus, then you remain lawless and you perceive Jesus as nothing more than fire (hell) insurance.* But the Son of God was not crucified to become your fire insurance, He died to destroy the works of the evil one. 1 John 3:8: "The Son of God appeared for this purpose, that He might *destroy* the works (lawlessness or sin) of the devil."

On the other hand, the Greek word for repentance in our Bible is *metanoeo* which is a composite word made up from *noeo* (to know), and *meta* (after). Therefore, the biblical definition for the word repentance literally means to completely change one's mind after receiving a mind changing revelation. Or you can say it this way: After hearing God's Word you have a moment of spiritual insight—a spiritual unveiling—so as to become exceedingly aware of the depraved nature and sinfulness of sin itself. Consequently, you no longer embrace the world's view of right and wrong, but thoroughly and completely embrace God's view. No longer are you restrained by the repercussions (punishment) of sin, but you are repulsed by sin itself. *You now have such a disdain for the depravity and sinfulness of sin you groan within wishing to be cleansed (forgiven) of its defilement. You groan within for your old spirit, which is*

dead to God, to be replaced with a new spirit which is alive to God.
You earnestly wish to change kingdoms, i.e., you wish to leave the
realm of Satan's kingdom and leadership, and be reborn (born-
again) into God's kingdom and leadership. *This type of true biblical
repentance will prepare the way for Jesus to do His work within you.*
By His death, He paid the price for your sin, thereby, cleansing
(forgiving) you of sin's defilement. Now cleansed by the blood of
Jesus, you are prepared to receive God's Holy Spirit. Prepared to be
reborn (born-again), causing you to become alive to God, and vic-
toriously ushered into God's kingdom.

Now let's look at the difference between works and fruit. The
definition of works is: To apply personal effort in order to achieve
a desired personal outcome. God gave us His law to show us the
work that must be done in *perfection* in order to achieve the desired outcome of heaven. But works lost its power to achieve this
desired outcome as we lost our *perfection* with the fall of Adam.
Consequently, all that God's law accomplished was to expose the
lawlessness which now dwells within us. In essence, God's law
made sin come alive, inasmuch as it exposed sin to be sin. *God's
law also exposed the immense distance we had traveled from God's
image, the image we were originally created to reflect.* Now the best
that the Law can hope to accomplish is to act as a restrainer until
our *perfection* could be reclaimed by the blood of God's only Son,
wiping our account (past, present, and future) clean of sin's defilement. Through His sacrifice, we now have the opportunity to receive His *perfection* as our own, thereby, delivering us from the
hopelessness of our works.

But you might ask, "Did you not start this commentary with a
quote from Jesus saying, 'And then I will declare to them, I never
knew you; depart from Me, you who practice (whose lifestyle is)
lawlessness.' Therefore, how can you now say works of the Law

are done away with?" I can say this because of the context of the Scripture where it was taken. *The entire scriptural context was about fruit and not works.* I understand on the surface both works and fruit appear to be the same, but in reality they are immeasurably different.

Fruit is an expression of a work already accomplished, ergo, we have the expression, "The fruit of our labor." But the fruit we'll be talking about is the fruit produced by the work of God, Jesus. *As we are born-again with God's Holy Spirit through the work (death and resurrection) of God's only Son, is it too difficult to believe that the very natural expression (fruit) of the born-again believer (reborn with God's Holy Spirit) is holy fruit?* Therefore, Jesus was saying, "If you identify yourself as a Christian, reborn with God's Holy Spirit, do not deceive yourself; if your lifestyle remains lawless, where then is the evidence (fruit) of the indwelling Holy Spirit? Does the Holy Spirit produce bad fruit? God forbid!" 1 John 3:8–10: "The Son of God appeared for this purpose, that He might destroy the works of the devil. No one who is born of God practices (a lifestyle of) sin, because His seed (Holy Spirit) abides in him; and he cannot sin, because he is born of God. By this the children of God and the children of the devil are obvious."

So then, fruit is an expression of salvation, but not *the means of salvation.* Let me ask you something in regard to works. Before you were born-again, did you lie in bed worrying if you were a bad enough sinner that day to get into hell? Of course not! That would be absurd! The fact is that you were already in Satan's kingdom and the natural fruit you produced was sin (lawlessness), restrained only by society's "*current*" set of moralities; a fruit increasing in lawlessness as God's influence is removed from society. In the same way, neither should Christians lie in bed worrying if they were a good enough saint (holy one) that day to get into heaven. The fact is, if you are born-again, you are already in God's kingdom and the natural fruit produced is righteousness (holiness), restrained only by our still fallen (depraved) flesh; a fruit increasing in holiness as we crucify the influence in our lives of the depraved nature of our flesh.

And finally, let's talk about God's *amazing grace*. Let's discover how God's amazing grace not only can coexist with His law, but how grace works to establish God's law. Paul tells us in Titus 2:11–14, "For the grace of God has appeared, bringing salvation to all men, *instructing us to deny ungodliness and worldly desires and to live sensibly, righteously and godly in the present age*, looking for the blessed hope and the appearing of the glory of our great God and Savior, Christ Jesus; who gave Himself for us, *that He might redeem us from every lawless deed and purify for Himself a people for His own possession, zealous for good deeds.*" That's right, it is grace's job to make us zealous for good deeds and purify us from sin. When grace finds us in sin, grace will with great tenacity convict our hearts. Grace is the hound from heaven that will not let go until we relent. Grace will bring upon us discipline, even severe discipline if needed to get us to relent from our sin and say yes to God. Grace is also extremely patient in its work of sanctification. If needed, grace will patiently reprove us several times a day in order to accomplish the work of God's Son within us. *Hence, grace will never, never become our apologist for sin!*

But brother, are you not painting a very harsh picture of grace? God forbid! I paint a picture of an exceedingly loving grace that *refuses* to allow you and me to be judged and condemned with the world. In fact, if this is the grace you find at work within you, it's proof positive of God's love for you, and it's confirmation of your adoption into God's family. *It's proof positive that you have the right— no, the privilege—to cry out to God using the words Abba (my) Father.* The writer of the book of Hebrews puts it this way in Hebrews

12:5–10, "My son, do not regard lightly the discipline of the Lord, nor faint when you are reproved by Him; for those whom the Lord loves He disciplines, and He scourges every son whom He receives. It is for discipline that you endure; *God deals with you as with sons; for what son is there whom his father does not discipline?* But if you are without discipline, of which all have become partakers, then you are illegitimate children and not sons. Furthermore, we had earthly fathers to discipline us, and we respected them; shall we not much rather be subject to the Father of spirits, and live? For they disciplined us for a short time as seemed best to them, *but He disciplines us for our good, that we may share His holiness.*"

But wait! I'm not done! What makes grace truly amazing is grace's awesome ability to remove the defilement of sin so completely, it's just as if we had never sinned at all. In other words, once we relent and say yes to God and no to our sinful depraved flesh, grace picks us up, embraces us, and empowers us to press on to the finish line. Grace will remove all traces of condemnation and reaffirm our place in God's family. There is a verse in the song "Amazing Grace" which expresses this truth in awesome brevity and beauty. It goes something like this: "It's grace that taught my heart to fear, and grace my fears relieved." Please allow me to elaborate. Grace teaches us to fear (reverence) and desire God's holiness, while at the same time, relieves our fears of condemnation. Grace will establish a peace within our hearts based on the security of knowing that God will never leave us nor forsake us. It was grace that allowed the Apostle Paul to say in Philippians 3:12–14, "Not that I have already obtained it, or have already become perfect, but I press on in order that I may lay hold of that for which also I was laid hold of by Christ Jesus. Brethren, I do not regard myself as having laid hold of it yet; but one thing I do: forgetting what lies behind and reaching forward to what lies ahead, I press on toward the goal for the prize of the upward call of God in Christ Jesus."

At first, I was going to use this commentary to point out the evidence (fruit) I saw to confirm that we are indeed living in the age that the Apostle Paul called the great *apostasy*. But our Lord stopped me. He reminded me that He called me to heal and restore, not to criticize and condemn. God asked me to simply point out the cause and to forget about the symptoms (evidence), inasmuch as pointing out the symptoms would truly accomplish nothing. However, if I would point out the cause, it would also make known to all the way to be restored. Therefore, I endeavored to place before you a warning to watch out for wolves in sheep's clothing, who see you as nothing more than an asset to devour. Ravenous wolves who will tickle your ears, and even entertain you, in order to maintain their fame, fortune, and church size. I also endeavored to place before you a way to re-evaluate your own heart to see if God is in you, and if you are in Him. For it's my heart-felt desire that everyone who identifies himself/herself as a Christian and says, "Lord, Lord," would be a Christian indeed. For if you are a Christian in name only, you will most assuredly be *left behind!*

Chapter Eight

The Sound of the Trumpet

Jeremiah 4:19: "My soul, my soul! I am in anguish! Oh, my heart! My heart is pounding in me; I cannot be silent, because you have heard, O my soul, *the sound of the trumpet,* the alarm of war."

On September 11, 2001, we heard *"The Sound Of The Trumpet,"* the call to war, when the World Trade Towers were mercilessly and savagely attacked by terrorists. The loss of innocent human life was both devastating and tragic. *In consternation, we all beheld the face of pure evil!* With tears and in horror we all watched as a few of the innocent victims of this evil chose to leap to their death to avoid the horror of death by fire. As I was watching this horror unfold, God reminded me that Satan was the administrator of all terror and deceptive propaganda (lies) in the world. John 8:44: "He (Satan) was a *murderer* from the beginning, and does not stand in the truth, because there is no truth in him. Whenever he speaks a lie, he speaks from his own nature; for he is a *liar,* and the father of lies."

Nevertheless, as it should be, the world's passion and focus were on the temporal needs of the sorely afflicted, and the discharge of justice upon Osama bin Laden and other terrorists like him. But on the other hand, we Christians must *not* abandon our passion and focus to overcome and defeat the author and father of all terrorism, the terrorist of our *eternal* spirit and soul, Satan. Satan incites killing for no other reason but hate, hatred for God and God's prize creation, mankind, whom God made in His own image. Satan's weapons of war are lies, deception, and seduction which all conspire together to inflame the hatred and to conceal God's love for mankind. Whereas, our weapons of war are truth (God's Word), empowered by the Holy Spirit and love—God's love which now dwells within us as we are born-again with His Holy Spirit. *Hence, the repercussions of us (God's Church) taking lightly our terrorist (Satan) are immeasurably greater than the World Trade Towers tragedy, inasmuch as eternity is immeasurable greater than the temporal.*

Matthew 11:12: "And from the days of John the Baptist until now the kingdom of heaven suffers violence (or is forcibly entered), and violent men take it by force (or seize it by force)." The word "force" in this quote from Scripture is the Greek word *harpazo* from which we get our word rapture. In other words, Jesus was telling us that Satan will not give up his captives without a fight. We must forcibly snatch his captives away and set them free. We cannot—we must not remain apathetic as we alone hold the keys (knowledge) to enter heaven. This does not mean we can "force" someone to accept the key to heaven, i.e., Jesus; but we must forcibly (actively) proclaim the gospel and God's Word in the face of Satan's hindrances and hatred. We must be willing to lay down our lives to get the key to heaven (the gospel) to Satan's captives, even if only one will accept it. *If God the Son was willing to leave heaven and all its blessings to suffer the excruciating pain of the cross to give you and me the key to heaven, setting us free from an eternity in hell, what are we willing to give up to get this key to heaven, this gospel, this freedom to another captive of Satan's terrorism?*

This is not to say that the World Trade Towers were not immensely horrible and grievous, but God also wants His Church to have an eternal perspective over and above the temporal perspective of the world. Nor is it unloving for us (Christians) to maintain our eternal perspective in the face of such a grievous tragedy; unless you think Jesus, God forbid, was unloving when He made the following statements: Luke 12:4–5: *"And I say to you, My friends, do not be afraid of those who kill the body, and after that have no more that they can do. But I will warn you whom to fear: fear the one who after He has killed has authority to cast into hell; yes, I tell you, fear Him!"* And John 6:27: "Do not work for the food which perishes, but for the food which endures to eternal life, which the Son of Man shall give to you, for on Him the Father, even God, has set His seal." And John 6:49–50: "Your fathers ate the manna in the wilderness, and they died. This is the bread which comes down out of heaven, so that one may eat of it and not die." And finally John 6:57–58: "As the living Father sent Me, and I live because of the Father, so he who eats Me, he also shall live because of Me. This is the bread which came down out of heaven; not as the fathers ate, and died, he who eats this bread shall live forever."

But concerning the temporal, I was both astonished and tremendously impressed by how the world responded to this grievous terrorist attack. Their passion and focus on the temporal should be both applauded and praised. However, as I was dwelling on the world's remarkable response to the temporal, my sense of admiration for the world's response was changed to tears of sorrow when our Lord led me to read the following: Luke 16:8–15: *"And his master praised the unrighteous steward because he had acted shrewdly;*

for the sons of this age are more shrewd in relation to their own kind than the sons of light. And I say to you, make friends for yourselves by means of the mammon of unrighteousness; that when it fails, they may receive you into the eternal dwellings. He who is faithful in a very little thing is faithful also in much; and he who is unrighteous in a very little thing is unrighteous also in much. If therefore you have not been faithful in the use of unrighteous mammon, who will entrust the true riches to you? And if you have not been faithful in the use of that which is another's, who will give you that which is your own? No servant can serve two masters; for either he will hate the one, and love the other, or else he will hold to one, and despise the other. You cannot serve God and mammon."

I instantly knew in my heart what our Lord wanted me to do. Our Lord wanted me to rehearse the world's passionate response to terrorism in the temporal and place it side by side to our response to terrorism in the greater eternal. *To place the world's passionate response to the horrors of temporal death, beside our (the Church's) response to the greater horror of eternal death, i.e., hell.* To say the least, I did not want to do it, because in my heart of hearts I already knew the outcome of such a comparison. It would reveal a lukewarmness within God's Church. Revelation 3:15–16: "I know your deeds, that you are neither cold nor hot; I would that you were cold or hot. So because you are lukewarm, and neither hot nor cold, I will spit you out of My mouth." But then again, I thought, I would rather have it revealed to all this side of heaven so all would have an opportunity to change and repent. Therefore, I began to do even as my Lord directed me to do.

My heart was so warmed when I saw the outpouring and generosity of the secular world in response to the devastating disaster brought upon us by the terrorists. Even all of Hollywood came together to put on a fund raiser that raised somewhere around

$350 million. Tears came to my eyes as I saw little children emptying their precious little banks filled with coins in order to help the victims of this terrorism. *And the only motivation the secular world needed was to see their fellow humankind in need.* Not once did I hear anyone promise a hundredfold return on their donation to arouse their benevolent spirit and passion. All the secular world needed to see was a temporal need, or crisis to move their innermost bowels of compassion. *Are we (Christians) no longer aroused simply by people's need of eternal life and salvation from hell?* Must there always be something in it for us such as a hundredfold return, before our compassion is moved? The reality of hell and its eternal fiery horrors were enough to move Jesus' innermost compassion and motivated Him to leave heaven and embrace a cross. Do we need more of a motivation than the reality of hell to move our innermost compassion? Do we still need to know what's in it for me? *If we (God's Church) are so lukewarm and passionless on the reality of heaven and hell, should we be surprised if the world remains unimpressed and unresponsive?*

James 3:1: "Let not many of you become teachers, my brethren, knowing that as such we shall incur a stricter judgment." I've seen many in a leadership position, for the sake of expediency, appeal to a Christian's carnal nature (flesh) instead of appealing to and building up the new born-again spirit within. For example, to raise finances they will appeal to fleshly greed by promising a hundredfold return. The hideous outcome of these teachers that appeal to our greed (flesh) to raise funds is that many now equate being rich in this world for being blessed by God. Hence, without giving it a second thought, their disciples live in worldly opulence, boasting in their earthly treasures. The end result is less money for the gospel as they follow their teacher's instructions precisely and amass huge earthly treasures for themselves. *Satan is a shrewd enemy indeed as he knows that an unfunded ministry is no threat to him!*

As for me and this ministry, we'll just keep our eyes on the heavenly treasure, because we know it is also written: *"You cannot serve both God and mammon!"*

But, brother, are we not told in Malachi 3:10 that we could test God with our donation and He would multiply it back to us until it overflows? Well, you just made my point. Have you ever read all of Malachi? *Malachi was preaching to one of the most corrupt, lukewarm, carnal, worldly, and secular groups of people in the whole Bible.* Is that really the book you would like to be identified with when you see Jesus face to face? Yes, because of the hardness of the people's heart, God relented and allowed this group to test Him. Yet, we also know without a doubt that it is God's *perfect* will not to test Him at all. As for me, I do not study the Bible to see how close to the *imperfect* I can get; I study to find God's perfect will, and with help from the Holy Spirit, to do it. Therefore, instead of Malachi 3:10, let's go to 2 Corinthians 9:10, "Now He who supplies seed to the sower and bread for food, will supply and *multiply your seed for sowing,* (i.e., it's not for us to keep), and *increase the harvest of your righteousness."* I'll take increased righteousness over increased worldly wealth every time. Proverbs 11:4: "Riches do not profit in the day of wrath, but righteousness delivers from death." Or what about 2 Corinthians 8:3–4, "For I testify that according to their ability, and beyond their ability *they gave of their own accord, begging us with much entreaty for the favor of participation in the support of the saints."* Did they need a fleshly motivation to move their innermost bowels of compassion?

I then started to rehearse in my mind how the US government was giving *20 billion* of our tax dollars toward rebuilding and humanitarian aid. The insurance companies estimated a payout of over *15 billion.* And various secular corporations were giving *literally hundreds of millions.* Hollywood's effort brought in about *350 million.* And as I was contemplating the mind-numbing size of those numbers, our Lord brought the following Scripture to my heart: Luke 9:59–60: "And He (Jesus) said, 'Follow Me.' But he said, 'Permit me first to go and bury my father.' But He said to him, '*Allow the dead to bury their own dead; but as for you, go and proclaim everywhere the kingdom of God.*'" I immediately sensed the seriousness, the sternness, of our Lord. Not only did this verse by context convey both gravity and urgency, but it also made very clear that His Church needs to concentrate its finances and efforts on the eternal needs of mankind, not the temporal.

Our Lord was *not* saying the temporal was not important, but He was trying to convey that the spiritually dead (the world) had more than enough money to handle the temporal and humanitarian needs. Therefore, His Church needs to concentrate on the eternal, the preaching and teaching of the gospel of Jesus Christ. Ephesians 6:12: "*For our struggle is not against flesh and blood,* but against the rulers, against the powers, against the world forces of this darkness, against the spiritual forces of wickedness in the heavenly places." The world's corporations, foundations, and sometimes even the US government will give *billions* to humanitarian aid. But if you mention Jesus, heaven, or hell the world will not give you a dime. And I know that to be true, as I have been rejected more than once as I have sought financial help to preach the gospel.

Therefore, let's turn the table on Luke 16:8–15, so that the sons of the light become more shrewd than the sons of this age. If we as Christians see a need for humanitarian aid, let us create or contact a secular non-profit. One that can be funded by secular government grants, foundations, and corporations so we can free up 100% of the Church's funds for the Kingdom of Heaven. Christians are so few in number and means as compared to the world, yet God's Church is the *only* source we have to fund the gospel. Satan loves to tug on our *huge* heart with humanitarian causes in order to starve the gospel into silence. Remember the very first thing the USA did to defeat terrorism? Our first strike in the war against terrorism was against the terrorist's finances. *Satan is no fool; an unfunded ministry is no threat to him!* Are you saying we should turn our backs on the hungry and suffering? No! God forbid! We should be the first one to help someone in need, but let's use the secular world to fund it. For example, how many well-intentioned Christians gave to this disaster without first thinking, how many *billions* do they really need? Let's be sure we are not duplicating what the secular world is already doing very well, because the secular world will *not* help us with the gospel.

I also saw the secular world put aside their inconsequential differences in order to come together to defeat a common terrorist. *All of a sudden—in the twinkling of an eye—that which was once very important, became frivolous in the face of pure evil.* In order to keep God's Church as non-effective as possible, Satan's number one objective is to divide God's Church into as many factions as possible. Therefore, we must not allow frivolous doctrinal differences to fracture God's Church. However, there are lines in the sand we must draw, such as *"Jesus is the way, and the truth, and the life; no one comes to the Father, but through Him."* But to fracture over which Bible translation you read, or when the rapture of the church will occur is just frivolous. We must become much wiser as to where we draw our lines in the sand. You can continue to preach what you believe, but please do not divide and fight over things which do not lead to death. There are eternal lives which hang in the balance. Titus 3:8–11: "This is a trustworthy statement; and concerning these things I want you to speak confidently, so that those who have believed God may be careful to engage in good deeds. These things are good and profitable for men. But shun foolish controversies and genealogies and strife and disputes about the Law; for they are *unprofitable and worthless*. Reject a factious man after a first and second warning, knowing that such a man is perverted and is sinning, being self-condemned."

My heart was warmed once again as I saw the secular world's respect and appreciation for the efforts of the rescue workers as they placed their lives in jeopardy to save total strangers from certain death, and/or help them escape from the entangled web of debris. The world also showed their appreciation in a tangible way by fulfilling the rescue worker's financial needs. Pastors, teachers, and evangelists at one time also commanded great respect as they also put aside their worldly wants and desires in order to save total strangers from eternal death, i.e., the flames of hell. And yes some, actually many, not only lost their lives figuratively, but also physically.

And as with all rescue workers, as a minister myself, I can tell you with certainty that there is also an emotional aspect to our rescue work. *Hell and eternal death to us is as real and hot as the fire that consumed the World Trade Towers, only the fire we seek to rescue people from has a ponderous eternal consequence.* Oh, how we are grieved when we try to point people to the fire escape (Jesus) and they just ignore us and run directly into hell's eternal fire. Or how emotionally draining it is as we try to rescue someone from the entangled debris of the web of Satan's deception with the truth of God's Word, but again they refuse to listen. Consequently, we are forced to watch their lives slowly drain away, languishing in the entangled web of Satan's deceptions. Brokenhearted and in tears, we know that we cannot force anyone to accept God's plan of salvation (Jesus), to be set free, to be born-again with God's Holy Spirit into His Kingdom.

It's likely that the world's selfless passion will fade away as the terrorists and temporal needs fade away; but what can our excuse be as Satan, the terrorist of all mankind, continues to kill, to destroy, and to hold his grip of hell and death over a myriad of souls through deception? *How can we ever justify allowing our selfless passion to fade away?* We must always guard our hearts from becoming apathetic and lukewarm, because if we don't, the advantage will go to Satan. Look at lives lost when the USA became lukewarm to the threats of terrorism from just man. *God forbid if we, the Church—God's Ambassador—ever become lukewarm concerning the threat to an individual's eternal life from the author of terrorism, Satan.* Think of the lives that could have been saved if God's Church would become the salt and light again. Think of the havoc we could have done to Satan's lies and deceptions that motivated the terrorists who hit the World Trade Towers.

Lord, please never let my passion become lukewarm for the eternal lives of mankind. But even as the world's passion needed a catalyst (seeing the World Trade Towers burning) to ignite their fleshly passion, I need a catalyst (a touch from You) to ignite the spiritual—the eternal passion within my heart. Open my eyes to the reality of the eternal horrors that await the victims of the terrorist, Satan. And God forbid that it could ever be said again, *"The sons of this age are more shrewd in relation to their own kind than the sons of light."* Help me Lord to hear *the sound of the trumpet*, the alarm of war. In Jesus' name, Amen!

Chapter Nine

The Best in Satan's Arsenal

Genesis 3:14–15: "And the Lord God said to the serpent, 'Because you have done this, cursed are you more than all cattle, and more than every beast of the field; on your belly shall you go, and dust shall you eat all the days of your life; and I will put enmity between you and the woman, and between your seed and her seed; *he shall bruise (crush) you on the head,* and you shall bruise (crush) him on the heel.'"

Satan succeeded in his quest to corrupt God's creation. He managed to corrupt God's most cherished and precious creation, mankind, whom God fashioned into His own image. Satan defrauded Adam and Eve into exchanging God's glory for his corruption. They immediately found not only that they themselves, but also that which God gave them, dominion over the earth, had entered into Satan's corrupt kingdom of self-centeredness. *Adam and Eve were defrauded by Satan into thinking that moving from the position of a servant to that of a god was a step forward in their evolution.* Instead, all they found was the consummate peril of nakedness!

The corruption of self-centeredness, or godhood, had now permeated God's creation. The corruption of self-centeredness immediately began to bare its fruit of anger, strife, jealousy, covetousness, selfishness, envy, greed, lust, hatred, vengeance, etc. From mankind on down, the law of the land was now the survival of the fittest. *Instead of a kingdom of servants, we now have a kingdom that delights in devouring one another, just so we can say in a spirit of egotistical pride, "I am my own god!"* Even today mankind continues down the same path of godhood, by deciding for himself what is good and what is evil, without perceiving his own pathetic nakedness. From time to time mankind is willing to help his fellow man, if he can derive from it a sense of self-satisfying condescension, or gain some future advantage for himself. Mankind may even obey God Himself if he sees a self-serving advantage in it. But then, his shameless naked attitude of godhood is exposed as he becomes enraged at God if he perceives his act of obedience, or benevolence resulted in personal loss instead of gain. *Is it no wonder that we who are Christians perceive this corrupt creation to be as close to hell as we will, or ever want to be.*

From time to time I hear people say that they would rather be a god in hell than a servant in heaven. *What a profound display of spiritual blindness or ignorance, and/or a consummate display of perverted logic!* As a god in a kingdom of gods, in other words hell, the only person you have to look after you is yourself, within a world where there is a vast myriad of other gods lusting for power and dominion over you. At the same time you're lusting and waiting for the opportunity to pay back in kind for evil done to you and/or gain dominion over someone else. *Now to me that would be hell!* Whereas, in a kingdom of servants, you will indeed have to give up your godhood—your self-centeredness—your self-concern, and begin to treat others as you would treat yourself. But you may say, "If I don't look out for myself, who will?" Well, in a kingdom of servants you would indeed no longer be looking out for yourself, but you would gain a vast myriad of other servants who would be looking out for you. In other words, in Satan's kingdom you'll be alone amidst a vast myriad of enemies, but in God's kingdom you'll be laying your life down in exchange for a vast myriad of servants, anxiously waiting to pick up your life. *As for me, I see great gain in God's kingdom.*

Accordingly, now the sayings of Jesus begin to sound incredibly wise, and not nearly as foolish as we had once thought. Luke 9:23–24: "And He (Jesus) was saying to them all, 'If anyone wishes to come after Me, let him deny himself, and take up his cross daily, and follow Me. For whoever wishes to save his life shall lose it, but whoever loses his life for My sake, he is the one who will save it.'" And Luke 12:29–34: "And do not seek what you shall eat, and what you shall drink, and do not keep worrying. *For all these things the nations of the world eagerly seek;* but your Father knows that you need these things. But seek for His kingdom, and these things shall be added to you. *Do not be afraid,* little flock, for your Father has chosen gladly to give you the kingdom. Sell your possessions and give to charity; make yourselves purses which do not wear out, an unfailing treasure in heaven, where no thief comes near, nor moth destroys. For where your treasure is, there will your heart be also." And finally Luke 22:24–27: "And there arose also a dispute among them as to which one of them was regarded to be greatest. And He (Jesus) said to them, 'The kings of the Gentiles lord it over them; and those who have authority over them are called 'Benefactors.' But not so with you, but let him who is the greatest among you become as the youngest, and the leader as the servant. For who is greater, the one who reclines at the table, or the one who serves? Is it not the one who reclines at the table? *But I am among you as the one who serves.*'"

In other words, we must let go and let God handle our affairs and concerns. We must deny ourselves and let God, our creator, become God of our lives once again. *What a scary thing to do!* I guess that's why it is written in Hebrews 11:6, "And without faith it is impossible to please Him, for he who comes to God must believe that He is, *and that He is a rewarder of those who seek Him.*" Only then can we have the courage and freedom to become a servant to all. To have the courage and freedom to love someone even if they do not love us back, to do good to those who persecute us, to take up our cross and follow Jesus, to regard another as more important than ourselves, to let go of a suffered wrong, forgive, and then love our enemy. Otherwise, we will remain a slave to self-centeredness, concerned only for others if we can perceive a benefit for ourselves. Hence, we will quickly become embittered when we perceive *"an unfairness"* in our lives which seems inharmonious to our labor of *"love,"* if we can call it love. Hebrews 12:15: "See to it that no one comes short of the grace of God; that no root of bitterness springing up causes trouble, and by it many be defiled." And who do we usually end up getting mad and/or embittered at? *None other then God Himself!* Ergo, Satan wins another battle.

Although Satan won the first battle, God declared the victory, *"He shall bruise (crush) you on the head, and you shall bruise (crush) him on the heel."* Accordingly, God moved quickly and cut mankind off from the tree of life and allowed death to reign so mankind's fate (corruption) would not become sealed in perpetuity. Then God placed in motion His plan of redemption for His most cherished and precious creation, mankind. In the fullness of time, when our redemption was at hand, Satan knew this meant his head would soon be crushed. This would mean that Satan would have no choice but to set free those prisoners of corruption (mankind) who accepted God's plan of redemption. Therefore, Satan used *"the best in* his arsenal" of deception to thwart God's plan of redemption. Hence, God's Lamb—God's only Son—Jesus, the restorer of the breach, became the recipient of Satan's best deceptions. Now we know where to look to familiarize ourselves with his deceptive tactics. And now we also have insight to some of the characteristics that are present in both God's kingdom and in Satan's kingdom. *All of which can now be used to help us discern and consequently avoid the snares and deceptions of our enemy, Satan.*

Matthew 4:1–4: "Then Jesus was led up by the Spirit into the wilderness to be tempted by the devil. And after He had fasted forty days and forty nights, He then became hungry. And the tempter came and said to Him, 'If You are the Son of God, command that these stones become bread.' But He answered and said, *'It is written, Man shall not live on bread alone, but on every word that proceeds out of the mouth of God.'"* The Scripture Jesus quoted originated from Deuteronomy 8:1–3, "All the commandments that I am commanding you today you shall be careful to do, that you may live and multiply, and go in and possess the land which the Lord swore to give to your forefathers. And you shall remember all the way which the Lord your God has led you in the wilderness these forty years, that He might humble you, *testing you, to know what was in your heart, whether you would keep His commandments or not.* And He humbled you and let you be hungry, and fed you with manna which you did not know, nor did your fathers know, that He might make you understand that man does not live by bread alone, but man lives by everything that proceeds out of the mouth of the Lord." Why would the Spirit of God lead both Israel and Jesus out into the wilderness and allow them both to become hungry? *To test their hearts (spirits) to see if obedience was from their lips only, or truly genuine and steadfast within their hearts!*

Hebrews 5:8: *"Although He was a Son, He learned obedience from the things which He suffered."* Unfortunately, there is no other way to test the genuineness of your obedience than to be placed in a situation where you have the power to say *no*, and to say *yes* would mean saying no to your own desires and/or needs. You place two plates in front of your child. One plate has a cookie placed upon it, but the other has a vegetable placed upon it. Being much wiser than the child, and therefore knowing what's best, you say to the child, eat the vegetable and leave the cookie alone. And if the child eats the vegetable and walks away from the cookie, you have indeed found a genuine heart of obedience. But, if you say to the child, eat the cookie and leave the vegetable alone, and the child does so, you still have not proven genuine obedience. Why? Because, you were actually in agreement with the child; therefore, all that was proven was that the child could be obedient to himself. *And being obedient* only *to self is actually nothing more than the definition of rebellion.* And if this rebellion (self-centeredness) continues unabated, the child will grow up as a god, determining right and wrong solely on the basis of what's best for him personally. Therefore, concerned only for himself, the concerns and the desires of anyone else simply vanish. The only thing in his heart that now has any value or significance is that which he sees in the mirror.

Hebrews 12:26–27: "And His voice shook the earth then, but now He has promised, saying, 'Yet once more I will shake not only the earth, but also the heaven.' And this expression, 'Yet once more,' denotes the removing of those things which can be shaken, as of created things, in order that those things which cannot be shaken may remain." *There will be no created being in the new heavens and new earth that has not been tested for this spirit of rebellion.* The new heavens and new earth will be unshakable (rebellion free) for eternity. Revelation 20:7–8: "And when the thousand years are completed, Satan will be released from his prison, and will come out to deceive the nations which are in the four corners of the earth." God held Satan in reserve so he could be used once again, at the end of times, to test the genuineness of obedience within the hearts of mankind. Why? Because there is *no* other way.

Satan's temptation toward Jesus was exceedingly cunning when he started his sentence with, "*If You are the Son of God*, command that these stones become bread." Satan knew the second Jesus used His power to satisfy His own desire, it would in fact prove just the opposite, that He was not God's Son. Remember the characteristic seen in God's kingdom is that of a servant whose concerns and desires are always expressed outward, and never, never inward. John 7:38: "He who believes in Me, as the Scripture said, 'From his innermost being shall flow rivers of living water.'" The living waters, a.k.a. the Holy Spirit, will *always* flow outward, never inward. Why then are people perplexed when someone filled with the Holy Spirit of God, and has the gift of healing, cannot use the gift upon himself? In the same way, why were people perplexed by Jesus in Mark 15:31–32, "In the same way the chief priests also, along with the scribes, were mocking Him among themselves and saying, '*He saved others; He cannot save Himself.* Let this Christ, the King of Israel, now come down from the cross, so that we may see and believe!'" *Ah! But if He did come down from the cross, would He not have proven just the opposite?* This time Satan lost.

Matthew 4:5–7: "Then the devil took Him into the holy city; and he had Him stand on the pinnacle of the temple, and said to Him, 'If You are the Son of God throw Yourself down; for it is written, He will give His angels charge concerning You; and on their hands they will bear You up, lest You strike Your foot against a stone.' Jesus said to him, 'On the other hand, it is written, You shall not put the Lord your God to the test.'" Jesus was referring to

Exodus 17:2–3, "Therefore the people quarreled with Moses and said, 'Give us water that we may drink.' And Moses said to them, 'Why do you quarrel with me? Why do you *test* the Lord?' But the people thirsted there for water; and they grumbled against Moses and said, 'Why, now, have you brought us up from Egypt, to kill us and our children and our livestock with thirst?'" And Exodus 17:7: "And he named the place Massah and Meribah because of the quarrel of the sons of Israel, and because they *tested* the Lord, saying, *'Is the Lord among us, or not?'*"

Was Jesus actually going to trust God's Word without testing it first? *If Satan could tempt Jesus into mistrusting and doubting God's Word enough to feel the need to test it, would it not have caused an erosion to take place in Jesus' obedience?* Accordingly, if Jesus would have given in to Satan's temptation, how then could Jesus face the excruciating pain of the cross that awaited Him? After all, how could Jesus become obedient to God the Father and allow Himself to suffer the excruciating death of the cross if God the Father could not be absolutely trusted? However, Jesus remembered a time in Israel's history when they doubted God's presence due to their circumstances. But then Israel soon discovered that God was not only with them, but was trying to prepare them for the battles which lay ahead; inasmuch as it was impossible to enter the "Promised Land" and defeat their enemies without a deep abiding faith and trust in God.

If Israel had gone into the "Promised Land" without this deep abiding faith and trust in God, they would have turned back at the first sign of any suffering from the hands of their enemies, and/or found their nation annihilated from the face of the earth, and ultimately would have thwarted God's plan of redemption. Remembering Israel's mistake, Jesus was able to say with complete confidence, faith, and trust, "On the other hand, it is written, You shall not put the Lord your God to the test."

Remember what Jesus said to Thomas in John 20:29, "Jesus said to him (Thomas), 'Because you have seen Me, have you believed? Blessed are they who did not see, and yet believed.'" *God did not want to reveal His hand to Israel in their time of tribulation, because if He did, their faith and trust in Him would not grow sufficient enough to face their enemies.* On the other hand, we found that Jesus was able to face His cross even when His circumstances demanded a verdict of abandonment, because Jesus was able to trust God at His Word without seeing. Otherwise, how could He have made a statement of *abandonment* one moment in Matthew 27:46, "*My God, My God, why hast Thou forsaken Me?*" And yet at the very next moment make a statement of absolute *trust* in Luke 23:46, "*Father, into Thy hands I commit My spirit.*" Like Jesus, we *must* learn to trust God without seeing, inasmuch as our Lord God tells us in Isaiah 55:8–9, "For My thoughts are not your thoughts, neither are your ways My ways. For as the heavens are higher than the earth, so are My ways higher than your ways, and My thoughts than your thoughts."

Matthew 4:8–10: "Again, the devil took Him to a very high mountain, and showed Him all the kingdoms of the world, and their glory; and he said to Him, 'All these things will I give You, if You fall down and worship me.' Then Jesus said to him, 'Begone, Satan! For it is written, You shall worship the Lord your God, and serve Him only.'" Now panic stricken, Satan was willing to give up his possession of the whole world in the hope to thwart God's plan of redemption. And all Jesus had to do to worship Satan and gain the whole world was to put Himself first and God the Father second. *Now, if Satan was willing to give up the whole world to keep us out of heaven, would that not strongly suggest to us that we should be equally willing to give up this world to gain heaven?* That's why Jesus said in Mark 8:36, "For what does it profit a man to gain the whole world, and forfeit his soul?" Well, Jesus did not have to think twice about it as He declared: "Begone, Satan! For it is written, You shall worship the Lord your God, and serve Him only."

Finally, in an act of shear desperation, Satan pleaded with Jesus to be merciful to Himself through one of His disciples. Satan even used the disciple who Jesus just hours before said that he was blessed because God revealed to his heart that He (Jesus) was indeed the Son of God. Satan thought, just maybe, he could deceive Jesus into thinking it was God once again speaking to Peter's heart in Matthew 16:22–23, "And Peter took Him aside and began to rebuke Him, saying, *'God forbid it (or God be merciful to You), Lord!* This shall never happen to You.' But He turned and said to Peter, 'Get behind Me, Satan! You are a stumbling block to Me; for you are not setting your mind on God's interests, but man's.'" But Satan's last desperate attempt to deceive Jesus was to no avail. As soon as Jesus heard that He should take thought of Himself, He immediately knew that it was just that old tempter Satan again. *Because the characteristic—the nakedness—of self-centeredness, and selfishness can only be found in Satan's kingdom—hell!*

My most precious brothers and sisters in the Lord, the shaking of our Lord's Church as quoted above in Hebrews 12:26–27, has begun. This shaking *must* take place before the second coming of our Lord for His Church—His bride. 1 Peter 4:17: "For it is time for judgment to begin with the household of God; and if it begins with us first, what will be the outcome for those who do not obey the gospel of God?" Our Lord is at the door and will be coming back soon for those who cannot be shaken. Therefore pray, "Lord keep me from temptation and the evil one. And deliver me safely into Your Kingdom according to your Word." 1 Corinthians 10:13:

"No temptation has overtaken you but such as is common to man; *and God is faithful,* who will not allow you to be tempted beyond what you are able, but with the temptation will provide the way of escape also, that you may be able to *endure* it." *Amen!* And to God be the glory!

Chapter Ten

Burn the Plow to Cook the Oxen

1 Kings 19:19–21: "So he (Elijah) departed from there and found Elisha the son of Shaphat, while he was plowing with twelve pairs of oxen before him, and he with the twelfth. And Elijah passed over to him and threw his mantle on him. And he left the oxen and ran after Elijah and said, 'Please let me kiss my father and my mother, then I will follow you.' And he said to him, 'Go back again, for what have I done to you?' *So he returned from following him, and took the pair of oxen and sacrificed them and boiled their flesh with the implements (plow) of the oxen,* and gave it to the people and they ate. *Then* he arose and followed Elijah and ministered to him."

Because Elijah was battle-worn, disillusioned, and dispirited, God commanded Elijah to seek out Elisha and transfer his calling to him. Upon finding Elisha, Elijah briefly tossed his mantle on Elisha to symbolize the transfer of Elijah's calling to Elisha. But afterward, Elijah kept walking without saying even one word to Elisha. Consequently, Elisha had to drop everything and run after Elijah. Then Elijah said to Elisha something very extraordinary,

"Go back again, for what have I done to you?" That's right, immediately Elijah did his best to discourage Elisha from following God's will for his life, i.e., to succeed Elijah as God's prophet. *In other words, God's testing of Elisha had begun!*

Would Elisha let Elijah's words question and dissuade him from his call? How precious was God's call to Elisha? How strong was Elisha's faith? Did Elisha have the *"right stuff"* to succeed Elijah? Obviously, there was not any pleading, nor any encouragement of any kind from Elijah to help motivate Elisha. What would Elisha do? When he caught up with Elijah would he then thank Elijah, worship God, and just go back to work as if nothing supernatural had happened to him? Would he just go back to the cares and concerns of this world? After all, it is conceivable that this was just one of many milestones in his life! Or did Elisha inherently know within his heart that the life he once knew was forever changed in that very brief moment when Elijah's mantle touched him? *Would Elisha be willing to pay the considerable price to be God's prophet?* Would Elisha be willing to literally lay down his life for God?

As it turned out, Elisha did have the right stuff. Elisha by faith, immediately destroyed the implements of his past profession so he could serve God *undivided* within his heart. Elisha knew the moment God touched him through Elijah, his life would never be the same. In that instant, Elisha was changed from a child of the earth consumed with temporal earthly concerns, to a child and prophet of God consumed with the eternal concerns of God. *In a very real sense, the old Elisha died and was born-again and entered into God's kingdom where God's will ruled and reigned!* (Although Elisha still needed to wait for the fulfillment via Jesus' death.) Without a second thought, by faith, Elisha made a very public declaration by burning his plow to cook the oxen that pulled it: I have lost and destroyed my old life in order to gain my new life in God!

By so doing, Elisha had removed the temptation of ever look-ing back. There was now nowhere else to go but to follow God's will and calling. The decision Elisha made at the very beginning of his call to burn his plow to cook his oxen, which he then fed to the people, turned out to be the wisest decision that he would ever make, inasmuch as Elijah continued to discourage Elisha. 2 Kings 2:2: "And Elijah said to Elisha, 'Stay here please, for the Lord has sent me as far as Bethel.' *But Elisha said, 'As the Lord lives and as you yourself live, I will not leave you.'* So they went down to Bethel." And again in 2 Kings 2:4, "And Elijah said to him, 'Elisha, please stay here, for the Lord has sent me to Jericho.' *But he said, 'As the Lord lives, and as you yourself live, I will not leave you.'* So they came to Jericho." And for a third time in 2 Kings 2:6, "Then Elijah said to him, 'Please stay here, for the Lord has sent me to the Jordan.' *And he said, 'As the Lord lives, and as you yourself live, I will not leave you.'* So the two of them went on." In essence, Elisha was saying, I burned my plow and fed my oxen to the people so now there is nowhere else for me to go, but to follow God and His call. Therefore, in the face of Elijah's ambiguity, Elisha remained unwa-vering in his commitment.

Many may say, "But Elisha was called to be a prophet of God, I'm just a normal everyday Christian." But inherent in that answer is found the root of our apathetic and dispassionate attitude to-ward our calling to be saints, the holy-ones of God. Let us first establish that becoming a Christian is not only a calling from God, but it *must* be a calling from God. As with Elisha, first the call must come: John 6:42–45, "And they were saying, 'Is not this Jesus, the son of Joseph, whose father and mother we know? How does He now say, 'I have come down out of heaven'?' Jesus answered and said to them, 'Do not grumble among yourselves. *No one can come to Me, unless the Father who sent Me draws him;* and I will raise him up on the last day. It is written in the prophets, 'And they shall all be taught of God.' Everyone who has heard and learned from the Father, comes to Me.'" And Romans 1:6–7: "Among whom you also are the *called* of Jesus Christ; to all who are beloved of God in Rome, *called* as saints (holy-ones)."

Second, let us establish the preciousness of our calling as compared to Elisha's to become a prophet of God. Jesus said in Matthew 11:11, "Truly, I say to you, among those born of women there has not arisen anyone greater than John the Baptist; *yet he who is least in the kingdom of heaven is greater than he.*" Therefore, John the Baptist was greater than Elisha, but since Jesus said the *least* in the kingdom of God is greater than John the Baptist, we must then conclude that the calling on *all* Christians is indeed greater than Elisha's calling to become God's prophet. Inasmuch as our call is greater, does God require, or perhaps even expect more from us than He did from Elisha? *The answer is yes!* Luke 12:48: "And from everyone who has been given much shall much be required; and to whom they entrusted much, *of him they will ask all the more.*" So then, if Elisha enthusiastically left his earthly life behind to follow God, how much more does God expect from those who receive His call to be saints to also enthusiastically leave their old earthly lives behind. And if we do not, will not Elisha's act of courage and obedience admonish us before God?

Are you saying that we must lose (forfeit) our earthly life in order to gain our new life in God? *Yes!* But then again, I'm only agreeing with Jesus when He said in Matthew 16:24–25, "Then Jesus said to His disciples, 'If anyone wishes to come after Me, let him deny himself, and take up his cross, and follow Me. For whoever wishes to save his life shall lose it; but whoever loses his life for My sake shall find it.'" As with Elisha, if we do not willingly abandon our old earthly lives immediately upon receiving God's call and leave ourselves nowhere else to go, we may be tempted to return to the world as we *endure* Satan's discouragements as we wait for the fulfillment of God's promise. Hebrews 11:13–16: "All these died in faith, *without* receiving the promises, but having seen them and having welcomed them from a distance, *and having confessed that they were strangers and exiles on the earth.* For those who say such things make it clear that they are seeking a country of their own. And indeed if they had been thinking of that country from which they went out, *they would have had opportunity to return.* But as it is, they desire a better country, that is, a heavenly one. Therefore, God is not ashamed to be called their God; for He has prepared a city for them."

So then, we *must* count the cost of God's call to be saints, born-again holy-ones! Luke 14:28–34: "For which one of you, when he wants to build a tower, does not first sit down and calculate the cost, to see if he has enough to complete it? Otherwise, when he has laid a foundation, and is not able to finish, all who observe it begin to ridicule him, saying, 'This man began to build and was not able to finish.' Or what king, when he sets out to meet another king in battle, will not first sit down and take counsel whether he is strong enough with ten thousand men to encounter the one coming against him with twenty thousand? Or else, while the other is still far away, he sends a delegation and asks terms of peace. *So therefore, no one of you can be My disciple who does not give up all his own possessions [just like Elisha].* Therefore, salt is good; but if even salt has become tasteless, with what will it be seasoned?"

John 6:26–27: "Jesus answered them and said, 'Truly, truly, I say to you, you seek Me, not because you saw signs, but because you ate of the loaves, and were filled. Do not work for the food which perishes, but for the food which endures to eternal life, which the Son of Man shall give to you, for on Him the Father, even God, has set His seal.'" Let us *not* become one of those who seek God's call of salvation because we seek to have our earthly appetites well fed. But let us seek God's call simply because we have tasted and fell passionately in love with God's kingdom—even His holiness. *Therefore, with faith and enthusiasm, let us burn our plow to cook our oxen,* leaving our old earthly lives behind in order to gain the true treasure of God's divine nature. Matthew 13:44–46: "The kingdom of heaven is like a treasure hidden in the field, which a man found and hid; and from joy over it he goes and sells all that he has, and buys that field. Again, the kingdom of heaven is like a merchant seeking fine pearls, and upon finding one pearl of great value, he went and sold all that he had, and bought it."

Therefore, let us no longer consider ourselves a sinner saved by grace, but a saint, a holy-one *kept* by grace. The statement, "a sinner saved by grace," embodies that which the Nicolaitans embraced, which Jesus both warned and admonished His church to repent of in Revelation 2:15–16, "Thus you also have some who in the same way hold the teaching of the Nicolaitans. *Repent therefore;* or else I am coming to you quickly, and I will make war against them with the sword of My mouth."

The Nicolaitans believed they needed Jesus to be saved, inasmuch as they were sinners and needed God's grace. But the Nicolaitans believed, because they were sinners, they could continue to sin as Jesus' death and resurrection only saved their spirit. They believed they could shamelessly compromise with the world, because their flesh and spirit were completely separate and could coexist without any consequence. Therefore, they looked upon Jesus' sacrifice as keeping them safe from any repercussions of sin; in essence, believing Jesus' sacrifice gave them the freedom to sin. *But in actuality that blasphemous teaching of the Nicolaitans insulted God's Spirit of grace.* Hebrews 10:26–29: "For if we go on sinning willfully after receiving the knowledge of the truth, there no longer remains a sacrifice for sins, but a certain terrifying expectation of judgment, and the fury of a fire which will consume the adversaries. Anyone who has set aside the Law of Moses dies without mercy on the testimony of two or three witnesses. How much severer punishment do you think he will deserve who has trampled under foot the Son of God, and has regarded as unclean the blood of the covenant by which he was sanctified, *and has insulted the Spirit of grace?*"

In contrast, we who once *were* sinners and are *now* born-again with God's Holy Spirit, find ourselves to be saints, the holy-ones of God that are *kept* by grace. We find grace at work to cover our stumbling, but we also know in our heart that God's grace could never be used to accommodate our fleshly appetites. Titus 2:11–12: "For the grace of God has appeared, bringing salvation to all men, *instructing* us to deny ungodliness and worldly desires and to live sensibly, righteously and godly in the present age." And 1 John 3:7–9, "Little children, *let no one deceive you;* the one who practices (whose lifestyle is) righteousness is righteous, just as He is righteous; the one who practices sin is of the devil; for the devil has sinned from the beginning. The Son of God appeared for this purpose, that He might destroy the works of the devil. No one who is born of God practices (has a lifestyle of) sin, *because His seed (Holy Spirit) abides in him; and he cannot sin, because he is born of God.*"

That's right, as God's saints, i.e., holy-ones, we *cannot* continue to sin, because sin now vexes us from within as we are instructed by God's grace and Holy Spirit within to deny ungodliness and worldly desires. God's grace will indeed cover our sins and leave behind no regret; but only if we find ourselves to be one of God's holy-ones by virtue of God's awesome miraculous power of transformation, i.e., turning a *sinner* into a *saint* by means of the death and resurrection of God's only Son, Jesus. Unless that miraculous transformation takes place, you cannot enter into the kingdom of God as you *must* be born-again. Just as Elisha instinctively knew in his heart he could not keep his life and follow Elijah at the same time so he wisely burned his plow to cook his oxen; *should we not also instinctively know in our heart that we cannot keep our lives in this world and fulfill our earthly appetites—our flesh—and follow Jesus at the same time?* Luke 16:13: "No servant can serve two masters; for either he will hate the one, and love the other, or else he will hold to one, and despise the other. You cannot serve God and mammon." And Matthew 16:24–25, "Then Jesus said to His disciples, 'If anyone wishes to come after Me, let him deny himself, and take up his cross, and follow Me. For whoever wishes to save his life shall lose it; but whoever loses his life for My sake shall find it.'"

But so often I find many well-intentioned Christians invoking God's grace seemingly without their hearts being broken and vexed over the sin committed. And they also seem to so effortlessly explain it all away by using the excuse, I'm just a sinner saved by grace. Of course, the actual state of your heart is solely between you and God, but if the above describes you, please allow me to lovingly warn you. *If you are still a sinner, you are neither saved by grace, nor born-again!* John the Baptist put it this way in Matthew 3:7–8, "But when he saw many of the Pharisees and Sadducees coming for baptism, he said to them, 'You brood of vipers, who warned you to flee from the wrath to come? *Therefore bring forth fruit in keeping with repentance.*'" And Jesus said in Matthew 7:22–23, "Many will say to Me on that day, 'Lord, Lord, did we not prophesy in Your name, and in Your name cast out demons, and in Your name perform many miracles?' And then I will declare to them, 'I never knew you; depart from Me, *you who practice (whose lifestyle is) lawlessness.*'"

The word John the Baptist used for repentance in the above paragraph means to change one's mind solely due to the sinfulness of sin and *not* because you're worried about the potential consequences of sin. True repentance is born out of a genuine change of mind toward God's view of sin, and therefore acknowledges and adopts the same view as God has toward sin. And if you go on from there and become born-again with God's Holy Spirit by accepting God's plan of redemption, you have in fact become a saint, i.e., a holy-one. When you become a saint born-again with God's Holy Spirit, not only will your mind thirst and crave after God's holiness, but now even your spirit (heart) within will be repulsed, even nauseated by sin and begin thirsting and craving after God's holiness. If this describes you, then those times you find your spirit willing, but your flesh weak, thereby causing you to stumble, you will also find God's grace to be both abundantly and exceedingly sufficient to cover and forgive any and all of your sins.

Why did I write this commentary? I wrote this commentary to be a safeguard to you. I want to make sure you are rock-solid and born-again. That you have indeed *burned* your plow and *cooked* your oxen so you will never be tempted to look back to the profession, i.e., the world you left, as the time of our Lord's coming is near. Luke 17:28–33: "It was the same as happened in the days of Lot: they were eating, they were drinking, they were buying, they were selling, they were planting, they were building; but on the day that Lot went out from Sodom it rained fire and brimstone from heaven and destroyed them all. *It will be just the same on the day that the Son of Man is revealed.* On that day, let not the one who is on the housetop and whose goods are in the house go down to take them away; and likewise let not the one who is in the field turn back. *Remember Lot's wife.* (Genesis 19:26: "But his (Lot's) wife, from behind him, *looked back;* and she became a pillar of salt.") *Whoever seeks to keep his life shall lose it, and whoever loses his life shall preserve it.*"

As we see the day of our Lord approach, may the words of the Apostles Paul and John keep all of us firmly *in* the grace of our Lord and *dead* to the world. Galatians 6:14–15: "But may it never be that I should boast, except in the cross of our Lord Jesus Christ, *through which the world has been crucified to me, and I to the world.* For neither is circumcision anything, nor uncircumcision, *but a new (born-again) creation.*" And 1 John 2:15–17: "Do not love the world, nor the things in the world. If anyone loves the world, the love of the Father is not in him. For all that is in the world, the lust of the flesh and the lust of the eyes and the boastful pride of life, is not from the Father, but is from the world. *And the world is passing away, and also its lusts; but the one who does the will of God abides forever.*"

Chapter Eleven

The Signs of Life

Before we can figure out what *"The Signs of Life"* are we must first define the word "life." God, in His Word, clearly describes a life He calls "the abundant life." But Satan also has a counterfeit that he and the world call "the abundant life," which will aggressively appeal to our flesh. *As always our adversary, Satan, will place before us a very attractive counterfeit to tempt us away from the genuine.* In order to understand the difference and discern which "abundant life" to seek after, we must also define the words "happiness" and "blessedness" according to God's Word. *Satan desires us to pursue with all our heart a state of happiness, whereas God desires us to pursue with all our heart a state of blessedness.*

To help us understand the differences between a state of happiness and a state of blessedness, I'll use one of Jesus' parables. Luke 16:19–21: "Now there was a certain rich man, and he habitually dressed in purple and fine linen, gaily living in splendor every day. And a certain poor man named Lazarus was laid at his gate, covered with sores, and longing to be fed with the crumbs which were falling from the rich man's table; besides, even the dogs were coming and licking his sores." The world, and I'm sorry to say many Christians, would read these three verses of Scripture and immediately conclude that the rich man had *"the abundant life"* and was obviously blessed by God; whereas, Lazarus had no life and none of God's blessings.

There is no doubt that the rich man lived out his life here on earth in *"a state of happiness,"* i.e., what Satan and the world would describe as the abundant life. But according to Scripture, did the rich man ever have what God calls *"the abundant life"*? Did the rich man ever live in *"a state of blessedness"*? To answer these questions let's read a little further in Luke 16:22–25, "Now it came about that the poor man (Lazarus) died and he was carried away by the angels to Abraham's bosom; and the rich man also died and was buried. And in Hades he (the rich man) lifted up his eyes, being in torment, and saw Abraham far away, and Lazarus in his bosom. And he cried out and said, 'Father Abraham, have mercy on me, and send Lazarus, that he may dip the tip of his finger in water and cool off my tongue; for I am in agony in this flame.' But Abraham said, *'Child, remember that during your life you received your good things, and likewise Lazarus bad things; but now he is being comforted here, and you are in agony.'"*

According to Scripture, Lazarus was the one who actually lived here on earth in a state of blessedness, and always had what God calls "the abundant life." *What a conundrum for the world, and unfortunately for many Christians!* How could God ever consider Lazarus' life as abundant, or blessed? Because when God considers the words "abundant life," He looks exclusively to the eternal and never to the temporal! *Inasmuch as everyone's spirit will live forever, both good and evil, would it not be wise for all of us to embrace the same view as God and pursue the eternal with all our heart?* Therefore, the question for us is, should we pursue with all our heart the temporal state of happiness which consists of about eighty years which Satan and the world call abundant life; or should we pursue with all our heart the eternal state of blessedness which God calls abundant life? The Apostle Paul knew the right answer, 2 Corinthians 4:16–18, "Therefore we do not lose heart, but though our outer man is decaying, yet our inner man is being renewed day by day. *For momentary, light affliction is producing for us an eternal weight of glory far beyond all comparison,* while we look not at the things which are seen, but at the things which are not seen; for the things which are seen are temporal, but the things which are not seen are eternal."

Am I trying to say we must choose between blessedness and happiness? *No!* What I'm trying to say is that being in a state of blessedness and/or being in a state of happiness, not only can be, but are completely independent of each other. Can you be happy in this world and not blessed? *Yes!* Can you be happy in this world and blessed? *Yes!* Can you be unhappy in this world and be blessed? *Yes!* So then the question for us remains, which do we pursue with all our heart? Do we pursue with *all* our heart a state of blessedness which God and Holy Scripture call abundant life? Or do we pursue with *all* our heart a state of happiness which is based solely on our temporal circumstances, which is Satan's and the world's counterfeit?

Satan's and the world's view of abundant life is: *The one who dies with the most toys wins!* That may indeed aggressively appeal to our flesh, but that view of abundant life would only be valid if our existence ended at the grave. *But the truth is, our existence is eternal!* And if we would be honest with ourselves, we do know intuitively that even though our bodies and this world grow old and decay, our spirit within does not, because it is indeed eternal! So what are *"the signs of life"* that authenticate being in a state of blessedness, i.e., God's abundant life; since the evidence cannot be based on our worldly circumstances, the abundance of our adult toys, nor even worldly success? Who then is the one that we can say with certainty is blessed?

Matthew 5:3: *"Blessed are the poor in spirit, for theirs is the kingdom of heaven."* Of all the *"signs of life"* there is none greater than a poor spirit, inasmuch as a poor spirit is where the state of blessedness must begin. *A poor spirit is the only incubator where our abundant life can be conceived and grow until death is swallowed up in victory!* There is *no* other incubator which can conceive the kingdom of heaven, also known as God's abundant life! Therefore, just as a poor spirit is the greatest sign of heaven and life, the absence of a poor spirit (a haughty spirit) becomes the greatest sign of hell and death! There is no greater example of this profound truth in God's Word than the account of Lucifer whose name was later changed to Satan. Isaiah 14:12–15: "How you have fallen from heaven, O star of the morning (Lucifer), son of the dawn! You have been cut down to the earth, You who have weakened the nations! But you said in your heart, 'I will ascend to heaven; I will raise my throne above the stars of God, and I will sit on the mount of assembly in the recesses of the north. I will ascend above the heights of the clouds; I will make myself like the Most High.' Nevertheless you will be thrust down to *Sheol*, to the recesses of the pit." *Satan, also known as the devil, became the poster boy of the arrogant—the personification of the haughty in spirit—the embodiment of the anti-life—the antithesis of abundant life!*

As if to further confound the world, Matthew uses a Greek word for poor, which illustrates a state of complete and total helplessness. Not just poor as in going hungry and/or without shelter from time to time, but so poor that without some kind outside intervention you would die! Luke 16:20–21: "And a certain poor man named Lazarus was laid at his gate, covered with sores, and longing to be fed with the crumbs which were falling from the rich man's table; besides, even the dogs were coming and licking his sores." *What an antithesis, even moronic to the world's view of abundant life!* Which would undoubtedly cause many to ask, "How can someone in such a complete state of helplessness have any life? How can anyone in such a condition be considered as having the abundant life and/or be considered as blessed?"

To gain insight, let's look at the work John the Baptist had to do before Jesus could come on the scene with God's gospel message. Luke 3:3–6: "And he (John) came into all the district around the Jordan, preaching a baptism of repentance for the forgiveness of sins; as it is written in the book of the words of Isaiah the prophet, 'The voice of one crying in the wilderness, make ready the way of the Lord, make His paths straight. Every ravine shall be filled up, and every mountain and hill shall be brought low; and the crooked shall become straight, and the rough roads smooth; and all flesh shall see the salvation of God.'" *Before Jesus could bring God's gospel of abundant life to mankind, John the Baptist had to first make a path in the wilderness of mankind's brazen heart.* Therefore, in the power of the Holy Spirit, John had to expose the poorness, the complete helplessness of mankind's heart, or spirit. A heart in desperate need of cleansing, a cleansing which John the Baptist symbolized by baptizing in water. Yes, John went about in the power of the Holy Spirit, exposing a spirit within mankind that was so poor it was completely and thoroughly helpless to help itself, and therefore, was in desperate need of God's outside intervention. *Then, and only then, was mankind's heart prepared to receive the gospel from God's only Son—Jesus!*

It was no wonder that those who saw themselves as righteous (or at the very least not helpless) so hated John the Baptist and wanted to kill him. But John the Baptist was only the instrument; it was the Holy Spirit Himself which exposed the truth that their (the self-righteous) spirit was actually poor, impoverished, destitute, and in need of God's outside intervention. In other words, until you can acknowledge this need, you are in fact blaspheming the Holy Spirit by calling Him (God) a liar. A sin which leaves you without any hope, because why would you feel the need to ask God to do a *"work"* within your heart if you did not see a need. John 6:29: "Jesus answered and said to them, 'This is the *work* of God, that you believe in Him whom He has sent.'" John 14:6: "Jesus said to him, 'I am the way, and the truth, and the life; no one comes to the Father, but through Me.'" *Yes, as moronic as it may sound to the proud of spirit and/or the self-righteous of this world, it can only be the poor (completely helpless) in spirit who are blessed!*

Hence, the first and greatest *"sign of life"* must be a poor spirit, as only the poor in spirit can understand and see their need for salvation, ergo, willing to accept God's *"work"* of salvation through His Son Jesus! And this promise in Matthew 5:3 of the poor in spirit having the kingdom of heaven is written in the original Greek in the present tense, therefore, it is in the possession of the poor in spirit *now!* In other words, just as God rules and reigns within the kingdom of heaven, the poor in spirit are born-again and *now* have God ruling and reigning within their hearts, i.e., they *now* have God's kingdom within their hearts (Luke 17:20–21)!

Matthew 5:4: *"Blessed are those who mourn, for they shall be comforted."* The fact that God now rules and reigns within the hearts of the poor in spirit by virtue of being born-again, causes the next *"sign of life"* to manifest. As God begins His reign within our hearts, we begin to mourn, grieve, and even bewail over sin in not only our lives, but also in the lives of those around us. We mourn over sin as we would mourn over the loss of a loved one. We begin to see and understand the outcome of sin—how it separated us from our creator, our heavenly Father; and we begin to desperately desire the intimacy we once had with God to be restored. We mourn over the sin that surrounds us every day as we now see and understand that sin was the cause of our eternal separation from God. This is what the Scriptures identify as hell and/or the second death! *How can we not mourn over the death and destruction sin leaves behind?* Was it not God's own mourning heart (spirit), mourning over our death—our separation from Him—which compelled Him to send His only Son to restore the intimacy we had once enjoyed? To literally save us from hell, the second death! But this verse is written in the original Greek in the future passive, because we cannot be comforted until the promise we now possess is actually fulfilled and our intimacy with God, our heavenly Father, is fully restored!

Matthew 5:5: *"Blessed are the gentle (humble), for they shall inherit the earth."* A heart characterized by gentleness or humility is our next *"sign of life."* Humility is not a weakness, but a virtue born out of immense inner strength—the inward strength it takes to admit we are not always right, nor are we the center of our own universe. It takes immense inner strength to deny yourself and allow God's holy light to expose your weaknesses and imperfections. *Only the weak cannot allow their imperfections to come to light, because their fragile egos could not handle the perceived indignity of ever being wrong and/or in a state of helplessness!* Instead, as the light (Holy Spirit) attempts to expose their imperfections, they gnash their teeth and growl like a frightened animal that's backed into a corner. Agitated and provoked, they again look for the comfort of their familiar territory of self-deceit and sin, i.e., the world they were born into. Whereas, the humble are willing to accept God's dealings as good and do not dispute, nor resist His work within; as they have learned by experience to no longer question

God's love for them and they begin to trust implicitly God's wisdom over their own. And since humility is a "sign of life," and life is defined as being with God, and as this earth and all that's in it belong to God, how then can the humble not inherit the earth? But once again this verse is written in the original Greek in the future passive, as Satan is now the god of this world in its fallen state. Besides, there is nothing in this present fallen world that I could conceivably desire!

Matthew 5:6: *"Blessed are those who hunger and thirst for righteousness, for they shall be satisfied."* As the humble of heart allow God to rule and reign within their hearts, and they begin to experience the righteousness of God firsthand, they begin to display another *"sign of life,"* an ever-increasing hunger and thirst for more. These humble spirits crave to be filled with all the goodness and righteousness of God; they have tasted it and found it to be most desirable. In God's righteousness they found a peace and freedom that are far beyond the ability of mankind's imagination to conceive. But once again this verse is written in the future passive, so the promise of our hunger and thirst for God's righteousness to be fully satisfied must wait for the redemption of our body, when we will be no longer tempted, or hindered by our flesh. But until then, our hunger and thirst should cause an impassioned desire within to press in as hard as we can, and get as close as we can to God's righteousness, even though perfection is for now unobtainable.

Matthew 5:7: *"Blessed are the merciful, for they shall receive mercy."* This *"sign of life"* begins to manifest itself within our lives as the hunger and thirst for God's righteousness causes us to discover a need—no, an overwhelming necessity—for God's mercy. And in the course of seeking God's righteousness, we also discover we are to treat our neighbor as we wish to be treated; how then can we withhold mercy from our neighbor? This promise is also in the future passive; therefore, we should not expect the mercy we now show someone to always be returned in kind. But that's OK! We know that someday the promise associated with this "sign of life" will be fulfilled. Luke 6:36–38: "Be merciful, just as your Father is merciful. And do not judge and you will not be judged; and do not condemn, and you will not be condemned; pardon, and you will be pardoned. *Give (mercy), and it will be given to you; good measure, pressed down, shaken together, running over, they will pour into your lap.* For by your standard of measure it will be measured to you in return." As for me, I cannot wait to be abundantly merciful to someone, because I know how much I need God's *immeasurable* abundance of mercy for myself!

Matthew 5:8: *"Blessed are the pure in heart, for they shall see God."* This *"sign of life"* is about a heart that's sincere, without duplicity or hypocrisy. It is a heart that passionately seeks after God's righteousness and virtues just because it is hopelessly in love with God. And never—never does it ever enter into their heart to seek His righteousness for any kind of personal reward or advantage; nor do they pathetically try to gain esteem in the eyes of God and/or mankind. *Are the motives in your heart pure?* Then, as this "sign of life" is also written in the future passive, there will come a day you will see God face to face (1 Corinthians 13:12).

Matthew 5:9: *"Blessed are the peacemakers, for they shall be called sons of God."* The Greek word for son in this verse denotes maturity and not a small child. Therefore, this *"sign of life"* is a sign which confirms maturity within a Christian's heart. Inasmuch as, you have moved away from a childish one-upmanship and/or the desire to seek revenge, onto a heart desiring reconciliation and restoration. Just like God, with all your heart you wish for none to perish, not even your worst enemy, but you wish for all to come to a saving knowledge of God. Even if you find you must deny yourself to accomplish this objective! As this verse is also written in the future passive, you may be known as a fool in this present world, but there will come a day when it will become known to all that you were just acting as a mature son or daughter of God.

Matthew 5:10–11: *"Blessed are those who have been persecuted for the sake of righteousness, for theirs is the kingdom of heaven. Blessed are you when men cast insults at you, and persecute you, and say all kinds of evil against you falsely, on account of Me."* Finally, we have another *"sign of life"* that is written in the present tense. That's right, we can count on the people of this world to continuously persecute and hurl insults at us, since this world can only love its own. *So beware!* Luke 6:26: "Woe to you when *all* men speak well of you, for in the same way their fathers used to treat the false prophets."

It is very important for us to always remember and incorporate these *"Signs of Life"* within our everyday lives. They were obviously *very* important to Jesus as He immediately followed with Matthew 5:13–16, "You are the salt of the earth; but if the salt has become tasteless, how will it be made salty again? It is good for nothing anymore, except to be thrown out and trampled under foot by men. You are the light of the world. A city set on a hill cannot be hidden. Nor do men light a lamp, and put it under the peck-measure, but on the lampstand; and it gives light to all who are in the house. *Let your light shine before men in such a way that they may see your good works, and glorify your Father who is in heaven."*

Chapter Twelve

Neither Can Salt Water Produce Fresh

James 2:8–13: "If, however, you are fulfilling the royal law, according to the Scripture, 'You shall love your neighbor as yourself,' you are doing well. But if you show partiality, you are committing sin and are convicted by the law as transgressors. For whoever keeps the whole law and yet stumbles in one point, he has become guilty of all. For He who said, 'Do not commit adultery,' also said, 'Do not commit murder.' Now if you do not commit adultery, but do commit murder, you have become a transgressor of the law. *So speak and so act, as those who are to be judged by the law of liberty. For judgment will be merciless to one who has shown no mercy; mercy triumphs over judgment.*" And James 3:9–12: "With it we bless our Lord and Father; and with it we curse men, who have been made in the likeness of God; from the same mouth come both blessing and cursing. My brethren, these things ought not to be this way. Does a fountain send out from the same opening both fresh and bitter water? Can a fig tree, my brethren, produce olives, or a vine produce figs? *Neither can salt water produce fresh.*"

Wow! What a sobering few verses we have from the book of James! As I read the above few verses of Scripture, they reminded me of the very high standard our Lord has set before us. Yet how easily all of us seem to suspend God's instruction in order to give preeminence to our flesh, while simultaneously not giving a second thought to the grave repercussions of disobedience. I could not help but feel a bit humbled as I considered my own Christian walk in light of the above Scriptures. How is it that we can read such verses in James about our relationship toward mankind one moment, and in the very next, act so contentious—so irreconcilable—so capricious in our relationships toward one another? Perhaps that's why James was also inspired by the Holy Spirit to write in James 1:23–24, "For if anyone is a hearer of the word and not a doer, he is like a man who looks at his natural face in a mirror; for once he has looked at himself and gone away, he has immediately forgotten what kind of person he was."

I know for me, I desperately want to be a doer of God's Word and not just a forgetful hearer. I want to look *intensely* into the mirror of God's Word for the image of my Father in heaven so as His child I can accurately project my Father's image to the lost and dying world that surrounds me every day. And once I found His image, I want to be sure that I will retain His image within my heart by being a doer of His Word. I also believe in their heart of hearts, most born-again Christians want the same. Therefore, let's take a closer look at these verses that deal with our relationship toward one another. But this time, with God's help, let us not forget what kind of person we are supposed to be and firmly set our hearts to be a doer of His Word and not just a hearer.

James 2:8: "If, however, you are fulfilling the royal law, according to the Scripture, *'You shall love your neighbor as yourself,'* you are doing well." How often do we personally miss the mark (sin) and yet so effortlessly judge ourselves to be basically good. And how exceedingly willing we are to show mercy toward ourselves and be reconciled to ourselves. But you may say, *"But brother, in this we have no leeway! Do you expect us to separate ourselves from ourselves?"* Well, I guess that does sound kind of dumb! After all, can we damage a part of our own body (emotional or physical) without feeling the pain? Nevertheless, as dumb as that may sound, we are doing just that every day, inasmuch as, the body (Church) is one in Christ, even as a husband and wife are one in marriage. Every day we inflict damage and hurt through disparaging remarks and/or harsh words of condemnation. Every day we see husbands, wives, and church members become hardhearted, merciless, and irreconcilable toward one another and then so easily and capriciously separate. Yes, we would do very well indeed if we would remember that both a husband and wife, and the members of Christ's Body are one and say, *"But brother, in this we have no leeway! Do you expect us to separate ourselves from ourselves?"*

James wrote, *"For whoever keeps the whole law and yet stumbles in one point, he has become guilty of all."* What an astonishing statement! You mean a person who has been diligent in his Christian walk all his life, yet misses the mark (sin) just once, needs the same measure of mercy from our Lord as a criminal? Yes, as astonishing as that may sound, it is true! This is a very important point to remember as it will keep us humble in heart, and thereby, keep us from setting ourselves up as judges. James 4:11–12: "Do not speak against one another, brethren. He who speaks against a brother, or judges his brother, speaks against the law, and judges the law; *but if you judge the law, you are not a doer of the law, but a judge of it.* There is only one Lawgiver and Judge, the One who is able to save and to destroy; but who are you who judge your neighbor?" Once again, as for me, *I just want to be a doer!*

Becoming a judge and not a doer of the law is a very grievous trap that the religious community is always falling into; therefore, let's guard our hearts from such evil thoughts least we find ourselves disciplined (humbled) by our Lord. Luke 18:10–14 reads: "Two men went up into the temple to pray, one a Pharisee, and the other a tax-gatherer. The Pharisee stood and was praying thus to himself, 'God, I thank Thee that I am not like other people: swindlers, unjust, adulterers, or even like this tax-gatherer. I fast twice a week; I pay tithes of all that I get.' But the tax-gatherer, standing some distance away, was even unwilling to lift up his eyes to heaven, but was beating his breast, saying, 'God, be merciful to me, the sinner!' I tell you, this man went down to his house justified rather than the other; *for everyone who exalts himself shall be humbled,* but he who humbles himself shall be exalted."

So how are we to act? We can again look back to the writings of James for the answer. James 2:12–13: *"So speak and so act, as those who are to be judged by the law of liberty. For judgment will be merciless to one who has shown no mercy; mercy triumphs over judgment."* Here we also see an unbreakable link as God is not mocked, what we sow, we will also reap. *No* mercy shown! *No* mercy given! Knowing this, would it not be wise for us to always remember to treat others as we wish to be treated, i.e., *mercifully?* Therefore, it would be wise for us to view every merciless word of judgment we speak against someone as if we're actually speaking judgment upon ourselves! Hence, if we find ourselves ill-treated to the point of persecution without cause, it would be wise for us to say what Jesus said as He was being crucified, *"Father, forgive them; for they do not know what they are doing."* We must leave all judgment and vengeance in God's hands as He alone knows the heart. To you and me, it surely looks as if they knew exactly what they were doing as the crowds spit upon and mocked Jesus while they watched the Roman soldiers hammer the nails into His feet and hands. But again, that is exactly why we *must* leave *all* judgment and vengeance in God's hands!

There is yet another benefit to showing mercy toward our enemies and those who despitefully treat us. Matthew 7:1–5: "Do not judge lest you be judged. For in the way you judge, you will be judged; and by your standard of measure, it will be measured to you. And why do you look at the speck that is in your brother's eye, but do not notice the log that is in your own eye? Or how can you say to your brother, 'Let me take the speck out of your eye,' and behold, the log is in your own eye? You hypocrite, first take the log out of your own eye, and then you will see clearly to take the speck out of your brother's eye."

Wow! Look at the beautiful thing that happens to us as we project God's heart of mercy toward mankind; the beam in our eye is removed so we can see clearly to take the speck out of our brother's eye. That's right! *We become effective ministers of reconciliation, inasmuch as we can now see clearly enough to remove the speck!* And as we become effective ministers of reconciliation, we gain a peace within our own hearts, which is of inestimable personal value. 1 John 4:17: "By this, love is perfected with us, that we may have confidence (great peace) in the day of judgment; *because as He is, so also are we in this world.*"

1 John 4:10–11: "In this is love, not that we loved God, but that He loved us and sent His Son to be the propitiation for our sins. *Beloved, if God so loved us, we also ought to love one another.*" This ministry of reconciliation was of such importance to God, He was willing to have His Son leave heaven and suffer the excruciating pain of the cross for a people, shall we say, somewhat less than lovable. To say that God went the extra mile for you and me is a huge understatement! *God's overwhelming love for us simply could*

not bear the sorrow of broken fellowship and separation. Therefore, not willing to wait for mankind to come to Him, He reached out to a hardhearted, unloving, obstinate people seeking to restore the fellowship and the oneness He once had with Adam. In Genesis 3:9, you can almost hear the pain in God's voice as He called out to Adam, *"Where are you?"* And now that the wall of separation (sin) has been torn down by the blood of God's very own Son, God continues to this very day to call out to mankind, *"Where are you?"* And yet, to my dismay, due to their hard irreconcilable heart most will close their ears to God's continued call for His sons and daughters to come home. With His arms longingly outstretched, God yearns to enfold us once again within His loving embrace.

In 1 John 4:11, we were told, "Beloved, if God so loved us, we also ought to love one another." But do we? Or are we displaying an image of God to the world which is judgmental, irreconcilable, easily offended, unmerciful, temperamental, touchy, moody, capricious, and/or easily angered as we allow God's desire for reconciliation, fellowship, and oneness to take a backseat to the insatiable cravings of our flesh? Is it any wonder that the world remains so confused when we speak of a God who loved us so much He gave His only Son to restore us unto Himself, while simultaneously we display an irreconcilable, unmerciful, even a capricious God by our actions. *And then, if that was not enough, we further exasperate the world's confusion by saying we are born-again with God's Spirit!* Even as our children will learn by what we do and not by what we say, so the world learns of God by what we do and not by what we say.

Hebrews 12:14–17: *"Pursue peace with all men,* and the sanctification without which no one will see the Lord. *See to it that no one comes short of the grace of God; that no root of bitterness springing up causes trouble, and by it many be defiled; that there be no immoral or godless person like Esau, who sold his own birthright* for a single meal. For you know that even afterwards, when he desired to inherit the blessing, he was rejected, for he found no place for repentance, though he sought for it with tears." If God was willing to leave heaven and literally be nailed to a cross to restore fellowship and oneness, is it too much for God to ask us to nail our fleshly emotions (cravings) to the cross in order to restore peace and fellowship? Therefore, I implore you! Don't be an immoral or godless person like Esau and sell your birthright as a minister of reconciliation in order to satisfy some insatiable emotion (craving) of your flesh. Unfortunately, as with God, no matter what we do, due to their hard irreconcilable heart, there will be those who will both ignore and have disdain for our continued call for reconciliation. Nevertheless, that will not get us off the hook, as it is written, *we must pursue peace with all!*

1 John 4:20: "If someone says, 'I love God,' and hates his brother, he is a liar; for the one who does not love his brother whom he has seen, *cannot* love God whom he has not seen." Here, the Apostle John totally abandons any pretense of trying to be subtle, and through the inspiration of the Holy Spirit, makes a very bold sweeping statement. *Without question, our horizontal relationship with one another has a direct impact on our vertical relationship with God! We could even go as far as to say that our relationship with one another is a direct reflection of our relationship with God!* If we hold bitterness and unforgiveness within our heart toward mankind, who is made in the image of God, we remain in darkness. 1 John 2:9–10: "The one who says he is in the light and yet hates his brother is in the darkness until now. The one who loves his brother abides in the light and there is no cause for stumbling in him." As severe as that may sound, this passage of Scripture could be of great benefit to us if we use it as an *"early warning system"* of our overall spiritual health, thereby, avoiding personal judgment and discipline. I paraphrase the Apostle Paul in 1 Corinthians 11:31–32, "But if we judge

ourselves rightly, we should not be judged and thereby avoid our Lord's discipline." That is, if we are willing to humbly accept the Holy Spirit's admonishment.

James 3:9–12: "With it we bless our Lord and Father; and with it we curse men, who have been made in the likeness of God; from the same mouth come both blessing and cursing. My brethren, these things ought not to be this way." Here James makes it clear that our relationship with mankind in general (not just within the church) is also a direct reflection of our relationship with God. When it becomes possible for *salt water to produce fresh,* a fig tree to produce olives, or a vine to produce figs, then and only then, will the possibility exist that we can both bless God and curse our fellow man or woman with the same tongue, i.e., heart. But you say, *"Brother, salt water cannot produce fresh that would be impossible!"* And you would be right! It is impossible! Yet we try to do just that every day!

Did you ever have a quarrel with your wife or husband and then walk into church with a smile, raising your hands toward heaven to praise God? *You can do that only when a fig tree produces olives!* Was there ever a time when someone cut in front of you as you were driving to church? You then shook your fist at the other driver and just moments later walk into church with a smile, raising your hands toward heaven to praise God. *You can do that only when a vine produces figs!* Was there ever a time you harbored unforgiveness and bitterness within your heart and simultaneously walk into church with a smile, raising your hands toward heaven to praise God? *You can do that only when salt water produces fresh!*

But until then, may I humbly suggest that you go quickly to God's throne of grace in the spirit of repentance. In other words, be extremely quick to sow to the Holy Spirit and even quicker to crucify your flesh. As it is written in Galatians 6:7–10, *"Do not be deceived,* God is not mocked; for whatever a man sows, this he will also reap. For the one who sows to his own flesh shall from the flesh reap corruption, but the one who sows to the Spirit shall from the Spirit reap eternal life. And let us not lose heart in doing good, for in due time we shall reap if we do not grow weary. So then, while we have opportunity, let us do good to *all* men, and *especially* to those who are of the household of the faith."

I realize this commentary has the potential to bring with it great conviction, as no one has achieved perfection. But we must *never* allow our ever-present frailty and/or past deficiencies to mitigate our obligation to press into the very high calling of God. The day we stop growing in the virtues of God—the day we give preeminence to our flesh over God's Word—the day we give preeminence to cultural morality over God's Word—the day we will no longer welcome instruction and admonishment from God's Word— the day we no longer endure sound doctrine—the day we treat God's Word as just a book of suggestions—the day we give our reverence to the gifts and not the gift giver—the day we treat God and His Word with such contempt and disregard, will be the day our faith died and became totally useless! James 2:19–20: "You believe that God is one. You do well; the demons also believe, and shudder. *But are you willing to recognize, you foolish fellow, that faith without works is (dead) useless?"*

Finally, I'll end with the words penned by the Apostle Paul in Ephesians as they so beautifully communicate what was in my heart as I wrote this commentary. Ephesians 4:1–6: *"I, therefore, the prisoner of the Lord, entreat you to walk in a manner worthy of the calling with which you have been called,* with all humility and gentleness, with patience, showing forbearance to one another in love, being *diligent* to preserve the unity of the Spirit in the bond of peace. There is one body and one Spirit, just as also you were called in one hope of your calling; one Lord, one faith, one baptism, one God and Father of all who is over all and through all and in all."

Father, help me to never become complacent with mediocrity in my spiritual walk. Help me place and keep Your Word as the apple of my eye. Help me to always maintain in my heart the same attitude the Apostle Paul had when he penned, Philippians 3:13–14, "Brethren, I do not regard myself as having laid hold of it yet; but one thing I do: forgetting what lies behind and reaching forward to what lies ahead, I press on toward the goal for the prize of the upward call of God in Christ Jesus." *In Jesus' name—Amen!*

Chapter Thirteen

Be Not Ignorant of Satan's Schemes

2 Corinthians 2:11: *"In order that no advantage be taken of us by Satan; for we are not ignorant of his (Satan's) schemes."* Ephesians 6:10–12: "Finally, be strong in the Lord, and in the strength of His might. Put on the full armor of God, that you may be able to stand firm against the schemes of the devil. *For our struggle is not against flesh and blood,* but against the rulers, against the powers, against the world forces of this darkness, against the spiritual forces of wickedness in the heavenly places."

As I see darkness (evil) encroaching upon every aspect of our society, I had to ask myself this question, "Has God's Church become ignorant of Satan's schemes?" And as I prayed, God placed this commentary on my heart. What makes Satan's schemes particularly hideous is the fact that in reality he is completely powerless. In fact, we, God's Church, have the keys (knowledge) to heaven and are instructed by God Himself to give that key to all who will listen. This knowledge (key) is so awesome in power that even the gates of hell (Hades), Satan himself, *cannot* prevail against it. Matthew 16:17–19: "And Jesus answered and said to him, 'Blessed are you, Simon Barjona, because flesh and blood did not reveal this to you, but My Father who is in heaven. And I also say to you that you are Peter, and upon this rock (foundation of revelation) I will build My church; *and the gates of Hades shall not overpower it.* I will give you the keys (knowledge) of the kingdom of heaven; and whatever you shall bind on earth shall be bound in heaven, and whatever you shall loose on earth shall be loosed in heaven.'"

Please allow me to take a brief, but needed departure to comment on the above line of Scripture, "I will give you the keys (knowledge) of the kingdom of heaven; and whatever you shall bind on earth shall be bound in heaven, and whatever you shall loose on earth shall be loosed in heaven." A more accurate translation of this line of Scripture would be: "I will give you the keys (knowledge) of the kingdom of heaven; and whatever you shall bind on earth (has first been) bound in heaven, and whatever you shall loose on earth (has first been) loosed in heaven." This more accurate translation meets the critical rule of interpretation by context, as Jesus' statement started with, "Blessed are you, because flesh and blood did not reveal this to you, but My Father who is in heaven." And again in John 6:44–45, "No one can come to Me, unless the Father who sent Me draws him; and I will raise him up on the last day. It is written in the prophets, 'And they shall all be taught of God.' Everyone who has heard and learned from the Father, comes to Me." *Hence, although God commanded us to proclaim the gospel (key), God maintains His sovereignty as revealer and initiator.* This is very important for us to remember as it will keep us from becoming haughty, inasmuch as, *"flesh and blood did not reveal this to you!"* Where is boasting? It is excluded!

1 Corinthians 1:18: "For the word of the cross is to those who are perishing foolishness, *but to us who are being saved it is the*

power of God." Since we, God's Church, hold this key (knowledge) to the power of God, Satan, the father of lies and deceit, had to devise a scheme (plan) to cause us (God's witness on earth) to self-destruct, or repress our effectiveness by manipulating us into rejecting the truth of God for a lie. *Inasmuch as, if Satan, through his schemes, could succeed in repressing, or even silence the gospel message (i.e., hide the key), God's power to save would not be released.* Romans 10:13–15: "Whoever will call upon the name of the Lord will be saved. How then shall they call upon Him in whom they have not believed? And how shall they believe in Him whom they have not heard? And how shall they hear without a preacher? And how shall they preach unless they are sent? Just as it is written, 'How beautiful are the feet of those who bring glad tidings of good things!'" *Therefore, we must not be ignorant of Satan's schemes, as Satan's power is* only *derived and kept through ignorance!* Because to know his schemes would cause his schemes to fall upon deaf ears! Inasmuch as we could then add our voices to Jesus' and say, Matthew 16:23, "Get behind Me, Satan! You are a stumbling block to Me; for you are not setting your mind on God's interests, but man's."

So what are these diabolical schemes of Satan that can render us ineffective? We can come to understand the evil one's schemes by examining the two names given to him in the Holy Scriptures, i.e., Satan and Devil. As we know, names were often used in the Bible to illustrate a revelation from God. For example, Abram's name, which meant "exalted father," was changed by God to Abraham which meant "the father of a multitude," which practically illustrated God's revelation for Abram. In the same way, God uses the names Satan and Devil to practically illustrate to us a revelation of the evil one's diabolical schemes.

The name Satan means "adversary," someone who stands in opposition to you or your plans. Even if an adversary cannot stop your plans, he will derive great pleasure in causing a hindrance to your work. Satan's desire is to be a hindrance to God's gospel message, which is the plan and work of God. Satan's hindrances to God's work (gospel) can take on many forms, i.e., fear, intimidation, anxiety, discouragement, depression, despair, discontent, unforgiveness, the love of money, greed, covetousness, selfishness, the cares of this world, criticism, slander, gossip, envy, jealousy, and so on. Do you see a common thread? Yes, Satan will appeal directly to our corruptible flesh in order to hinder God's gospel message. *Therefore, we must not allow our emotions or carnal reasoning to ever triumph over God's Word within our hearts.*

We can gain further insight as to how Satan will use his adversarial schemes against God's work by considering how he used his schemes against Jesus. Emmanuel (God with us) was in a body made of flesh and blood, and therefore, was also subject to the same temptations we are, yet He did not sin (Hebrews 4:15). In Matthew 4:1–11, Satan used Jesus' hunger and emotions to question God's love and faithfulness, he used the seductiveness of pride and ambition to get Jesus to test God, and finally he used the seductiveness of power and money to get Jesus to turn a deaf ear to God. Then incredibly in Matthew 16:21–23, Satan used Jesus' closest friends, His most intimate inner circle, to bring in carnal reasoning to thwart God's plan of salvation. *And yet, Jesus was able to stand against all of Satan's schemes through prayer, the power of the Holy Spirit, and the knowledge of God's Word.* Which are the very same safeguards we have at our disposal today to stand against all of the schemes of the evil one.

Not so long ago Satan tried to hinder me through a brother in Christ by using him to dampen my zeal and enthusiasm with the statement, "We must not become too bold as it could offend, and we run the risk of coming across as judgmental. And in so doing, we would not be exhibiting God's love." But in fact, contrary to that carnal reasoning, it would actually be the antithesis to agape love if I kept silent; as I would be allowing someone to go to hell for the selfish carnal desire to be liked by the world, i.e., appeasement. However, I would be the first to acknowledge that we need to pray to be sure our heart is right before God and our attitude is right toward man, i.e., to save and not to judge. *Nevertheless, to say the absence of offense should be our goal simply cannot be supported by Holy Scripture!*

Matthew 10:32–39: "Everyone therefore who shall confess Me before men, I will also confess him before My Father who is in heaven. But whoever shall deny Me before men, I will also deny him before My Father who is in heaven. *Do not think that I came to bring peace on the earth;* I did not come to bring peace, but a sword. For I came to set a man against his father, and a daughter against her mother, and a daughter-in-law against her mother-in-law; and a man's enemies will be the members of his household. He who loves father or mother more than Me is not worthy of Me; and he who loves son or daughter more than Me is not worthy of Me. And he who does not take his cross and follow after Me is not worthy of Me. He who has found his life shall lose it, and he who has lost his life for My sake shall find it." And again in 2 Corinthians 2:15–16, "For we are a fragrance of Christ to God among those who are being saved and among those who are perishing; *to the one an aroma from death to death,* to the other an aroma from life to life." And again in John 15:18–19, "If the world hates you, you know that it has hated Me before it hated you. If you were of the world, the world would love its own; but because you are not of the world, but I chose you out of the world, therefore the world hates you." *If you are in Christ, you are an offense to the world!*

John 16:8: "And He (the Holy Spirit), when He comes, will convict the world concerning sin, and righteousness, and judgment." *The power of the Holy Spirit was given to us to convict the world of sin in order to save, which in reality, is a consummate display of God's agape love.* Allow me to explain. You cannot come to Jesus unless you see a need, and you cannot see a need without first being convicted of sin. But afterward, the humble of heart will then be convicted of righteousness and we gain a friend. On the other hand, the proud of heart will then be convicted of judgment and they will begin to gnash their teeth and commence to hate us with every ounce of their being.

Therefore, to him who said I should temper my zeal for the harvest of souls in order to appease and not offend, I'll just echo what Jesus said in Matthew 16:23, "Get behind Me, Satan! You are a stumbling block to Me; for you are not setting your mind on God's interests, but man's." However, also like Jesus, my anger will be solely directed at Satan's diabolical scheme to silence my zeal for souls and not at the man whom Satan used; as I remember Jesus' agape love for Peter remained intact, inasmuch as, our warfare is not against flesh and blood, but spiritual. Nevertheless, Jesus had to deal sternly with the temptation Peter's words caused within His heart, i.e., the temptation to use carnal reasoning to avoid the excruciating pain of the cross. Even as I had to deal sternly with my heart when that brother's words neutralized my zeal for the harvest of souls as I initially wanted to use his carnal reasoning to justify my silence. *After all, it sounded so good!* Who would want to offend and/or be seen as judgmental? That can't be love, can it?

This spiritual warfare is real and we must fight against it with all of our heart and in the power of the Holy Spirit. For example, did God lay on your heart to give to a ministry, but then later back away thinking to yourself, "I need the money more than they do? After all, I worked hard for it and I should spend and enjoy it on myself!"? Or did God lay on your heart to pray for someone, but then you thought, "I do not have the time, besides it's probably just me and everything is OK!"? Or did God tell you to forgive someone, but the shrill of your emotions from deep within your heart kept you from saying yes to God? Or did God tell you to overcome evil with good and that vengeance was His, but you could not let go, because your carnal reasoning said, "If I do nothing that person will get away with it!"? I could go on, but I think you get the point.

All of the above situations are adversarial to God's work and/or plans. So we must learn to say within our heart and in the power of the Holy Spirit, "Get behind Me, Satan (Adversary)! You are a stumbling block to Me; for you are not setting your mind on God's interests, but man's." You may say, "That's too hard brother!" *But you must also remember, obedience is defined by doing something you do not wish to do!* Hebrews 5:8: "Although He was a Son, He learned obedience from the things which He suffered."

The evil one's other name, Devil, means "one who casts himself, or something, between two for the sole purpose to separate and divide," as demonstrated in the Garden of Eden. As the evil one slandered God before Adam and Eve, he caused doubt to grow within their hearts about God's love and motivation. This drove a wedge between them, which consummated in division, separation, and finally death. Therefore, we must not be found doing the same to each other by means of slander and gossip, as it would be an antithesis to our collective calling as ministers of reconciliation. 2 Corinthians 5:18–19: "Now all these things are from God, who reconciled us to Himself through Christ, *and gave us the ministry of reconciliation,* namely, that God was in Christ reconciling the world to Himself, not counting their trespasses against them, and He has committed to us the word of reconciliation."

Indeed what an insidious devilish scheme this is, as the evil one all ready knows! It's written in Luke 11:17, *"Any kingdom divided against itself is laid waste; and a house divided against itself falls."* But what makes this scheme exceedingly insidious is that at the same time we slander, demonize, and gossip, we can also be made to feel righteous, superior, and even pious. But we must remember that in reality, all we're doing is the Devil's work. And in so doing, we now have hundreds (perhaps thousands) of different denominations which have served only to water down, conceal, and even bring disrepute to God's immutable, unalterable, consistent gospel message of reconciliation.

Jesus gave us very explicit instructions concerning this in Matthew 13:28–30, "And he said to them, 'An enemy has done this!' And the slaves said to him, 'Do you want us, then, to go and gather them up?' But he said, *'No; lest while you are gathering up the tares, you may root up the wheat with them. Allow both to grow together until the harvest;* and in the time of the harvest I will say to the reapers, "First gather up the tares and bind them in bundles to burn them up; but gather the wheat into my barn."'" And again in Mark 9:38–40, "John said to Him, 'Teacher, we saw someone casting out demons in Your name, and we tried to hinder him because he was not following us.' But Jesus said, 'Do not hinder him, for there is no one who shall perform a miracle in My name, and be able soon afterward to speak evil of Me. For he who is not against us is for us.'"

Even the Apostle Paul had much to say about internal division, which he denounced severely! 1 Corinthians 3:1–4: "And I, brethren, could not speak to you as to spiritual men, *but as to men of flesh,* as to babes in Christ. I gave you milk to drink, not solid food; for you were not yet able to receive it. Indeed, even now you are not yet able, for you are still fleshly. *For since there is jealousy and strife among you, are you not fleshly, and are you not walking like mere men?* For when one says, 'I am of Paul,' and another, 'I am of Apollos,' are you not mere men?" And again in Titus 3:9–11, "But shun foolish controversies and genealogies and strife and disputes about the Law; for they are unprofitable and worthless. Reject a *factious man* after a first and second warning, knowing that such a man is perverted and is sinning, being self-condemned."

This in no way suggests that we should compromise the truth and/or the immutable gospel message, nor allow blatant—flagrant—unabashed sin within the Church for the sake of peace. But concerning matters that do not lead to death, if separation occurs, let them be the one who separates. But as for you and I, let us allow the Word of God to be a lamp unto our feet. Romans 12:18: "If possible, *so far as it depends on you*, be at peace with all men." And Jesus said in Mark 9:50, *"Have salt in yourselves, and be at peace with one another."*

Therefore, let us no longer be ignorant of the evil one's schemes, but fight against them by putting on the full armor of God and be filled with God's Holy Spirit. As we find ourselves completely powerless to stand against Satan's schemes without God's direct intervention. For example, it is impossible to forgive someone, *from within your heart*, without God's help. And pray without ceasing to be kept from temptation, i.e., the evil one's schemes. So we can again become the salt and light, holy and distinctive from the world. And no longer be just a *"noisy"* gong, or a *"clanging"* cymbal, for we are commanded to make a "noise" which can be easily distinguishable from the "noise" of the world as described in 1 Corinthians chapter thirteen.

But you may say, "Are we not to put on the full armor of God to fight evil spiritual forces in heavenly places?" No! We are informed by Ephesians 6:10–20 where our spiritual battle originates, but our battle is waged from within. Indeed, it may be more exciting, and can even puff you up thinking you're doing battle in heavenly places, but it's time to become humble enough to associate this warfare with the battle which wars within. When Jesus taught us to pray, He did not tell us to war in the heavenly places, but to pray that we will be kept from the evil one and temptation. *Although this battle is very personal and is waged within, we do have outside help as we seek God in prayer and put on His heavenly armor!*

Lord, I now see the schemes of the evil one and how he has used me in the past by manipulating me in becoming an adversary to Your work by acting in accordance with my flesh and not Your Word. But I also know that I do not have the power to change, nor can I recognize Satan's schemes without Your help. *Father, will You help me put on Your full armor and fill me with Your Holy Spirit so I may be one of the ones who will stand firm against the schemes of the evil one.* And allow Your light to burn brightly by allowing Your treasure within this earthly vessel to shine through, to pierce through the darkness, bringing glory to You. All the while remembering it is written, "There is no condemnation in Christ." Amen!

Chapter Fourteen

Have This Attitude in Yourselves

Philippians 2:5–8: *"Have this attitude in yourselves which was also in Christ Jesus,* who, although He existed in the form of God, did not regard equality with God a thing to be grasped, but emptied Himself, taking the form of a bond servant, and being made in the likeness of men. And being found in appearance as a man, He humbled Himself by becoming obedient to the point of death, even death on a cross."

In my commentary, "The Spirit of the Lord is upon Me," I wrote of the motive which caused Jesus, the very Son of God, to leave heaven to suffer the excruciating pain of death via the cross. In the Britannica-Webster dictionary, the word "motive" is defined as, "something (as a need or a state of mind) that leads or influences a person to do something." We discovered that the only motive Jesus needed to leave heaven was His awe-inspiring love for mankind. *Jesus saw mankind's need for salvation and He became exceedingly motivated to do something about it, even unto leaving heaven and suffering an excruciating death on the cross.* There is no other motivation mentioned in the Holy Scriptures that provoked Jesus' awe-inspiring actions except His unfathomable selfless love for mankind!

That being the case, I made the argument that whatever we do as Christians should also have just one motive, an awe-inspiring selfless love for mankind. A love so powerful that we wish for none to perish, but for all to come to a saving knowledge of Jesus Christ. *A love so powerful that we endure all things, setting aside our own wants and desires by crucifying them on our cross.* The Apostle Paul wrote in 2 Timothy 2:10, "For this reason I endure all things for the sake of those who are chosen, that they also may obtain the salvation which is in Christ Jesus and with it eternal glory." And in Colossians 1:24: *"Now I rejoice in my sufferings for your sake,* and in my flesh I do my share on behalf of His body (which is the church) in filling up that which is lacking in Christ's afflictions."

The Apostle Paul, born-again and filled with the Holy Spirit, not only rejoiced in his sufferings, but was honored to be a partaker of Christ's afflictions for mankind. Paul became one with Christ Jesus, inasmuch as, he was born-again with the Spirit of Christ—even the Spirit of God. The only motive Paul needed was his selfless love for mankind, a love placed within his heart by God, the Holy Spirit. *Paul wishing for none to perish, took up his cross daily, laid his life aside—even his desires, to deliver the gospel message to mankind.*

"Have this attitude in yourselves which was also in Christ Jesus . . ." Now, by the grace of God, I wish to write about the attitude you and I should have, which was also in Christ Jesus. The word "attitude" has to do with position. For example, a plane's attitude is its position relative to some fixed reference point. In the same way, our attitude is determined by the way you and I see our position relative to another person. For example, if we see ourselves in a higher position than someone else, our attitude would reflect a

superiority and our demeanor would come across to others as judgmental. On the other hand, if we see ourselves in a lower position, our attitude becomes submissive and our demeanor would come across to others as that of a servant, i.e., a minister. Our attitude has a profound impact on everything we do or say. It will even have a profound effect on our perspective, i.e., how we evaluate any given situation.

For example, I often hear it said in the Church today that if God doesn't judge the USA, He would have to apologize to Sodom and Gomorrah. In doing so, are we, as God's ambassadors of reconciliation, not acting a little like the Pharisee in Luke 18:10–12, "Two men went up into the temple to pray, one a Pharisee, and the other a tax-gatherer. The Pharisee stood and was praying thus to himself, 'God, I thank Thee that I am not like other people: swindlers, unjust, adulterers, or even like this tax-gatherer. I fast twice a week; I pay tithes of all that I get.'" *And if we are acting a bit "holier-than-thou," are we then expressing to the unsaved (the world) the attitude which was in Christ Jesus?* Are we expressing an attitude to the unsaved consistent with our role as God's ambassadors of reconciliation? Luke 9:54–56: "And when His disciples James and John saw this, they said, 'Lord, do You want us to command fire to come down from heaven and consume them?' *But He (Jesus) turned and rebuked them, and said, 'You do not know what kind of spirit you are of; for the Son of Man did not come to destroy men's lives, but to save them.'* And they went on to another village."

And if we are standing in judgment, how then can we evaluate, anyone or anything, clearly enough to be God's ambassadors of reconciliation to the unsaved? Luke 6:39–42: "And He also spoke a parable to them: 'A blind man cannot guide a blind man, can he? Will they not both fall into a pit? A pupil is not above his teacher; *but everyone, after he has been fully trained, will be like his teacher. And* why do you look at the speck that is in your brother's eye, but do not notice the log that is in your own eye? Or how can you say to your brother, 'Brother, let me take out the speck that is in your eye,' when you yourself do not see the log that is in your own eye? You hypocrite, first take the log out of your own eye, and then you will see clearly to take out the speck that is in your brother's eye." And in James 4:11–12, "Do not speak against one another, brethren. He who speaks against a brother, or judges his brother, speaks against the law, and judges the law; *but if you judge the law, you are not a doer of the law,* but a judge of it. There is only one Lawgiver and Judge, the One who is able to save and to destroy; but who are you who judge your neighbor?"

On the other hand, I see the situation we have here in the USA as evidence of our (God's Church) failure to be the salt and light we are called to be. Matthew 5:13–16: "You are the salt of the earth; but if the salt has become tasteless, how will it be made salty again? It is good for nothing anymore, except to be thrown out and trampled under foot by men. *You are the light of the world.* A city set on a hill cannot be hidden. Nor do men light a lamp, and put it under the peck-measure, but on the lampstand; and it gives light to all who are in the house. Let your light shine before men in such a way that they may see your good works, and glorify your Father who is in heaven."

Could the USA's moral decline be evidence of our light growing dim, or being completely out? After all, we know by experience that darkness can *never* put out the light, but light will always conquer darkness. If you doubt it, try to go into a lit room and turn on the darkness to put the light out. On the other hand, we can *always* defeat darkness by turning on a light. *But if the light grows dim, or goes out, darkness will always fill the vacuum.* Therefore, do we continue to blame the darkness, or should we be looking to see if we (God's Church) are putting out any light at all? 2 Chronicles 7:14: "And *my people* who are called by My name humble themselves and pray, and seek My face and turn from their wicked ways, then I will hear from heaven, will forgive their sin, and will heal their land."

Therefore, I humbly submit to you that along with motivation, attitude needs to be an equal and active participant in molding us Christians into the image of Christ Jesus. Where motive may be the potter's right hand, attitude is his left. Can you image what a vessel being formed on a potter's wheel would look like if the potter *only* used his right or left hand? *I can image a very lopsided, unbalanced, even a disfigured vessel, which could never resemble the image the potter was trying to produce.* Which in our case would be a vessel that would reflect the potter himself. With that in mind, fully grasping Philippians 2:5–8, becomes both pivotal and critical before we can reflect a proper image of Christ to a lost and dying world. 2 Corinthians 5:20: "Therefore, we are ambassadors for Christ, as though God were entreating through us; we beg you on behalf of Christ, be reconciled to God." Therefore, let's take a look at this pivotal, even critical attitude we are instructed to have within us.

"Who, although He existed in the form of God, did not regard equality with God a thing to be grasped . . . ." Yet we (God's Church) are so zealous to lay claim to (grasp) so much just because through Jesus Christ we have been *adopted* into God's family. And now that we are adopted, do we automatically know good from evil and know all things? Do we no longer have to ask God for His will? I recently heard a minister with a *very* large TV ministry say, "We cannot ask God for His will when we pray, because it would destroy our faith." I don't know about you, but I have not yet arrived to the place where I'm all knowing and all seeing. All of our faith must be directed at God's love and faithfulness toward us, includ-

ing God's wisdom when dealing with the dilemmas in our daily lives. It is imperative for us to do so, because at best, until perfection comes, we see through a glass darkly. Therefore, using the power of our faith to acquire our will, outside the confines of God's will, would at best be foolish and at worst, Satanic. *For even a mustard seed of "ungodly" faith can indeed move mountains.*

Genesis 3:2–5: "And the woman said to the serpent, 'From the fruit of the trees of the garden we may eat; but from the fruit of the tree which is in the middle of the garden, God has said, 'You shall not eat from it or touch it, lest you die.' And the serpent said to the woman, 'You surely shall not die! For God knows that in the day you eat from it your eyes will be opened, and you will be *like God*, knowing good and evil.'" Can you image what it would have been like if Adam and Eve had this attitude within them—". . . *did not regard equality with God a thing to be grasped"?* Why, we could have avoided all of this present-day suffering! Adam and Eve could have said, "Get behind me, Satan! Not my will, but God's will be done!" *Having the right attitude is an awesome safeguard from being tempted to do evil, and it will even give us eyes to see through Satan's deception!*

We are to have a holy fear (respect) for God, an awesome fear and respect for God's wisdom over and above our own. Have we not heard that we are to lean not to our own understanding and trust in God with all of our heart? *How can we have trust and faith in our God, even the God of Jacob, Isaac, and Abraham, concerning our eternity, and yet seem to mistrust Him so effortlessly with our day-to-day lives?* God forbid if I do not rely on His wisdom over my own by adding to my prayer, "Yet not my will be done!" Even when I find myself in an affliction that I cannot understand. *After all, that is when we find out if our faith and trust in God are truly genuine!*

Psalm 78:40–42: "How often they rebelled against Him (God) in the wilderness, and *grieved* Him in the desert! And again and again they tempted God, and *pained* the Holy One of Israel. They did not remember His power, the day when He redeemed them from the adversary." *All of us Christians have been delivered from our adversary, Satan!* And we were delivered with an even greater display of power than God displayed in Egypt. *Will we now question God in our wilderness experience?* Are we so distrustful of God that we have become afraid to end our prayers with, "Nevertheless, Your will be done"? Would it not have grieved and pained you if you have proven to be faithful time and time again, and yet in a time of crisis, your love and faithfulness were questioned? Psalm 106:13–15: "They quickly forgot His works; *They did not wait for His counsel (plan), but craved intensely in the wilderness,* and tempted God in the desert. So He gave them their request, but sent a wasting disease among them." God's ways will always be higher than our ways! But will we trust God?

Philippians 2:27: "For indeed he was sick to the point of death, but God had *mercy* on him, and not on him only but also on me, lest I should have sorrow upon sorrow." By using the word mercy, does that sound like the Apostle Paul both demanded and expected God to heal Epaphroditus? As there can be so many ramifications to one answered prayer (desire), do we really want to take on the responsibility of imposing our own will? Genesis 3:6: "When the woman saw that the tree was good for food, and that it was a delight to the eyes, and that the tree was desirable to make one wise, she took from its fruit and ate; and she gave also to her husband with her, and he ate." *Yes, even a desire which seems good, proper, and righteous in our eyes can turn cataclysmic, not only for us, but also for future generations.*

"But emptied Himself, taking the form of a bond servant . . . ." Jesus emptied Himself, no one forced Him. His act was completely voluntary. So a non-Christian has nothing to fear, we (Christians) cannot force you to accept Jesus as your savior. *So relax! Unless, perhaps, it is the truth itself you fear.* The Greek word used for bond servant is very interesting. It describes one who is in a permanent relationship of servitude to another. The bond servant's will is altogether consumed in the will of the other. The bond servant is completely devoted to another's will, even unto the disregard of one's own interests, i.e., not my will, but Your will be done. Dear friends, we Christians are *all* called to be bond servants to God!

"And being made in the likeness of men. And being found in appearance as a man . . . ." 2 Corinthians 5:2–4: "For indeed in this house we groan, longing to be clothed with our dwelling from heaven; inasmuch as we, having put it on, shall not be found naked. For indeed while we are in this tent, we groan, being burdened, because we do not want to be unclothed, but to be clothed, in order that what is mortal may be swallowed up by life." *Isn't this incredible and amazing?* We're groaning to be clothed, while Jesus laid all aside to become like us. And Jesus did it for a people, shall we be kind and say, who was somewhat less than alluring. The only way we know if we have this same attitude within us, is if we see the salvation of this somewhat uncomely world as being *much* more important than getting our own desires and needs fulfilled, i.e., taking up our cross and following Jesus.

"He humbled Himself by becoming obedient to the point of death, even death on a cross." Deuteronomy 8:3: "And He humbled you and let you be hungry, and fed you with manna which you did not know, nor did your fathers know, that He might make you understand that man does not live by bread alone, but man lives by everything that proceeds out of the mouth of the Lord." How

do we know when we have the same attitude as Jesus had? *When in the midst of our severest wilderness experience, even our severest trial, we forsake the use of all of our God-given powers for our temporal relief for God's eternal purpose.* In other words, using none of our power until we see our Father do it first. Yes, asking God for His will to be done over and above our own. Laying down our lives, our will, for His!

Matthew 4:2–4: "And after He had fasted forty days and forty nights, He then became (extremely) hungry. And the tempter came and said to Him, 'If You are the Son of God, command that these stones become bread.' But He answered and said, *'It is written, Man shall not live on bread alone, but on every word that proceeds out of the mouth of God.'"* What if Jesus had given in and used His power to deliver Himself from hunger? We know Jesus had the power, being the Son of God. But Jesus would not use His power unless He heard from God Himself. If Jesus had given in to this temptation of the flesh, would He have not also used His power to avoid the even greater suffering of the cross? We all know Jesus had the power to extricate Himself from this most excruciating trial via the cross. But if He did, where would you and I be? *At the time, do you think anyone understood God's plan?*

God forbid that any of us should suffer, because now we have Holy Spirit *power*—right? *Wrong!* Allow me to answer this in the same way Jesus did in Matthew 16:23, "But He turned and said to Peter, 'Get behind Me, Satan! You are a stumbling block to Me; for you are not setting your mind on God's interests, but man's.'"

Father, as it is written, "Man shall not live on bread alone, but on every word that proceeds out of the mouth of God," help me to have the same *attitude* as was in my Lord Jesus. Help me to trust and wait on You, even in my severest trial. Especially when I do not understand! For Your ways will always be higher than my ways. Help me to remember the prayer Jesus taught us to pray, *"Thy kingdom come, Thy will be done, on earth (and in my life) as it is in heaven."* Fill me with faith and power from above so I may know Your will, and be able to place Your will over and above my own. In Jesus' name, Amen!

Chapter Fifteen

The Spirit of the Lord Is Upon Me

Luke 4:17–21: "And the book of the prophet Isaiah was handed to Him (Jesus). And He opened the book, and found the place where it was written, '*The Spirit of the Lord is upon Me, because He anointed Me to preach the gospel to the poor. He has sent Me to proclaim release to the captives, and recovery of sight to the blind, to set free those who are downtrodden, to proclaim the favorable year of the Lord.*' And He closed the book, and gave it back to the attendant, and sat down; and the eyes of all in the synagogue were fixed upon Him. And He began to say to them, '*Today this Scripture has been fulfilled in your hearing.*'"

I believe the above passage of Scripture to be one of the most profound and pivotal passages in the New Testament. I can think of no other Scripture that so clearly and distinctly defines the objective of Jesus' life and ministry while He was with us. This was the reason God sent His only Son to die for us. This was the reason Jesus willingly sacrificed His life and suffered the excruciating pain of the cross. This was the reason Jesus left heaven. *The Father, Son, and Holy Spirit were in one accord—in complete agreement, and with great tenacity, proceeded to accomplish this awe-inspiring objective.*

This awe-inspiring objective was the controlling influence in Jesus' life. Everything Jesus said and did was motivated with this one objective in mind. Jesus' eyes always remained focused and fixed on this one objective. The Holy Spirit came upon Jesus, without measure—with all power—in order to equip Jesus to fulfill this one objective. *Since this awe-inspiring objective necessitated the full attention and power of the Father, Son, and Holy Spirit, would it not also be wise for us to give it our full attention?* Let's take a closer look at this profound passage of Scripture.

"The Spirit of the Lord is upon Me, because He anointed Me . . . ." The word "anointed" in this quote from Scripture simply means to equip, to furnish someone with the necessary equipment for the administration of the specified objective. From this quote we are also told that it's the Holy Spirit's job to do the equipping. This is extremely important to understand, because from this Scripture we get a very clear and distinct picture of the Holy Spirit's role in God's divine and awe-inspiring plan. We are made aware that the responsibilities of Jesus and Holy Spirit differ, i.e., Jesus becomes the sacrifice and the Holy Spirit supplies the power, but the objective remains the same. Which should be no surprise to us, as we know the Father, Son, and Holy Spirit have always been one. Therefore, it is reasonable for us to come to the conclusion that the anointing—the power you and I receive from the Holy Spirit should also be focused on this same objective. *In other words, the only reason we should be seeking and asking for the Holy Spirit to come upon us with power is so we can accomplish this same awe-inspiring objective, the proclamation of the gospel message.*

Seeking to be anointed by the Holy Spirit with another objective, or with an agenda of our own creation, would not only be foolish, but would also set us up for deception. *Satan would be happy to masquerade in the Holy Spirit's place with a myriad of signs, wonders, and other displays of power to keep us deceived and rendered useless in God's objective.* Therefore, it becomes imperative for us to fully understand God's awe-inspiring objective, inasmuch as, God wants us also to become one with Him. John 17:22: "And the glory which Thou hast given Me I have given to them; that they may be one, just as We are one." Let's now begin to unveil God's awe-inspiring objective.

"To preach the gospel to the poor . . . ." To gain insight, we must accurately define the word "poor" as it is used in this quote. In society today the image that immediately comes to mind by the word "poor" is someone who does not have the financial means to reach society's arbitrary standard of living. However, this Greek word for poor simply means someone who is completely and totally destitute, helpless, and powerless to accomplish any desired aspiration without some kind of outside intervention.

Remember how John the Baptist was sent by God to prepare the way for Jesus? John traveled about the countryside preaching in the power of the Holy Spirit, bringing conviction into the hearts of many, in order to bring about repentance. This caused many to realize their need to be cleansed of their defilement—their sin. Hence, we get the external symbolism of water baptism, which symbolizes the need for cleansing, a cleansing which now became so essential as the Holy Spirit supernaturally exposed our need.

But now we have a huge problem! Washing our flesh with water cannot change who we are (our heart), or remove our sin. We now find ourselves in a position where we are completely and totally destitute, helpless, and powerless to accomplish this essential need. What a dilemma we now find ourselves in! The Holy Spirit exposed our need and at the same time we found ourselves to be completely helpless and powerless to do anything about it. We find ourselves in the very precarious position of being completely destitute and *poor!* Who will intervene to help us?

Jesus now comes on the scene preaching the gospel, the good news *that God Himself will intervene on our behalf.* Inasmuch as, we found ourselves to be completely helpless and powerless, God sent His only Son to intervene on our behalf. Jesus sacrificed His life to cleanse us from our defilement—our sins. *But this gospel, this good news, was only good news to the* poor! To the proud of heart and self-righteous, this gospel was not good news at all; it was extremely offensive. After all, they were in need of no one—not even God! The gospel message became so offensive to the proud and self-righteous they spit upon and killed the messenger—Jesus. We now know God used the proud and self-righteous as unwilling pawns to ultimately fulfill His plan of intervention.

"He has sent Me to proclaim release to the captives . . . ." Once again, we find a message which only the poor of heart can embrace and can only offend the proud of heart. In order to admit a need to be set free, you would have to also admit to a loss of control over your own life. In other words, a slave! John 8:33–36, "They answered Him, 'We are Abraham's offspring, and have never yet been enslaved to anyone; how is it that You say, 'You shall become free?' Jesus answered them, 'Truly, truly, I say to you, everyone who commits sin is the slave of sin. And the slave does not remain in the house forever; the son does remain forever. *If therefore the Son shall make you free, you shall be free indeed.'"*

But it goes far beyond the basic concept of the inability to say no to sin, as some will undoubtedly say, "I'm not out of control! I have the ability to exercise self-control!" Nevertheless, if you sin just once, you are no longer a freeman, but a slave, a captive to sin's punishment. Since no one can ever look into a mirror and say,

"I have never in my life missed the mark (sin)," then all of us are in desperate need of a pardon. The Greek word translated "release" in the above quote is the same word used for remission, forgiveness, pardon, and deliverance. Proclaiming release to the captives, is *very* good news (gospel) to me!

"And recovery of sight to the blind . . . ." Revelation 3:17–18: "Because you say, 'I am rich, and have become wealthy, and have need of nothing,' you do not know that you are wretched and miserable and poor and blind and naked, I advise you to buy from Me gold refined by fire, that you may become rich, and white garments, that you may clothe yourself, and that the shame of your nakedness may not be revealed; and eye salve to anoint your eyes, *that you may see."* Here Jesus gives to us a clear indication of the blindness He came to take away—the blindness to our spiritual condition. As the Holy Spirit convicts us of sin, He is in reality empowering us to see for the first time our true spiritual condition. *The Holy Spirit is indeed enabling the blind to see.* In the above verse, Jesus also gives us insight to the cause of our spiritual blindness. It is a proud, hard, arrogant heart which will cause this spiritual blindness.

John 9:39–41: "And Jesus said, 'For judgment I came into this world, that those who do not see may see; and that those who see may become blind.' Those of the Pharisees who were with Him heard these things, and said to Him, 'We are not blind too, are we?' Jesus said to them, 'If you were blind, you would have no sin; but since you say, 'We see,' your sin remains.'" With this verse we come to understand that if we continue to reject the efforts of the Holy Spirit to convict us of sin, there remains no hope. If in the arrogance of our heart we continue to reject the Holy Spirit's definition of right and wrong for our own definition (in essence calling evil, good and good, evil), we will never see a need for a savior and our spiritual blindness becomes *terminal*. Mark 3:28–30: "Truly I say to you, all sins shall be forgiven the sons of men, and whatever blasphemies they utter; but whoever blasphemes against the Holy Spirit never has forgiveness, but is guilty of an eternal sin, because they were saying, 'He has an unclean spirit.'"

"To set free those who are downtrodden . . . ." The word downtrodden in the Greek language display's an image of not only brokenness, but a shattering into small pieces. And since everything so far in this gospel message has dealt with our spiritual condition, we can reasonably conclude this passage does also. We also find the word downtrodden to be in the passive voice. In other words, this shattering of our spirit was done to us by an outside force.

Even as our spirit was shattered by an outside force, God sent an outside force to restore it. Our shattered, downtrodden spirit came through the disobedience of someone other than ourselves and is now bound up, made whole, and restored through the obedience of another. 1 Corinthians 15:22: "For as in Adam all die, so also in Christ all shall be made alive." And again in Romans 5:17–19, "For if by the transgression of the one, death reigned through the one, much more those who receive the abundance of grace and of the gift of righteousness will reign in life through the One, Jesus Christ. So then as through one transgression there resulted condemnation to all men, even so through one act of righteousness there resulted justification of life to all men. For as through the one man's disobedience the many were made sinners, even so through the obedience of the One the many will be made righteous."

"To proclaim the favorable year of the Lord . . . ." Here Jesus announced to mankind that for a fixed period of time God was willing to extend His hand of mercy toward His creation—you and me. This is a time when God would allow mankind the unprec-

edented gift of unmerited favor—the gift of salvation and freedom from His righteous judgment, allowing mankind, His prodigal sons and daughters, an opportunity to come home. Read Luke 15:11–32.

In the Greek, the word for "year" used in this passage represented something we must never forget. It illustrates an image of time with both a beginning and a definite end, while at the same time not being specific as to its length. In other words, this time period of God's mercy, compassion, and grace toward mankind will *definitely* come to an end sometime in the future.

When Jesus stood up in the synagogue and started to read Isaiah chapter sixty-one, He abruptly stopped without finishing the rest of Isaiah's prophecy. Instead He closed the book and said in Luke 4:21, "Today this Scripture has been fulfilled in your hearing." In so doing, Jesus made it extremely clear that this was all of Isaiah's prophecy to be fulfilled at this time, or season. The very next line in Isaiah is bone-chilling, foretelling God's next item of business with mankind after this "Favorable year of the Lord." The next line in Isaiah reads, *"And the day of vengeance of our God!"* This should bring a sense of urgency within our hearts for the proclamation of the gospel toward mankind.

The Father, Son, and Holy Spirit placed such a high value on the above gospel message, They literally held nothing back, even unto the sacrifice of God's own Son. If that is the case, what does God expect from us? We find the answer to our question in John 17:18, *"As Thou didst send Me into the world, I also have sent them into the world."* And again in John 17:20, "I do not ask in behalf of these alone, but for those also who believe in Me through their word." Jesus makes it very clear that His prayer in John 17 was directed at all believers in Christ Jesus. The same mission objective Jesus started was now to be handed over to us to finish, giving the gospel message to mankind to proclaim to mankind.

John 17: 14– 16: "I have given them Thy word; and the world has hated them, because they are not of the world, even as I am not of the world. *I do not ask Thee to take them out of the world,* but to keep them from the evil one. They are not of the world, even as I am not of the world." What an incredible prayer Jesus offered up to God the Father! Could Jesus leave us in the world if He knew we were going to be mistreated and hated by the majority of people around us? John 16:1–4: "These things I have spoken to you, that you may be kept from stumbling. They will make you outcasts from the synagogue, but an hour is coming for everyone who kills you to think that he is offering service to God. And these things they will do, because they have not known the Father, or Me. But these things I have spoken to you, that when their hour comes, you may remember that I told you of them. And these things I did not say to you at the beginning, because I was with you."

Jesus expected us to have the same passion and love for the gospel message and for mankind that He had, a passion and love so great that we would be willing to endure personal sacrifice and hardship. Jesus' love for mankind was so great that He actually left heaven to suffer here on earth. How many of us would be willing to pray, "God, keep me out of heaven a little longer so I can touch one more soul with your gospel, or help one more weary soul to stand"? Jesus endured all kinds of insults and indignities for the gospel's sake, because of His love and passion for mankind. How much personal sacrifice and hardship are we willing to endure for the gospel's objective?

When we asked for the Holy Spirit to come upon us, what objective did we have in mind? Was it for a selfish, self-serving objective, or was the objective the gospel message? When you asked for a miracle, was it for the gospel's sake, or to fulfill your own desires? Acts 4:29–31: "And now, Lord, take note of their threats, and grant that Thy bond servants may speak Thy word with all confidence, while Thou dost extend Thy hand to heal, and signs and wonders take place through the name of Thy holy servant Jesus. And when they had prayed, the place where they had gathered together was shaken, and they were all filled with the Holy Spirit, and began to speak the word of God with *boldness!"*

When I speak of the objective of the gospel message, I'm not restricting it only to the evangelistic point of view, but from every needed area pastors, prophets, teachers, and so on. All ministry areas are needed and equally important to the fulfillment of God's gospel objective, or why would God place them in the body of Christ—the Church. Not all can be pastors, prophets, or teachers, nonetheless, we all have a role in fulfilling God's gospel objective with such things as prayer, financial support, encouragement, obedient life style, and so on. *And we must maintain a sense of urgency, for now is the favorable year of the Lord!*

Matthew 25:14: "For it is just like a man about to go on a journey, who called his own slaves, and entrusted his possessions (mankind) to them." And again in Matthew 25:24–27, "And the one also who had received the one talent came up and said, 'Master, I knew you to be a hard man, reaping where you did not sow, and gathering where you scattered no seed. And I was afraid, and went away and hid your talent in the ground; see, you have what is yours.' But his master answered and said to him, 'You wicked, lazy slave, you knew that I reap where I did not sow, and gather where I scattered no seed. Then you ought to have put my money in the bank, and on my arrival I would have received my money back with interest.'" *Are we willing to risk (sacrifice) our God given talents and/or assets to give God His heart's desire?*

Lord, baptize, even immerse us in the Holy Spirit to give us the faith and courage to place the objective that is so close to Your heart, the gospel, first and foremost in ours. Pour the Holy Spirit upon us to take away our fear of man, our anxiety for tomorrow's bread, that we may give freely—even sacrificially to bring to bear all our God given talents and/or assets to accomplish Your heart's desire—Your awe-inspiring objective, to proclaim Your gospel to mankind. In Jesus' name, Amen!

Chapter Sixteen

I Want to Be Just Like You

I cannot think of any more precious words in the human language than, *"I want to be just like you,"* when the words are directed to a father from the lips of his children. Although my Lord has never blessed me with children, it will in no way disqualify me from knowing how precious, even priceless, those words would be to hear from my child. Likewise, I also know in my heart of hearts it would be just as precious to our Father in heaven to hear these words, *"I want to be just like you"* from His children. These words would be as precious to God as the fragrance of a rose in the cool and stillness of midnight. A fragrance of such delight— of such preciousness—would cause us to have an involuntary impulse to expand our lungs to a point our lungs would feel as if they were about to burst within us. We would not be willing to allow one precious molecule of that fragrance to escape from us. And when we finally exhale, it would be accompanied with a sigh of inexpressible delight.

On the other hand, these same seven innocent words have the potential to become so corrupt that the only fragrance, which would be emanating from the words would be akin to rotting flesh. In fact, the words have the potential to become so offensive that the only impulse you would have is to exhale, not willing to allow one molecule of that corrupt fragrance to invade your senses. *What could cause these seven innocent words to have such a profound dissimilarity, i.e., to be so precious or so corrupt?* It is the yearning in your heart at the time you say, "I want to be just like you" which will produce this profound dissimilarity. In other words, what god-like attribute are you actually seeking after? What is the yearning of your heart which caused those seven innocent words to fall from your lips?

There are times in my life when a subject matter is of such significance that mere words seem totally inadequate to convey its seriousness; so it is with this subject. Therefore, would you just take a moment and pray for the Holy Spirit to come upon you and become your teacher? That He would go beyond the total inadequacy of my words and ability to give to you a personal revelation of this subject's profound significance. Nevertheless, I will do my best to explain to you how the yearning of your heart could have such a profound effect on seven such innocent words.

I will begin with the yearning heart that truly makes the words, *"I want to be just like you,"* both fragrant and precious to our Father in heaven—the God of Jacob, Isaac, and Abraham. So what is this yearning that produces such a precious fragrance, a fragrance that God could take such a delight in? *It is the yearning that seeks the inheritance of His glory; a yearning within our hearts so great that it supersedes—even supplants—our own desire and self-will in order to secure His glory!*

But now we have a problem. We must establish an accurate definition of God's glory because it is this definition of God's glory which will cause the profound dissimilarity. For example, if someone tells you they love you, it could just mean that the person finds you attractive and merely wishes to have an affair with you. I'm sure you would agree that such a definition of the word "love" would dreadfully corrupt such a precious and fragrant word. Unfortunately, you and I need both time and experience before we would know what was on the person's heart when he spoke this most fragrant word, "love," whereas, God knows what's in our heart before we even say a word. *That being the case, would it not be prudent for us to first judge our own heart by defining His glory even as God Himself defines His glory? Of course it would!*

First, it would be beneficial for us to understand the symbolism the Hebrew language gives to the word we translate into English as "glory." In Hebrew it symbolizes a weightiness, something which is esteemed, something which is majestic, something which is awesome, something which is superior, something worthy of all consideration. In Scripture, God's glory is described to be so brilliant that heaven itself has no need for a sun to give it light (Revelation 21:23), a glory so powerful, so awesome, that no man can look directly at it and remain among the living. When Moses asked God to see His glory, God only allowed Moses to see His glory's afterglow, as it meant sure death for Moses to look directly at it; a glory so fragrant and precious it would instantly bring extreme delight to God's heart, causing Him to deeply inhale, not willing to allow one precious molecule of glory's fragrance to escape. *What could this breathtaking glory be?* Actually, in the Holy Scriptures, God answers this most significant question directly from His own lips.

In Exodus 33:18–19, "Then Moses said, *'I pray Thee, show me Thy glory!'* And He said, *'I Myself will make all My goodness* pass before you, and will proclaim the name of the Lord before you.'"

Notice that what Moses calls God's "glory" and what God calls "His goodness" are one and the same. We know both God and Moses are speaking of the same thing when God switches back to the word "glory" in Exodus 33: 20–23, "But He said, 'You cannot see My face, for no man can see Me and live!' Then the Lord said, 'Behold, there is a place by Me, and you shall stand there on the rock; and it will come about, while My *glory* is passing by, that I will put you in the cleft of the rock and cover you with My hand until I have passed by. Then I will take My hand away and you shall see My back, but My face shall not be seen.'" *Once again we see this glory as being so powerful, so awesome, so brilliant, that in order for Moses to remain alive he was only allowed to see this glory's afterglow.*

Now we get from God's own lips His definition of glory. Exodus 34:5–7: "And the Lord descended in the cloud and stood there with him as he called upon the name of the Lord. Then the Lord passed by in front of him and proclaimed, 'The Lord, the Lord God, is compassionate and gracious, slow to anger, and abounding in lovingkindness and truth; who keeps lovingkindness for thousands, who forgives iniquity, transgression and sin; yet He will by no means leave the guilty unpunished, visiting the iniquity of fathers on the children and on the grandchildren to the third and fourth generations.'"

God's glory consists of both compassion and grace. God, through His compassion, has the ability and will to empathize with us, to fully understand and feel our pain. He has the ability and will to both cry and rejoice along with us. As a matter of fact, our tears are so precious to Him, He saves them in a bottle (Psalm 56:8). But God does not stop there! He then applies His grace to our wound as a fragrant balm for our healing. He pledges His favor when no one else will even approach us. And even if all abandon you, His grace allows Him to meet you with peace in His left hand and acceptance in His right hand.

In God's glory we can find perfect patience as He is slow to anger. God is willing, for a time, to set aside His anger at a sinful world, wishing for none to perish, but for all to come to repentance and salvation.

God's glory is also abounding in lovingkindness (mercy). God's glory does not just contain mercy; His glory is abounding in mercy; so much so that it becomes an absolute delight for God to envelop us in forgiveness. But the word mercy goes even further. Mercy forgives even when you cannot forgive yourself. Mercy envelops you in more kindness than you could even hope or dream of receiving. Mercy lifts you up when you are so far down that you cannot escape the mud and mire under your own power.

God's glory is the embodiment of truth. Therefore, God's glory is inherently faithful. It keeps its lovingkindness for thousands, faithfully forgiving iniquity, transgression, and sin. Yet, God's glory will not leave the guilty unpunished, but visit the iniquity of fathers on the children and on the grandchildren to the third and fourth generations. In other words, God's glory is so awesome that we may be tempted to use it as a reason to indulge sin, as many now do. Hence, we get the quote, "If God is love, there cannot be a hell." But the fact remains that sin will be judged and there is a hell. *However, God's glory was also the very thing that created the door which we use to escape His judgment. And that door is* Jesus!

God's definition of glory is awesome, but do you see something which seems to be missing? I'll give you a hint. It's something the world would highly esteem and would readily include in the definition of God's glory. Nevertheless, this something obviously merits no consideration to God as He chooses to completely omit it from His definition of glory. What is so highly esteemed among mankind, but of no consideration to God? It was God's *display of power* as He delivered His people from Egypt. Therefore, since God did not consider His *display of power* as part of His glory, should we not also eliminate it from our list? Instead let's reconsider Jesus' words in Matthew 6:33, "But seek first His kingdom and His righteousness; and all these things shall be added to you." In other words, the *"power"* is inherently found in God's righteousness, goodness, i.e., *glory*, but if we are found seeking power, we end up losing it all. *Yes, another biblical paradox!*

Which brings me to the corruption which can also be found in the words, *"I want to be just like you."* If by saying the words "I want to be just like you," you are actually yearning in your heart for power: power to gain personal control over your life and circumstances; power to lord over someone, or to have control over their life; power to exalt yourself in the eyes of mankind; power to determine your own rules, i.e., to determine for yourself what is good and what is evil. If this is the yearning from your heart, then the words, "I want to be just like you" are as corrupt as rotting flesh, and the fragrance is immeasurably repulsive to God.

In Scripture, we are given two very tragic examples of this corruption of the heart in both Lucifer (Satan) and Adam. First we'll take a look at the account of Lucifer in Isaiah 14:12–17, "How you have fallen from heaven, O star of the morning (Lucifer), son of the dawn! You have been cut down to the earth, you who have weakened the nations! *But you said in your heart,* 'I will ascend to heaven; I will raise my throne above the stars of God, and I will sit on the mount of assembly in the recesses of the north. I will ascend above the heights of the clouds; *I will make myself like the Most High.*' Nevertheless you will be thrust down to Sheol (Hell), to the recesses of the pit. Those who see you will gaze at you, they will ponder over you, saying, 'Is this the man who made the earth tremble, who shook kingdoms, who made the world like a wilderness and overthrew its cities, who did not allow his prisoners to go home?'"

Now let's take a look at Adam in Genesis 2:15–17, "Then the Lord God took the man and put him into the garden of Eden to cultivate it and keep it. And the Lord God commanded the man, saying, 'From any tree of the garden you may eat freely; but from the tree of the knowledge of good and evil you shall not eat, for in the day that you eat from it you shall surely die.'" And again in Genesis 3:4–6, "And the serpent said to the woman, 'You surely shall not die! For God knows that in the day you eat from it your eyes will be opened, *and you will be like God,* knowing good and evil.' When the woman saw that the tree was good for food, and that it was a delight to the eyes, and that the tree was desirable to make one wise, she took from its fruit and ate; and she gave also to her husband with her, and he ate." *Having "power" has always been and will always be extremely seductive!* But the real tragedy was that both Adam and Eve were already like God in every way until they lost God's *glory* in their pursuit of *power.* God's glory, which was once their covering, was now gone and they found themselves to be naked.

In contrast, we have Jesus as an example as one who is seeking God's true glory. Speaking of the cross and His approaching sufferings, Jesus said in John 12:27–28, "Now My soul has become troubled; and what shall I say, 'Father, save Me from this hour'? But for this purpose I came to this hour. Father, glorify Thy name." And again in John 13:31–32, "When therefore he had gone out, Jesus said, 'Now is the Son of Man *glorified,* and God is *glorified* in Him; if God is *glorified* in Him, God will also *glorify* Him in Himself, and will *glorify* Him immediately.'"

You may ask, "How can we find God's glory in Jesus suffering excruciating pain on a cross?" The answer becomes crystal clear as you come to understand the definition of God's glory. The sufferings Jesus was about to undergo perfectly illustrated God's definition of glory because it publicly exposed to the world God's mercy, grace, and forgiveness toward mankind. At the same time the glory of God's justice was revealed as the judgment for sin is death. In God's glory, mankind found forgiveness and gained salvation through the sacrifice of His only Son. In God's glory, our judgment for sin was placed upon God's only Son (if you're willing to accept it). And in God's glory, we can also clearly see the inherent power contained within God's glory as the grave could not hold Jesus.

Jesus did not sacrifice Himself on the cross to empower us to arrogantly display all kinds of signs and wonders. After all, even Satan has the ability to display power (Mark 13:22–23). But Jesus died to restore God's glory, God's nature, God's Spirit to mankind. By repenting (turning away from sin) and accepting Jesus' sacrifice for the forgiveness of our sins, we once again regain God's glory, God's nature, God's Spirit as we are "born-again" into His image. John 17:22–26: *"And the glory which Thou hast given Me I have given to them;* that they may be one, just as We are one; I in them, and Thou in Me, that they may be perfected in unity, that the world may know that Thou didst send Me, and didst love them, even as Thou didst love Me. Father, I desire that they also, whom Thou hast given Me, be with Me where I am, in order that they may behold My glory, which Thou hast given Me; for Thou didst love Me before the foundation of the world. O righteous Father, although the world has not known Thee, yet I have known Thee; and these have known that Thou didst send Me; and I have made Thy name known to them, and will make it known; that the love wherewith Thou didst love Me may be in them, and I in them."

2 Corinthians 3:18: "But we all, with unveiled face beholding as in a mirror the *glory* of the Lord, are being *transformed into the same image from glory to glory,* just as from the Lord, the Spirit." And what is this image, this glory, we are being transformed into?

It is God's glory! God's glory is compassionate and gracious, slow to anger, and abounding in lovingkindness and truth; who keeps lovingkindness for thousands, who forgives iniquity, transgression and sin (the glory of God's justice no longer has a part as justice was fulfilled in Jesus' sacrifice. If you're willing to accept it). *Yes, as fantastic as it might sound, God wishes to share His glory with us.* 1 John 3:2–3: "Beloved, now we are children of God, and it has not appeared as yet what we shall be. We know that, when He appears, we shall be like Him, because we shall see Him just as He is. And everyone who has this hope fixed on Him purifies himself, just as He is pure." Moses could look only at the afterglow of God's glory for fear of dying, whereas, we who are born-again will actually be able to see God as He is, because we will be partakers of that same awesome glory.

It is no wonder that Satan wishes to conceal God's true glory from us. Unfortunately, he seems to be doing a really good job of it. You tell me: what do you see manifested in abundance throughout God's Church, an arrogant display of power or a reflection of God's true glory? And what do the majority in God's Church seem to seek after? Is it the power or God's true glory? *Let us no longer be defrauded from our inheritance in Christ Jesus.* God forbid that any of us would hear Matthew 7:21–23, "Not everyone who says to Me, 'Lord, Lord,' will enter the kingdom of heaven; but he who does the will of My Father who is in heaven. *Many* will say to Me on that day, 'Lord, Lord, did we not prophesy in Your name, and in Your name cast out demons, and in Your name perform many miracles?' And then I will declare to them, '*I never knew you;* depart from Me, you who practice lawlessness.'"

It is the tangible reality of the born-again experience which secures our place in heaven. It is the yearning heart of God's Spirit within us for God's true glory that assures us of our heavenly inheritance. It is the yearning heart for God's true glory which is the earnest—the down payment—of our dwelling place in heaven. It is the heart yearning for God's true glory which confirms that this world is not our home; in fact, we are just wandering pilgrims yearning for the redemption, the transformation of our body (flesh), so we can finally be home. And yet at the same time this same yearning heart wishes to stay a little longer so we can share this remarkable heritage—this awesome glory—with others. It is this yearning heart within for God's true glory which assures us that now we are the children of God, causing us to cry out, Abba Father. So, what does your heart yearn after when you say to God, *"I want to be just like you"*?

We must come to understand what makes heaven, heaven. It is not God's display of power, for even Satan can display power; but it is God's glory that makes heaven so heavenly!

Chapter Seventeen

Christian Heroism

The words "Christian heroism" are two words we seldom see associated together in society. As a matter of fact, in the eyes of society, that particular word association would be looked upon as an oxymoron. In society, Christians are portrayed as weak, meek, and cowardly. *However, in reality, the biblical Christian should be defined as heroism personified and be revered in society!* But regrettably, because of a societal ignorance of Scripture and/or simple intellectual dishonesty, the expression "Christian heroism" has become known to the majority in society as a contradiction in terms.

Society has actually redefined the word "hero" as one who has wealth, power, and/or a comely physical appearance. Whereas, character should be the defining attribute which creates and establishes our heroes. We can see this trait throughout our society today from sports to politics. As society continues to elevate physical appearance, money, and/or power over character to define our heroes, do we really need to spend millions on a commission to find out why society is losing its conscience, or why children are killing children without remorse? Could it be that the one thing that is truly heroic, biblical Christianity, is made fun of, even demonized, to the point of rejecting the Holy Bible as an evil influence? As a consequence of this attitude, society has become blind to the fact that the Holy Bible is actually filled from cover-to-cover with acts of unprecedented character-based heroism.

Therefore, I believe it's time we once again reestablish—even trumpet to society—that the words "Christian heroism" can indeed have an impeccable association. To do this we must first establish, even reestablish, a proper definition of heroism. We can start with the actual definition that I found in my Britannica-Webster dictionary: *"Great self-sacrificing courage—see courage. Courage, greatness of heart in facing danger or difficulties. Hero, a person admired for achievements and qualities."* In other words, we need to see if we can associate biblical Christianity with self-sacrifice, showing courage in the midst of dangers or difficulties, and/or having admired qualities, i.e., character. As we make that association, perhaps society will then find the courage to reexamine who they are holding up as heroes for our children to emulate?

As we examine heroism in the Holy Scriptures, I want you to notice that the acts of Christian heroism were birthed by a deep, abiding faith and trust in God. A good place to start our examination of Christian heroism would be in the Old Testament with King David. King David gives us a unique opportunity not only to see his heroism in action, but also see his failure to act heroically. In King David's story we also get to see clearly the momentous consequences of both his heroism and his lack of heroism.

David's act of heroism, 1 Samuel 17: Goliath was more than nine feet tall and so gigantic in stature that all of Israel lost heart at the sight of this giant. Even King Saul, who himself was of sizeable stature, lost heart and was afraid to come face to face with Goliath. On the other hand, there was David, the youngest son of Jesse, still just a youth, who was willing, even eager, to confront this gigantic Goliath. David, motivated by a strong faith and trust in God, placed himself in harm's way for his countrymen. After making it abundantly clear that his act of heroism was birthed by his faith and trust in God, David went out to face this giant eye to eye. Armed with only a shepherd's sling, David slew Goliath. David's act of courage caused the Philistines to flee and thereby he saved the lives of perhaps tens of thousands of his countrymen.

David's failure to act heroic, 2 Samuel 11–12: Here King David fails to act heroically by taking the path of least resistance and consequently gives in to the lust of his flesh: David takes to himself a married woman named Bathsheba. Unlike the heroism he displayed in facing Goliath, now he thought only of himself and gave no thought to the effect his actions would have on others. Did King David, who was now wealthy and powerful as the King of Israel, act courageously and heroically by thinking only of what was expedient and beneficial to himself? *No! On the contrary, those are the kind of self-indulgent thoughts only a coward would have!* The price of his cowardly act cost the life of both Bathsheba's innocent husband Uriah, and an innocent newborn baby. You may ask, "Why did the innocent have to die for David's act of weakness—his act of cowardice?" The answer is elementary: the innocent always suffer at the hands of a coward.

You may recoil at my associating the word coward with King David, but if I am going to call his courage, heroism, as I should, then I must call his lack of courage, cowardice. For me to do anything less would be intellectually dishonest. *We cannot—must not— try to become politically correct by trying to avoid hurting someone's feelings by using a more palatable description of King David's weak-*

ness, such as, "King David was a victim of his lust." Do you not realize by affording King David this leeway we are actually setting up a defense for our own weaknesses, thereby, eliminating our greatest restrainer—shame? And if you claim to be a "victim," where then is the motivation for you to change or repent? Remember, Jesus clearly teaches that without repentance there is no forgiveness.

Nevertheless, King David again shows us another true act of heroism by coming clean and taking responsibility for his act of cowardice/weakness and thereby stops the bleeding. Most of the time you cannot reverse the damage that has already been done; but, by taking the heroic step of confession and repentance, you can stop the proliferation of any more damage. On the other hand, if you continue to act cowardly by justifying your weakness, the circle of your innocent victims will only become enlarged.

Let us now move on to the greatest hero who has ever walked on this earth. Remember the definition I found in the Britannica-Webster dictionary for hero, i.e., "Great self-sacrificing courage. Greatness of heart in facing danger or difficulties. A person admired for achievements and qualities." I believe in my heart of hearts that Jesus Christ is the greatest hero who has ever walked on this earth. I'm sure the reaction from a majority of the secular world would be to ridicule my statement. Nevertheless, the fact remains that Jesus Christ does indeed thoroughly fulfill even the secular world dictionary's definition for both courage and heroism.

As far as Jesus fulfilling the attribute of "a person admired for achievements and qualities," there is little or no conflict. Most religions of this world will tell you that they think of Jesus as a good man, but then reject Him as Savior. What about great self-sacrificing courage? To answer that, all we have to do is go to the account of Jesus in the Garden of Gethsemane in Luke 22:39–44. In this account of Jesus we have the most remarkable display of both courage and self-sacrifice this world has ever seen—or ever will see. I say this for two reasons. First, Jesus had to not only face the most excruciating death that mankind has ever conceived, but He faced this painful death for the same people who despised Him and actually spit in His face. Second, Jesus had both the power and ability to walk away from His cross and completely avoid personal suffering. It was no wonder that as Jesus faced this dilemma, His emotions, His feelings, His body (flesh) suffered such overwhelming violence as to cause His sweat to become as drops of blood.

Today, society would look at Jesus as a fool—not a hero—to suffer for those who despised and spit in His face. And why would today's society think Jesus to be a fool? To answer that, all I have to say are two words: *situational ethics!* With situational ethics you will never have to suffer violence to your own feelings, emotions, or body (flesh). *What a gutless, cowardly position to take! No values, no rights, no wrongs, just whatever feels good*—do it! Looking out only for yourself, without the slightest thought for anyone else, whereas, biblical Christianity is exhorted to follow Jesus' example. 1 Peter 4:19: "Therefore, let those also who suffer according to the will of God entrust their souls to a faithful Creator in doing what is right." *Doing the right thing in spite of personal suffering is heroism personified! Conforming to godliness in a godless world* defines *courage!* No situational ethics found here!

When society makes a statement like, "Christianity is for the weak, or for those who need a crutch," it only exposes society's profound and willful ignorance of Christianity. The very first act of a Christian is in itself an act of great courage. To admit that you are a sinner (not perfect) and are in need of a savior is a very courageous thing to admit. Finding humility within yourself is much more difficult than saying, "I have need of no one!" Pride comes to us naturally; therefore, in order to find humility, we must first do violence to our pride. True humility comes only by way of crucifying our pride, i.e., taking up our cross; *does this not make humility itself intrinsically heroic and courageous?* Perhaps that is why Jesus said in Matthew 7:13–14, "Enter by the narrow gate; for the gate is wide, and the way is broad that leads to destruction, and many are those who enter by it. For the gate is small, and the way is narrow that leads to life, and *few* are those who find it." *Have not heroes always been in the minority?*

Do we have a problem in the church today manifesting Christianity to society as both courageous and heroic? Have we allowed the word "overcomer" to be redefined as free from trials, hardships, pain, or self-denial, *thereby, avoiding* our *cross?* Have we allowed phases like "spirit of lust" or "generational curse" to enter into the church to avoid personal responsibility, *thereby, avoiding* our *cross?* It is not unlike the way society avoids personal responsibility by using the word "victim." However, the Bible describes an overcomer as one who actually *perseveres* through personal hardship and pain, willing to suffer violence to their pride and/or emotions, even unto death, to accommodate godliness.

Biblical Christianity will not allow us to avoid our cross. Luke 14:25–35: "Now great multitudes were going along with Him; and He (Jesus) turned and said to them, 'If anyone comes to Me, and does not hate his own father and mother and wife and children and brothers and sisters, yes, and even his own life, he cannot be My disciple. Whoever does not carry his own cross and come after Me cannot be My disciple. For which one of you, when he wants to build a tower, does not first sit down and calculate the cost, to see if he has enough to complete it? Otherwise, when he has laid a foundation, and is not able to finish, all who observe it begin to ridicule him, saying, this man began to build and was not able to finish. Or what king, when he sets out to meet another king in battle, will not first sit down and take counsel whether he is strong enough with ten thousand men to encounter the one coming against him with twenty thousand? Or else, while the other is still far away, he sends a delegation and asks terms of peace. So therefore, no one of you can be My disciple who does not give up all his own possessions. Therefore, salt is good; but if even salt has become tasteless, with what will it be seasoned? It is useless either for the soil or for the manure pile; it is thrown out. He who has ears to hear, let him hear.'"

Could Jesus make it any clearer that being a Christian would, out of necessity, require both courage and heroism on our part? *Jesus makes it abundantly clear that Christianity, without self-denial and the cross, is not even good enough for the manure pile.* Because of the severity of Jesus' words in this verse, we will at first instinctively try to avoid it. No wonder Jesus concluded His statement with the words, "He who has ears to hear, let him hear!" It takes an act of courage even to read the above verse, and an even greater act of personal heroism to fulfill it.

Why does biblical Christianity include self-denial and the cross? It is because the salvation that Jesus has made available to us has not yet come to its compete fulfillment. 1 Corinthians 15:50–53: "Now I say this, brethren, *that flesh and blood cannot inherit the kingdom of God;* nor does the perishable inherit the imperishable. Behold, I tell you a mystery; we shall not all sleep, but we shall all be changed, in a moment, in the twinkling of an eye, at the last trumpet; for the trumpet will sound, and the dead will be raised imperishable, and we shall be changed. For this perishable must put on the imperishable, and this mortal must put on immortality." In other words, through our acceptance of Jesus' sacrifice for our sins, our spirit is reborn into God's image, whereas our soul (mind) must be continually renewed by God's Word and our body (flesh) remains dead to God and a slave to sin. Therefore, there is a continual warfare between our body (flesh) and our born-again spirit. Since our body (flesh) is not and cannot be redeemed, we have no choice but to crucify our body (flesh) by way of our born-again spirit and by the renewing of our mind. *Our cross is clearly unavoidable (Romans 12:1–2)!*

As the cross is unavoidable in our daily walk as a Christian and since Jesus as He faced His cross had to exhibit both great courage and heroism unto sweating blood why then should we think it to be any easier for us to say "yes" to God and "no" to our body (flesh)? This point is very important to understand for us to achieve victory. *If you do not have an accurate diagnosis, how can you apply the proper cure?* Denying yourself and taking up your cross daily will indeed take an act of great courage and heroism. You will have to do great violence to your emotions, feelings, and/or desires, i.e., crucifying your body (flesh) in order to conform to godliness. This is no small feat! In fact, many will try to avoid the pain of the cross by blaming a spirit of lust, anger, fear, and/or anxiety, when in reality these are all deeds of an unredeemed body (flesh). Therefore, the proper cure is *death by way of the cross* (Galatians 5:16–24).

By understanding this you will also avoid Satan's condemnation. Allow me to explain. Let's say you harbor anger or unforgiveness toward someone, but you know by the renewing of your mind and witnessed from within by your born-again spirit that this is unacceptable to God. You begin to do violence to your emotions. *The battle becomes intense!* Your mind and spirit says "yes" to God, but your flesh—your emotions are screaming, "No, I will never forgive!" Satan, the accuser, comes to you saying, "You hypocrite! How can you say you're a Christian while still harboring anger and unforgiveness." Without condemnation you respond, "In my heart I desire God's will. The battle with my flesh may not be over, but a hypocrite I am not. I will persevere and do violence to my emotions until my flesh is crucified" (Romans 7:14–8:1).

This is a daily battle we all will have until the day of our final redemption. Romans 8:18–25: "For I consider that the sufferings of this present time are not worthy to be compared with the glory that is to be revealed to us. For the anxious longing of the creation waits eagerly for the revealing of the sons of God. For the creation was subjected to futility, not of its own will, but because of Him who subjected it, in hope that the creation itself also will be set free from its slavery to corruption into the freedom of the glory of the children of God. For we know that the whole creation groans and suffers the pains of childbirth together until now. *And not only this, but also we ourselves, having the first fruits of the Spirit, even we ourselves groan within ourselves, waiting eagerly for our adoption as sons, the redemption of our body.* For in hope we have been saved, but hope that is seen is not hope; for why does one also hope for what he sees? But if we hope for what we do not see, with *perseverance* we wait eagerly for it." Can the words *"Christian"* and *"heroism"* have an impeccable association? *Yes and amen!*

If you have acted cowardly by giving in to your weakness, can you once again become heroic? Yes, just as King David did by taking the heroic step of confession and repentance, becoming once again salt and light to a dying world, even unto seventy times seven times (Matthew 18:22 and Luke 17:4)! Where do you find the courage to be both heroic and persevering? The same place Jesus found it—in prayer! Luke 22:45–46: "And when He rose from prayer, He came to the disciples and found them sleeping and said to them, 'Why are you sleeping? Rise and pray that you may not enter into temptation.'" And again Matthew 6:13, "And do not lead us into temptation, but deliver us from evil." *This highway of holi-*

ness is not for the timid, nor the cowardly, but at the end of our pilgrimage is found rapturous joy.

Isaiah 35:8–10: "And a highway will be there, a roadway, and it will be called the *Highway of Holiness.* The unclean will not travel on it, but it will be for him who walks that way, and fools will not wander on it. No lion will be there, nor will any vicious beast go up on it; these will not be found there. But the redeemed will walk there, and the ransomed of the Lord will return, and come with joyful shouting to Zion, with everlasting joy upon their heads. They will find gladness and joy, and sorrow and sighing will flee away."

Chapter Eighteen

The New Testament Tithe

Realizing people can get really touchy when you talk about money, and knowing I will be going against conventional wisdom—in some eyes, even being radical—your first inclination may be to dismiss this commentary altogether. But, I implore you to do as the people in Berea did in Acts 17:10–11 and examine God's Word to see if what I say is true or not. If true, it then becomes another one of those times where we must *endure* sound doctrine.

We begin where Jesus was about to become so radical in His teaching about the Law that He had to preface His teaching with Matthew 5:17–18, "Do not think that I came to abolish the Law or the Prophets; I did not come to abolish, but to fulfill. For truly I say to you, until heaven and earth pass away, not the smallest letter or stroke shall pass away from the Law, until all is accomplished." Jesus was about to show everyone who was willing to listen that, in reality, following the letter of the Law was in fact *not* fulfilling the heart of the Law. Jesus' teaching was about to become so radical—so hard to follow—that the religious community of His time would actually accuse Him of trying to abolish the Law. This allowed them to turn a deaf ear to what Jesus had to say, while at the same time, in their own eyes, retain their piety. What was this radical teaching? It was that the Law could only truly be fulfilled by a change in our heart, i.e., having the Kingdom of God within us. To illustrate the *enormous* difference between following the *letter* of the Law and fulfilling the *heart* of the Law, Jesus proceeded to give us several examples. I'll cite just one:

Matthew 5:21–22: "You have heard that the ancients were told, 'You shall not commit murder' and 'Whoever commits murder shall be liable to the court.' But I say to you that everyone who is angry with his brother shall be guilty before the court; and whoever shall say to his brother, '*Raca* (empty headed),' shall be guilty before the supreme court; and whoever shall say, 'You fool,' shall be guilty enough to go into the fiery hell." Here Jesus allows us to see the enormous difference by exposing that the mere outward application of the *letter* of God's Law came nowhere near the actual fulfillment of the *heart* of the Law.

Actually, to say this was an enormous difference would be an understatement! No wonder Jesus had to preface His teaching with, "I'm not abolishing the Law, but fulfilling it!" No wonder the religious community was up in arms! *Why, if this teaching were accepted, it would totally destroy their self-proclaimed piety. This was an impossible teaching! Who then could be saved? Who then could boast? This was just unacceptable!* Therefore, the religious community proclaimed that Jesus was trying to do away with the Law of Moses and labeled Jesus, in essence, a heretic. This enabled the religious community to continue to deceive themselves and turn a deaf ear to Jesus' teaching, allowing their self-proclaimed "piety" to remain intact.

The religious community completely missed the purpose of the Law. The Law was not given to us so we may have something to boast in, or so we could save ourselves, but rather to allow sin to become utterly sinful, and alive within us to make us conscious of its existence. Romans 7:9–10: "And I was once alive apart from the Law; but when the commandment came, sin became alive, and I died; and this commandment, which was to result in life, proved to result in death for me."

Allow me to explain. If you were driving down a road at eighty miles per hour and saw no posted speed limit, you would continue to drive without fear—without condemnation. Nevertheless, what if the posted speed limit was seventy and you simply missed the sign? Since you missed the sign, you remained without condemnation or fear. But were you innocent? No! You were still going over the speed limit. Now what if you saw the sign with a posted speed limit of seventy, would not the sin you were committing immediately come alive (conscious) within you? Would you not begin to feel an expectation of judgment? Therefore, although the posted speed limit caused the sin to come alive within you and allowed you to feel condemned, its purpose was to ultimately save you from judgment.

Galatians 3:23–26: "But before faith came, we were kept in custody under the law, being shut up to the faith which was later to be revealed. Therefore the Law has become our tutor to lead us to Christ that we may be justified by faith. But now that faith has come, we are no longer under a tutor. For you are all sons of God through faith in Christ Jesus." This is exactly what Jesus was trying to tell those who were trusting the letter of the Law for their salvation when He said, "Whoever commits murder shall be liable to the court. But I say to you that everyone who is angry with his brother shall be guilty before the court; and whoever shall say to his brother, 'Raca (empty headed),' shall be guilty." *Jesus was say-ing, it was now time for us to mature, tossing aside our tutor—the Law—and by way of our rebirth, begin to aspire, begin to press to-ward the very heart of the Law.*

The Law of Moses was given to us as a restrainer, to restrain our madness, to restrain the depravity of our corrupt nature, to keep in check our natural inclination for self-destruction. It was to be a road sign in our life to *slow down* our eighty-miles-per-hour descent into total destruction. Nevertheless, the Law being weak inasmuch as it could not change our nature; it only succeeded in making us conscious of sin. *Jesus was trying to point out that it was our corrupt nature that produced the need for the Law in the first place.* It was our corrupt nature which produced the corrupt seed, enticing us to say to our brother, "Raca, (empty headed)." Left unrestrained, such an attitude would grow into hate—and hate into murder; hence, the need for the Law.

Because of our corrupt nature, the Law of Moses could only truly be fulfilled by changing that nature, i.e., being born-again. The Kingdom of God could now reside within us through the blood of Jesus. Therefore, those who are born-again have no need for the external Law, since the Law is now residing within us, *teaching us to say no to sin at its conception.* In other words, our new spirit stops the corrupt seed—"*Raca*"—at its source and allows it no soil in which to grow. 1 John 3:8–9: "The Son of God appeared for this purpose, that He might destroy the works of the devil. No one who is born of God practices (or perpetually practices) sin, be-cause His seed (Spirit) abides in him; and he cannot sin, because he is born of God."

Those of us who are born-again should no longer have the need to be restrained by the Law because we are now restrained by God's

Holy Spirit who dwells within us. This moves us far beyond our tutor, the Law, unto the fullness—the maturity—of being God's sons and daughters. We are no longer content with just fulfilling the letter of the Law, but we strive, we press, into the fullness and perfection of the Law. Our new nature encourages us to press into God's holiness, and to heartily embrace the Spirit who gave birth to the Law—God's Holy Spirit. This fulfillment or perfection, according to Jesus, implied much more than just the application of the *letter* of Law in our lives.

Which brings me to the "law" of the tithe and why we cannot find the word "tithe" in the New Testament as defined as ten percent. Yet we seem to tenaciously cling to that definition. Luke 5:39: "And no one, after drinking old wine (Law) wishes for new; for he says, *'The old is good enough.'*" This is particularly true as it pertains to money, for the tithe—the ten percent—is *much* more palatable than its fulfillment—its *perfection*. Since the old is so much more palatable to us, we quickly cling to the Old Testament for our instruction, without giving much thought to why we cannot find the word tithe connected with the giving of our finances in the New Testament.

Keeping all this in mind, let's take a look at the word "tithe" in the last place it is mentioned in the Bible, except when Jesus used it as a reference to chastise the religious community. Malachi 3:10: "'Bring the whole tithe into the storehouse, so that there may be food in My house, and test Me now in this,' says the Lord of hosts, 'if I will not open for you the windows of heaven, and pour out for you a blessing until it overflows.'" You must admit the Church, as a whole, *really* likes this verse! But let us examine it in the light of New Testament fulfillment. This is where my commentary begins to get radical, deviating greatly from conventional teaching, even as Jesus did in Matthew 5:21–22 as He defined fulfilling the Law.

Many teachers of our day will point out with glee that this is the *only* place in the Bible where God allows us to test Him, as if we should be proud of the fact that God gives us permission here to test Him. But at the same time they turn a blind eye to the fact that throughout the Bible God actually deplores being tested. It is true that God's permissive will allows us to test Him in Malachi, but should His sons and daughters be content with God's permissive will instead of His perfect will? *As we read Malachi, we discover a time in history when all God was receiving from His people were their leftovers.* Therefore, in order to deal with their hardheartedness, God gave permission for His people to test Him. Yes, even today this remains a great verse to overcome hardheartedness and raise money. But now as His sons and daughters, should we be proud of the fact we still need to use this verse? Are we not in fact actually exposing our own hardheartedness by embracing God's permissive will of testing Him?

Let us compare this to another example in God's Word concerning His permissive will. Matthew 19:7–8: "They said to Him, 'Why then did Moses command to give her a certificate of divorce and send her away?' He said to them, *'Because of your hardness of heart,* Moses permitted you to divorce your wives; but from the beginning it has not been this way.'" Notice God's permissive will on divorce was formulated to deal with the problem of our hardheartedness. Certainly this is nothing for us to boast in. *So we find this duplicity today within God's Church.* We wisely teach against divorce, although it's permissible, yet shamelessly, and with glee, we continue to propagate the fact that we have God's permissive will to test Him as it concerns our finances.

What about the motivation God had to use, i.e., ". . . if I will not open for you the windows of heaven, and pour out for you a blessing until it overflows." Even today this will still pry open our checkbooks, but do we really want this to be our motivation? *Even the unbelievers will give in order to receive a return—a profit!* 1 Corinthians 13:3: "And if I give all my possessions to feed the poor, and if I deliver my body to be burned, but do not have love, it profits me nothing." When Jesus gave His life for us—literally everything He had—the only motivation He needed was His love for us. If Jesus now lives within us, through our rebirth, should we need a greater motivation than love?

What about the tithe as it is defined as ten percent of our income? The reason you will not find the word "tithe" in the New Testament to describe the giving of our finances to our Lord's work is that, as God's sons and daughters, we are to follow Jesus' example of complete surrender. Therefore, to fulfill the tithe unto perfection (maturity), we must be willing to move from God's *permissive* will into His *perfect* will; we must finance evangelism, the needs of others, and the teaching of God's Word selflessly without an imposed limit. Giving not under compulsion, but from a sincere heart, motivated only by love, a love birthed by God's Holy Spirit which now lives within us.

2 Corinthians 8:12–15: "For if the readiness is present, it is acceptable according to what a man has, not according to what he does not have. For this is not for the ease of others and for your affliction, but by way of equality, at this present time your abundance being a supply for their want, that their abundance also may become a supply for your want, that there may be equality; as it is written, '*He who gathered much did not have too much, and he who gathered little had no lack.*'" Here Paul clearly describes the perfection (maturity) of giving as being without a set limit. Could it be that God originally set a ten percent limit (tithe) as a way to deal with our old nature—our covetousness, our hardheartedness?

Because of the security money represents in this world, this concept may seem very radical; which is exactly why Jesus made it very clear that it would be *absolutely* impossible to serve both God and money. We would either serve (hold on to) our money and turn a deaf ear to God, or serve (hold on to) God and let go of our money. Jesus clearly stated that if we would be willing to seek God and His righteousness that He would take care of our daily needs, i.e., become our security in place of money. Jesus *never* taught us to pray for God to supply our future needs by increasing our bank accounts, thereby, exposing our trust in money instead of God.

Matthew 6:19–24: "Do not lay up for yourselves treasures upon earth, where moth and rust destroy, and where thieves break in and steal. But lay up for yourselves treasures in heaven, where neither moth nor rust destroys, and where thieves do not break in or steal; for where your treasure is, there will your heart be also. The lamp of the body is the eye; if therefore your eye is clear (single in focus), your whole body will be full of light. But if your eye is bad, your whole body will be full of darkness. If therefore the light that is in you is darkness, how great is the darkness! No one can serve two masters; for either he will hate the one and love the other, or he will hold to one and despise the other. You cannot serve God and mammon (money)."

Indeed, this may seem extremely radical but Jesus really does not leave us any leeway. *We cannot go before God boasting in our piety by either pointing to our fulfillment of the letter of the tithe, or having as the motivation of our heart to lay up even more treasure upon earth—can we?* Luke 12:20–21: "But God said to him, 'You fool! This very night your soul is required of you; and now who will own what you have prepared?' So is the man who lays up treasure for himself, and is not rich toward God." And Luke 16:8–9: "And his master praised the unrighteous steward [or steward of unrighteousness, i.e., steward of money] because he had acted shrewdly; for the sons of this age are more shrewd in relation to their own kind than the sons of light. And I say to you, make friends for yourselves by means of the mammon of unrighteousness; *that when it fails,* they may receive you into the eternal dwellings."

In combining the above two parables, Jesus clearly indicates that the fulfillment of the tithe unto perfection is to use everything you have to make friends (disciples) in the Kingdom of God. Mark 10:21: "And looking at him, Jesus felt a love for him, and said to him, 'One thing you lack: go and sell all you possess, and give to the poor, and you shall have treasure in heaven; and come, follow Me.'" And Mark 10:26: *"And they were even more astonished and said to Him, 'Then who can be saved?'"* Although both we and the disciples may read this verse with astonishment, we should not try to explain it away as some try to do.

Although I wrote this commentary, I know (perhaps along with you) that I have not arrived yet. Nevertheless, we should, with the help of God's Holy Spirit which now dwells within us, aspire to endure sound doctrine and press into the *very high* calling of God in Christ Jesus. Yet, as we continually strive to press toward perfection (maturity), we still have nothing to boast in, because we are only doing what we are suppose to do. Luke 17:9–10: *"He does not thank the slave because he did the things which were commanded, does he?* So you too, when you do all the things which are commanded you, say, 'We are unworthy slaves; we have done only that which we ought to have done.'"

Lord, as this ministry continues to grow, may I never use its increase to live in extravagance, but only to further Your Kingdom. May my eyes remain clear—single in focus, serving and trusting in You only—so no darkness may be found in either me or this ministry. 1 Timothy 6:5–8: ". . . men of depraved mind and deprived of the truth, who suppose that godliness is a means of gain. But godliness actually is a means of great gain, when accompanied by contentment. For we have brought nothing into the world, so we cannot take anything out of it either. And if we have food and covering, with these we shall be content."

I ended this commentary with a prayer that I would never use this ministry's increase to live in extravagance, but only to further God's Kingdom. I chose the word "extravagance" to establish a difference between living in *excess,* as compared with living *well.* Therefore, please don't misunderstand me; I'm not saying you must live in a mud hut in order to be perfect. But at the same time, I do not want you to turn a deaf ear to God, thinking that you have fulfilled your obligation; nor do I want you to become proud thinking you "fulfilled" the Law based on a percentage; nor should you feel condemned if you are not able at this time to give a certain percentage.

As far as defining the line between living in *extravagance* and living *well,* it is not something for me, nor anyone else, to judge; that is between you and God. What I am simply saying is, we should be open to God's direction in the matter of giving—giving *no* thought to percentages. Be willing to prayerfully examine your lifestyle, and continually ask God to examine your priorities in this life. If you do this simple thing, you would be amazed at how *"fulfilling"* this life can be. 2 Corinthians 9:10–12: "Now He who supplies seed to the sower and bread for food, will supply and multiply your seed *'for sowing'* and increase the harvest of your righteousness; you will be enriched in everything for *all liberality,* which through us is producing *thanksgiving* to God. For the ministry of this service is not only fully supplying the needs of the saints, but is also overflowing through many thanksgivings to God."

The main purpose of this ministry has been, and remains to be, to provoke Christians around the world to take a second look at their doctrine and lives. I have never wanted anyone to follow me in lockstep, but for everyone (including me) to take a long look at *what* we believe, and *why* we believe it. And then begin to live out what we believe in our day-to-day lives so all of us may hear one day from God the most sought after words in the human language, *"Well done!"* If indeed Jesus is coming back soon, as many of us believe, would He not admonish us beforehand and shake us up a bit in order to get us ready for His coming?

Chapter Nineteen

The Believer's Authority and Victory

2 Timothy 4:3: "For the time will come when they will not endure sound doctrine; but wanting to have their ears tickled, they will accumulate for themselves teachers in accordance to their own desires."

Oh how we love to sit under teaching that teach us about our authority and victory in Christ! We'll travel for miles, fill stadiums and churches to the max. We'll buy multiple tapes and books just to get our hands on this authority (power) and victory. How seductive it is to hear that we can have anything we desire and move mountains with just a mustard seed of faith. *Victory over our circumstances, authority over our lives, all so we can custom design our lives into our* own *desired image.* However, if we were to closely examine the Holy Scriptures, we would begin to see this teaching to be inconsistent with both God's Word, and the lives of God's faithful who are depicted in the Bible.

My purpose with this commentary is not to completely denounce the teaching on authority and victory, but to try to bring a proper perspective to it. Therefore, unlike some of the "Super-Apostles" of our day, I'll try to balance this teaching with a smidgen of stark reality. The one thing we all must be careful of is not to fall into the trap of putting on our rose-colored glasses and refusing to *endure* sound doctrine just because it is not what we want to hear. We must be very careful not to allow the cares of this world and the desire for other things, to obscure the truth.

Endure—what an interesting word the Apostle Paul chose to use in association with the phrase "sound doctrine." When I looked up this word in the Greek Lexicon, the word "endure" was in the middle voice. The middle voice implies an action taken by you in order to secure a desired outcome upon yourself. Therefore, when Paul said, *"endure sound doctrine,"* Paul implied that we must act upon ourselves in such a way as to cause ourselves to bear up with sound doctrine. In other words, we must act upon ourselves so we will not turn away from sound doctrine simply because it is hard for us to embrace. We must be willing to put aside that which we *want* to hear for that which we *need* to hear, i.e., sound doctrine. Paul, realizing this would be no easy thing for us to do, chose the word "endure," which demands much from us individually.

In the beginning, as I studied God's Word, the hardest thing for me to do was to lay aside my agenda in exchange for God's—to desire God's will more than my own. Matthew 16:24–25: "Then Jesus said to His disciples, 'If anyone wishes to come after Me, let him deny himself, and take up his cross, and follow Me. For whoever wishes to save his life shall lose it; but whoever loses his life for My sake shall find it.'" Therefore, all of us must be determined in our hearts not to interpret Scripture through the eyes of our desire (flesh), but through the eyes of God's Holy Spirit. 1 Corinthians 2:14: "But a natural man does not accept the things of the Spirit of God; for they are foolishness to him, and he cannot understand them, because they are spiritually appraised." From this verse of Scripture can we not come to the conclusion that the ways of the natural man are abhorrent to God, and God's ways are abhorrent to the natural man? Therefore, we need to pray every day that we will rightly divide His Word, i.e., pray for God to help us *endure* sound doctrine, understanding that our mind, the way we thought and reasoned up to the time of our "born-again" experience, was *hostile* to God's sound doctrine.

Keeping all this in mind, let us take another look at our authority in Christ. *Did you not immediately love this word authority?* Before you were saved, what did this word mean to you? In other words, when you were a natural man/woman and you heard this word "authority," what kind of thoughts were conjured up in your mind? Most likely your thoughts went right along with a definition I found in the Britannica-Webster dictionary: "The right to give commands." Can you not just close your eyes and imagine the power coursing through every ounce for your being? Slaying and casting out demons on your right and on your left, healing the sick, raising the dead, commanding prosperity to come to you, and rebuking poverty. I could go on, but I'm sure you get my point.

Not only is that what we see today in the church here in the USA, but we also see it propagated throughout churches all over the world. Christians congregate by the tens of thousands to hear how they can get their every desire fulfilled. Their ears *"itch"* to hear more as they rush in to gain this power, this authority. They are willing to do, or give, whatever it takes to receive this power. Just as Simon did in Acts 8:17–19, "Then they began laying their hands on them, and they were receiving the Holy Spirit. Now when Simon saw that the Spirit was bestowed through the laying on of the apostles' hands, he offered them money, saying, 'Give this authority to me as well, so that everyone on whom I lay my hands may receive the Holy Spirit.'" Simon was just *"itching"* for this power, this authority!

However, Simon did not get the response from Peter he hoped for. As a matter fact, Peter's answer was rather rude. Acts 8:20–23: "But Peter said to him, 'May your silver perish with you, because you thought you could obtain the gift of God with money! You have no part or portion in this matter, *for your heart is not right before God.* Therefore repent of this wickedness of yours, and pray the Lord that if possible, the *intention* of your heart may be forgiven you. For I see that you are in the gall of bitterness and in the bondage of iniquity.'"

What was that—his heart was not right before God? Full of wickedness? But all he wanted was the power to give whosoever the Holy Spirit. What could be wrong with that? The Holy Spirit is a good thing, right? Healing and miracles are good things, right? The more people with the Holy Spirit the better, right? Or could it have been he wanted this power—this authority—so he could do with it whatever he wished? You may say, "But Simon wanted to use the authority so he could profit by the Holy Spirit. That is *not* me!" Well, now would be a good time to ask yourself a very serious question. When you sought to obtain this authority, was it so you may receive this power to fulfill your wants, your desires, and your prosperity? If so, how does that really differ from Simon's motivations?

Let's take a look at what Jesus had to say about people using their authority with the wrong motive. Matthew 7:22–23: "Many will say to Me on that day, 'Lord, Lord, did we not prophesy in Your name, and in Your name cast out demons, and in Your name perform many miracles?' And then I will declare to them, *'I never knew you.'"* This is where we begin to understand what the right motivation should be. As you can see, everything these people were doing appeared to be righteous and good, even saying, "Lord, Lord," but evidently there was literally a *fatal* flaw in the exercising of their authority.

Remember, they did have authority and power; they were casting out demons and healing the sick. So what was this fatal flaw? We have in this Scripture two very important clues. First is the context that this portion of Scripture was placed in. The context, both before and after, pertains to obedience, i.e., the opposite of lawlessness—the opposite of fruitlessness. The second clue we have is Jesus' statement, "I never knew you."

You may ask, "What role does obedience play in the use of the power and authority given to the believer?" It has everything to do with it! Remember, power and authority was displayed in the verse above, but obviously that was not the mark of a believer. The mark of a believer is found in John 14:23–24, "Jesus answered and said to him, 'If anyone loves Me, he will keep My word; and My Father will love him, and We will come to him, and make Our abode with him. *He who does not love Me does not keep My words*; and the word which you hear is not Mine, but the Father's who sent Me.'" What an awesome statement! Jesus thought it so important that He added emphasis to it by saying, ". . . and the word which you hear is not Mine, but the Father's who sent Me." Yes, this came directly from God the Father, so do not even try to debate this point!

Why did Jesus place such importance on obedience? Because, the mark that God looks for in a believer is a heart-felt willingness to lay aside his/her life, "*crucifying*" personal desires for God's. John 14:30–31: "I will not speak much more with you, for the ruler of the world is coming, and he has nothing in Me; but that the world may know that I love the Father, and as the Father gave Me commandment, *even so I do.* Arise, let us go from here." Jesus had both the power and authority to avoid His cross, but *chose* to lay His desire aside for God's. Matthew 26:52–54: "Then Jesus said to him, 'Put your sword back into its place; for all those who take up the sword shall perish by the sword. Or do you think that I cannot appeal to My Father, and He will at once put at My disposal more than twelve legions of angels? How then shall the Scriptures be fulfilled (God's desire)?'"

Therefore, we must come to the conclusion that the only power and authority God recognizes is the power and authority which are placed in the confinement of His will. This brings me back to another definition of authority I found in the same dictionary, ". . . to carry out or enforce the commands of another." This is the definition we as Christians must cling to.

Matthew 8:8–9: "But the centurion answered and said, 'Lord, I am not worthy for You to come under my, roof, but just say the word, and my servant will be healed. For I, too, am a man *under* authority, with soldiers under me; and I say to this one, 'Go!' and he goes, and to another, 'Come!' and he comes, and to my slave, 'Do this!' and he does it.'" The word I want you to focus on in this Scripture is the word "under." To be *"under"* authority is having an authority under the authority of another. In other words, this authority given to us is to be used *exclusively* to fulfill the desires of the person from whom the authority originates. Which, in our case, is God Himself.

The following are some questions we can ask ourselves to see if we are operating *under* God's authority or our own. Do we start every day in prayer, asking God to lead us into His perfect will? Jesus said in John 5:19, "Jesus therefore answered and was saying to them, 'Truly, truly, I say to you, the Son can do nothing of Himself, unless it is something He sees the Father doing; for whatever the Father does, these things the Son also does in like manner.'" Jesus knew that His authority was only to be exercised in the *confinement* of God's will; therefore, He prayerfully and diligently sought His Father's will in everything. That's what the Bible means when it says the Father and the Son are one.

This brings me to our second clue, "I never knew you." Could it be that they never really knew God, because they sought Him with the wrong motive—to have their own desires fulfilled? They never really sought God; *they sought only the gift.* And since they never really knew God, then Jesus also claimed not to know them.

Are you willing to close your prayer, your request, your exercise of power and authority with the words, ". . . *nevertheless Your will be done?"* Luke 22:41–44: "And He withdrew from them about a stone's throw, and He knelt down and began to pray, saying, 'Father, if Thou art willing, remove this cup from Me; yet not My will, but Thine be done.' Now an angel from heaven appeared to Him, strengthening Him. And being in agony He was praying very fervently; and His sweat became like drops of blood, falling down upon the ground." Jesus choosing to resist using His power and authority to fulfill His own desire to escape His cross, sweated blood in order to say no to self, and yes to God. Hebrews 5:8: "Although He was a Son, He learned *obedience* from the things which He suffered." Jesus, *endured* sound doctrine!

Are you angry at, disappointed with, or quarreling with God right now because your wishes and/or desires are not being fulfilled? If you are, this is the clearest indication of all that you're trying to exercise your power and authority for your own pleasures and/or desires, and therefore, you have a wrong heart and motive. James 4:1–3: "What is the source of quarrels and conflicts among you? Is not the source your pleasures that wage war in your members? You lust and do not have; so you commit murder. And you are envious and cannot obtain; so you fight and quarrel. You do not have because you do not ask. You ask and do not receive, *because you ask with wrong motives, so that you may spend it on your pleasures."*

Now, let us define the word "victory." Luke 16:19–25: "Now there was a certain rich man, and he habitually dressed in purple and fine linen, gaily living in splendor every day. And a certain poor man named Lazarus was laid at his gate, covered with sores, and longing to be fed with the crumbs which were falling from the rich man's table; besides, even the dogs were coming and licking his sores. Now it came about that the poor man died and he was carried away by the angels to Abraham's bosom; and the rich man also died and was buried. And in Hades he lifted up his eyes, being in torment, and saw Abraham far away, and Lazarus in his bosom. And he cried out and said, 'Father Abraham, have mercy on me, and send Lazarus, that he may dip the tip of his finger in water and cool off my tongue; for I am in agony in this flame.' But Abraham said, 'Child, remember that during your life you received your good things, and likewise Lazarus bad things; but now he is being comforted here, and you are in agony.'"

If you were to come upon this situation today, would you not be tempted to look upon the one that is living in ease as having victory and the one who is poor and sick as the one who *needed* victory? However, the above story clearly indicates that Lazarus was the one who had victory all along. Don't get me wrong, I'm not saying you must be poor to have victory; I'm saying victory cannot be defined by outward appearances. *Victory in Christ has nothing to do with your portion in this life.*

In conclusion, using your power and authority outside the confinement of God's will—even if it appears on the surface to be good—is in reality rebellion; and rebellion is the same as *witchcraft.* 1 Samuel 15:22–23: "And Samuel said, 'Has the Lord as much delight in burnt offerings and sacrifices as in obeying the voice of the Lord? *Behold, to obey is better than sacrifice,* and to heed than the fat of rams. For rebellion is as the sin of divination (witchcraft), and insubordination is as iniquity and idolatry.'"

As far as defining victory in Christ, I could not define it more beautifully than King David did in Psalm 17:14–15, ". . . From men of the world, *whose portion is in this life;* and whose belly Thou dost fill with Thy treasure; they are satisfied with children, and leave their abundance to their babes. As for me, I shall behold Thy face in righteousness; *I will be satisfied with Thy likeness when I awake."* Do you, as with King David, define victory in your heart as standing before God in righteousness and being in God's likeness when you awake? If so, you already have your *victory!* 1 John 3:2: "Beloved, *now* we are children of God, and it has not appeared as yet what we shall be. We know that, when He appears, we shall be like Him, because we shall see Him just as He is."

Chapter Twenty

Let Not Your Heart Be Troubled

Psalm 11:1–4: "*In the Lord I take refuge;* how can you say to my soul, 'flee as a bird to your mountain; for, behold, the wicked bend the bow, they make ready their arrow upon the string, to shoot in darkness at the upright in heart. If the foundations are destroyed, what can the righteous do?' The Lord is in His holy temple; the Lord's throne is in heaven."

This Scripture is so fitting for today as we read headlines about shootings in churches and schools, where our teenagers are shot down for saying, "Yes, I believe in God." We are seeing first hand the wicked bending their bow at the upright in heart and our moral foundations are being destroyed. However, as we see this Scripture come alive in our headlines, we must also be equally aware that God remains on the throne and in control. What can the righteous do? *We can take refuge in God!* At first glance this may seem to be a paradox; how can God be on the throne, in control, and allow the wicked to bend their bow at the upright in heart?

This brings me to the following Email I received from Donat in Ufa, Russia, asking that very question. As you can see, these tragic events are not just a local phenomenon. The following is a portion of the Email I received on October 6, 1999: "God is in my heart, but sometimes I need something that can help me keep my faith stronger than it is now. We live in cruel, terrible times, especially here in Russia. As you know, in our country began a new wave of terrorism, children and old people are dying. And I'm asking myself, *How can God let it be?* That's why I need your tapes (sermons), perhaps listening to these tapes I can find the answer."

"How can God let it be?" Throughout my thirty plus years as a Christian this has been a question that I have encountered in believers and unbelievers alike. The believers struggle with the question concerning their faith, and unbelievers use it as an excuse to dismiss God altogether. I can certainly understand their trouble coming to terms with this question, because as a whole, the Church has backed away from answering it. *All we seem to hear any more are the pleasant things, but the more difficult parts of Scripture we happily ignore.* Isaiah 30:10–11: "Who say to the seers, 'you must not see visions;' and to the prophets, 'you must not prophesy to us what is right, speak to us pleasant words, prophesy illusions. Get out of the way, turn aside from the path, let us hear no more about the Holy One of Israel.'"

In my walk as a Christian, I've found myself around many pastors and Christians in general, from whom I have heard some amazing statements. For example, the number one response I get from Christians as to why they did not like a pastor was, "The pastor did not talk enough about the power and blessings that belong to us—he was way too gloomy." I would have thought the number one reason would have been, "He doesn't accurately teach the Word." I actually was told that a pastor of a rather large church said, "I cannot tell my church that truth—why, I would lose half my congregation." I could go on, but I think you get my point: Isaiah 30:10–11 seems to be as pertinent today as it was centuries ago.

Now back to the question, *"How can God let it be?"* In the beginning, God gave a lease (an allotted amount of time) for mankind to reign on this earth, with the hope that mankind would follow His will and ways. However, with Satan's prompting, mankind decided to turn away from God and follow Satan's advice to become as gods. It was at this time that sin and death entered into the world and the Garden of Eden was no more. Therefore, how can we blame God for the evils in this world, when it was brought about by our own hand? Yes, we did it to ourselves. You may then ask, "If God is all-powerful, why doesn't He just stop it?" Because God will not go back on His own Word. He gave the world to mankind, therefore, it will remain in mankind's hand until the allotted time is up.

Nevertheless, God did not abandon us. Time and time again throughout recorded history we see God, driven by His love and mercy, stepping in, keeping mankind from destroying himself before his allotted time was up. God did so by intervening in the affairs of mankind, intervening in such events as wars and natural calamities, which are generated by mankind's unwise decision in the Garden of Eden to turn our back on God, *deciding for ourselves between good and evil.* Nevertheless, from the beginning, God had a plan to rescue mankind from the mess we found ourselves in by not listening to Him in the first place. So once again, driven by His love and mercy, He sent His only Son to die for us so we may be freed from sin and death.

However, this redemption was for our spirit and not for the earth, or our flesh. Therefore, this earth and our bodies are still under the curse of sin and death where bad things will happen. So when evil happens, instead of blaming God, put the blame where it belongs: on our willful sin and Satan. And remember those times in our lives when God chose to intervene, or help us to endure—driven by His love and mercy—not because we deserved it. How then can we even ask the question, *"How can God let it be?"* when all God has done for us is good, even when we brought this evil upon ourselves by turning away from God in the first place. If God was not for us, sin and Satan would have brought mankind to extinction long before our earthly allotted time was up—destined for hell and death, remaining eternally separated from God. So when bad things begin to happen, before you curse God, remember He created us to live in the Garden of Eden; *we chose the thorns and thistles.* It is only because of God's grace and mercy toward us that we now have any hope at all.

Now with this in mind, let us look at something Jesus told His disciples in John 16:33, "These things I have spoken to you, that in Me you may have peace. *In the world you have tribulation,* but take courage; *I have overcome the world."* In the Scriptures preceding this verse Jesus was informing His disciples not only of God's love toward them, but also of the coming hardships they would have to endure. The reason Jesus gave for telling His disciples ahead of time was so they may have peace in the midst of their hardships. In other words, when things happen and you cannot understand why, remember, "I (Jesus) told you ahead of time so you will know I am still in control; and because I love you, I have told you both the good and the bad things which must come to pass so you may have peace." Are you beginning to see the absolute beauty of this Scripture?

Nevertheless, I still like the second part of the Scripture best, "In the world you have tribulation, but take courage; I have overcome the world." Many will concentrate on the word overcome, trying to infer that it means the triumph over tribulation itself. However, if that was what Jesus meant, would He not have said it? But instead Jesus said, ". . . in this world you *will* have tribulation." This world is still subject to Satan, sin, and death, therefore, you will have tribulation. You simply cannot avoid it.

Until mankind's allotted time is up and God returns the earth to His absolute control, both sin and death will continue to reign. However, we are to take courage: *Jesus has overcome the world.* Since Jesus has overcome Satan, sin, and death, proven by the fact of His resurrection, we through belief in Him, have also overcome Satan, sin, and death by our rebirth. In other words, we may still have to live in this world filled with sin and death, but through our rebirth we no longer belong to this world. John 17:16: "They are not of the world, even as I am not of the world." Through God's salvation (Jesus) we no longer belong to this world which remains in the grip of Satan, sin, and death. Instead, we now belong to God through Jesus' sacrifice. Therefore, the sin and death that now reign in this world may indeed plague us, but it has *no* hold on us. As it is written in 1 Corinthians 15:55, *"O death, where is your victory? O death, where is your sting?"*

God gets blamed for so much when it should be blamed on our sin of turning away from God and embracing Satan's advice in the Garden of Eden. Throughout mankind's history, about 6,000 years, God has consistently reached out to us. First, by giving us His Law to restrain the evil in this world so that mankind would not self-destruct, and later by making a way of escape by sending His only Son for our redemption. Yet today, in our "wisdom," we have outlawed God's law and as a result we are beginning to see our own destruction through the manifestation of lawlessness. So why do we accuse God for being unloving and uncaring when tribulation comes our way, when in fact, He has already done so much for us? John 17:15: "I do not ask Thee to take them out of the world, but to keep them from the evil one." By remaining in this world we may have tribulations, but we will never again be in Satan's control, nor suffer his outcome of the eternal separation from God in the Lake of Fire, where lawlessness reigns, made for Satan and those who chose his ways.

What I'm going to talk about now may label me as a "gloom-and-doom preacher" by some, but nothing could be further from the truth. I believe being forewarned is being forearmed. Jesus had some unpleasant things to tell His disciples in John 15:18–16:4, but also said in 16:1, "These things I have spoken to you that you may be kept from stumbling." Jesus would never hold anything back from His disciples for fear of losing their admiration; He loved them too much to be that selfish. His only concern was to forewarn in order to keep His disciples from stumbling. Therefore, what I'm about to say is not because I'm a "gloom-and-doom preacher" wanting to frighten people, but just the opposite. I love you and I want to keep you from stumbling.

It all started when by request I started praying that hurricane Floyd would turn away from the United States. However, every time I would begin to pray, God seemed to stop me. This went on for a day or two until I finally gave up and just started praying for God's people: for their protection, endurance, and steadfastness in the faith. When I switched my focus from the hurricane to God's people, I received great peace again with my prayer. As I continued to seek God for clarification, I believe His answer to me was that disasters will continue to come in ever increasing numbers, closer together, with greater intensity, and that these things must be. I'm not talking about just the weather, but war, earthquakes, famine, terrorism, shootings, and so on, not just in the United

States, but worldwide. Jeremiah 15:1–2: "Then the Lord said to me, 'Even though Moses and Samuel were to stand before Me, My heart would not be with this people; send them away from My presence and let them go!' And it shall be that when they say to you, 'Where should we go?' then you are to tell them, Thus says the Lord: 'Those destined for death, to death; And those destined for the sword, to the sword; And those destined for famine, to famine; And those destined for captivity, to captivity.'"

I do *not* believe this to be the start of the Great Tribulation, but instead, I do believe it to be the beginning of the birth pangs spoken of in Matthew 24:8. As with birth pangs, these tribulations will increase in both frequency and intensity, to the point where believers and unbelievers worldwide will begin to take notice and become concerned. And just like birth pangs, once they begin, they cannot be stopped. As for us Christians, we must remember not to blame God if we find ourselves in the midst of a trial. Instead, let us praise God knowing that both hell and death have been conquered. Remember, the things coming upon the world is nothing more than the wages of sin, which is death. God is only allowing mankind to reap the consequences of his own sin and lawlessness.

Therefore, let us embrace Jesus' admonition to us found in Matthew 24:9–13, "Then they will deliver you to tribulation, and will kill you, and you will be hated by all nations on account of My name. And at that time many will fall away and will deliver up one another and hate one another. And many false prophets will arise, and will mislead many. And because lawlessness is increased, most people's love will grow cold. *But the one who endures to the end, he shall be saved.*" Be careful not to fall away, or stumble, although you may find yourself in the midst of a severe trial. Instead say, "O death, where is your victory? O death, where is your sting?"—

knowing in your heart that Jesus has overcome the world; and therefore, *we who are in Him have also overcome the world.* And be careful not to let lawlessness cause you to grow cold in your love and become hardhearted, knowing that the one who endures to the end will be saved.

Remember what the Apostle Paul said in 2 Corinthians 4:16–5:1, *"Therefore we do not lose heart,* but though our outer man is decaying, yet our inner man is being renewed day by day. For momentary, light affliction is producing for us an eternal weight of glory far beyond all comparison, while we look not at the things which are seen, but at the things which are not seen; for the things which are seen are temporal, but the things which are not seen are eternal. For we know that if the earthly tent which is our house is torn down, we have a building from God, a house not made with hands, eternal in the heavens." Again Paul says in Romans 8:35–39, "Who shall separate us from the love of Christ? Shall tribulation, or distress, or persecution, or famine, or nakedness, or peril, or sword? Just as it is written, 'For Thy sake we are being put to death all day long; we were considered as sheep to be slaughtered.' But in all these things we overwhelmingly conquer through Him who loved us. For I am convinced that neither death, nor life, nor angels, nor principalities, nor things present, nor things to come, nor powers, nor height, nor depth, nor any other created thing, *shall be able to separate us from the love of God, which is in Christ Jesus our Lord."*

If trials do come your way, do not say in your heart, "How could You let this happen, God?" Instead, remember how God in His love and mercy, at just the right time, sent His Son to suffer and die that we also may overcome this world and live forever with Him, giving us His Holy Spirit as the guarantor and pledge of our redemption. Romans 5:3–6: "And not only this, but we also exult in our tribulations, knowing that tribulation brings about perseverance; and perseverance, proven character; and proven character, hope; and hope does not disappoint, *because the love of God has been poured out within our hearts through the Holy Spirit who was given to us.* For while we were still helpless, at the right time Christ died for the ungodly."

At times we may feel like God has abandoned us, but allow me to comfort you with Jesus' own words to His disciples when He told them that He had to leave them; I'm sure His disciples were feeling abandoned themselves. John 14:1–4: "*Let not your heart be troubled*; believe in God, believe also in Me. In My Father's house are many dwelling places; if it were not so, I would have told you; for I go to prepare a place for you. And if I go and prepare a place for you, *I will come again, and receive you to Myself; that where I am, there you may be also.* And you know the way where I am going."

Chapter Twenty-one

The Truth Shall Make You Free

Jesus said in John 8:32, "*. . . the truth shall make you free.*" But, how can you know what the truth is with so many voices saying so many different "truths" about God, and Christianity in general? *The first thing you must do is place such a great value in your heart for the truth that you will seek it with all your heart.* Matthew 13:44–46: "The kingdom of heaven is like a treasure hidden in the field, which a man found and hid; and from joy over it he goes and sells all that he has, and buys that field. Again, the kingdom of heaven is like a merchant seeking fine pearls, and upon finding one pearl of great value, he went and sold all that he had, and bought it."

The truth can only become that valuable to you if you come to understand that you have a need to be set free. For example, we see that the Pharisees thought they had no need to be set free in John 8:33, "They answered Him, 'We are Abraham's offspring, and have never yet been enslaved to anyone; how is it that You say, You shall become free?'" The Pharisees knew the Scriptures inside and out; they could quote volumes of Scriptures at the drop of a hat. Almost every day they spent the day debating the Scriptures but somehow they did not know they were *slaves to sin* and needed to be set free.

John 8:34–36: "Jesus answered them, *'Truly, truly, I say to you, everyone who commits sin is the slave of sin.* And the slave does not remain in the house forever; the son does remain forever. If therefore the Son shall make you free, you shall be free indeed.'" In the pride of their hearts the Pharisees thought they already had the truth; they were Abraham's offspring, holy, and God's chosen people. Therefore, Jesus' statement, "the truth will set you free" had no real value to them; upon seeing no value in the truth, (being unteachable—unyielding—stubborn) they turned away from the truth and embraced a lie. The Pharisees' pride blinded them to the truth. Jesus had said something to them that they did not want to hear; after all, they already knew the "truth"—or so they thought.

But you might say, "That was the Pharisees; what does that have to do with me?" The Apostle Paul, talking about the last days in 2 Timothy 4:3–4 said, "For the time will come when they will not endure sound doctrine; but wanting to have their ears tickled, they will accumulate for themselves teachers in accordance to their own desires; *and will turn away their ears from the truth, and will turn aside to myths."* If this is indeed the last days, should we not be careful that we do not reject the truth simply because it was not what we wanted to hear? Millions are going to hell, because they (like the Pharisees) don't like being called a sinner, and therefore, they accept the myth, "it's an alternative life style." Beware that you don't reject the truth for a lie because you are too proud and hardhearted to accept it. If you think that cannot happen to you, think again. Jesus told us—no, He *commanded* us—that we must forgive. But how many of us quickly reject that truth because that is the last thing we want to hear after someone has deeply hurt us?

Proverbs 1:7: "The fear of the Lord is the beginning of knowledge; fools despise wisdom and instruction." If you want to be blessed with the discernment to know the difference between truth and error, you must be humble and teachable. The word "fear" as used here just means you respect God enough to take His Word seriously. You need to fear (respect) God enough to esteem His Word even if it is not what you want to hear; allowing God's Word, and not your emotions, to be a lamp unto your feet.

I lent a book to a friend by Roy Hession, titled *The Calvary Road*. As you can tell by the title, the book was not going to be an easy read inasmuch as it was all about taking up your cross, i.e., denying yourself. My friend ended up becoming very angry, even throwing the book across the room a few times! It was very obvious my friend did not like what the book had to say. However, my friend did pick the book back up off the floor. You see, my friend feared (respected) God so much that even though the book contained things that my friend did not want to hear, if the book contained the truth; my friend wanted all of it. After getting past the emotions, my friend found the book to be full of God's truth. If we want to gain discernment between truth and error, we must at *all* times value the truth as a great treasure, being willing to give up everything to have it.

In our quest to recognize the truth from error we must learn to discern God's voice. In John 10:25–27, "Jesus answered them, 'I told you, and you do not believe; the works that I do in My Father's name, these bear witness of Me. But you do not believe, because you are not of My sheep. *My sheep hear My voice*, and I know them, and they follow Me.'"

When you are with people for a long period of time, you not only know their voice, but you begin to know their wants and desires. And those who have been married for many years will begin to say, "I know him; he would not do that," or "Yes, I can see him doing that." Or they may say, "Yes, that's something he would say," or "No, he would never say that." She would know her husband so well that she could make such statements and be correct, actually becoming one with her husband. *The bride could easily, at any time, pick her husband's voice out of a crowd.* How did she come by such an intimate relationship with her husband? It's simple— by spending time with him. Of course you already knew that was going to be the answer. And yet, we as the Bride of Christ, wanting an intimate knowledge of God, wonder why we don't have it when we just give God an hour on Sunday. You know, you cannot develop an intimate relationship with someone here on earth like that; so why then should we expect our relationship with God to be any different?

If you want to discern God's voice from among the myriad number of voices saying, "I have the truth," yet you know they cannot all be true since they contradict each other, then you are going to have to value your relationship with God as a pearl of great price, willing to sell everything to own it; spending time in prayer until you begin to recognize His voice. Spending time in His Word until you begin to understand His heart. There is no one else who can do it for you. Others can help by pointing you in the right direction, but it is up to you to get intimate enough with God to discern His voice from among the myriad number of voices that are constantly clamoring for your attention.

The Word of God is an exact representation of God Himself. We know this because in John 1:14, we find Jesus described as "the Word in flesh;" and in Hebrews 1:3 we also find Jesus defined as "the exact representation of God Himself." That being the case, we can come to the conclusion that if we want to learn to recognize God, then His Word would be the obvious place to go. *Since God is spirit, we cannot use our eyes to recognize Him, so we must allow His Word to form an image of God within our heart.* Whenever I begin to hear a myriad number of voices proclaiming that they have the truth, I begin looking for God. I can recognize God through the image I have within my heart, placed there by His Word. If I don't see God, I take what I hear with great skepticism, throwing out the chaff and keeping only the grain, if there is any grain to be found.

Since God is spirit and we cannot use our eyes to gain His image, we must become very diligent in our study of His Word to assure we attain an accurate image of God in our hearts. In our quest for God's image we can gain a very important lesson from the childhood fable about the three blind men and the elephant. One of the blind men, trying to gain an image of the elephant, grasped the elephant's tail. From that brief encounter, he came away thinking the image of the elephant was like a rope. The second blind man wrapped his arms around one of the elephant's legs and came away thinking the image of the elephant was like a tree. And finally the third blind man grasped the trunk of the elephant and became convinced the image of the elephant was like a snake. As you can see, all three actually did have hold of the elephant, but each came away with a very distorted view of the whole. Although all three blind men gained their knowledge directly from the elephant, the image they came away with was 100 percent wrong! *You cannot gain a true image of anything piecemeal!*

Just because someone uses a quote from the Bible, even if the Bible is quoted accurately, they can still be 100 percent wrong with their conclusion. Yes, exactly like the three blind men: 100 percent right inasmuch as they were touching an elephant, and yet 100 percent wrong with their conclusion. If you want to come away with a true image of God, you must study the *complete Word of God*, both the Old and New Testaments; and along with your teacher and helper the Holy Spirit, begin to harmonize every detail. I know of no one that can say, "I see God perfectly," but if you approach the Holy Scriptures in this way, over time your discernment of God's truth will be *greatly* enhanced.

Let me give you an example out of God's Word from Matthew 4:5–7, "Then the devil took Him (Jesus) into the holy city; and he had Him stand on the pinnacle of the temple, and said to Him, 'If You are the Son of God throw Yourself down;' for it is written, 'He will give His angels charge concerning You; and on their hands they will bear You up Lest You strike Your foot against a stone.' Jesus said to him, 'On the other hand, it is written, You shall not put the Lord your God to the test.'"

We must understand that Satan's most successful tactic in his war against the truth, is to quote God's Word to us, but have us come away with the wrong conclusion. This is no small thing; it can cause the falling away of many. When Satan tempted Jesus in the wilderness, this was the tactic he used against our Lord. Satan accurately quoted God's Word to Jesus, but with a 100 percent wrong conclusion. How did Jesus know the conclusion was wrong? *Because He knew the complete Word of God, and said in verse seven, ". . . on the other hand, it is written."* Jesus had to use a different part of God's Word in order to properly discern God's truth. Although both were true quotes from God's Word, they had to be combined in order to get to the whole picture—the whole truth. Whenever you do not understand something in the Bible, just keep reading; in time, you will find the answer in the Bible. In other words, the Bible needs no special or private interpretation; the Bible will interpret itself.

You may hear many different interpretations of Scripture, but the flaw is not with the Bible—it's with the interpreters. If you want to discern truth from error, you must treat the Scriptures as a hidden treasure and, with a sincere heart, search the Scriptures with diligence. There is no shortcut. However, your heart must be sincere, or you will only see what you want to see and become as blind as the men who thought the elephant was like a rope, tree, or snake. If your heart is *sincere*, ask God for your teacher and helper, the Holy Spirit, to help lead you into all truth, and with His help, *you will find it.*

Satan has yet another tactic he will use to cause you to accept whatever someone says about God without putting it to the test of God's Word—God's entire Word. It begins when you want something for yourself so bad that your desire causes you to have "tunnel vision." The only thing you wish to see is your miracle, the fulfillment of your desire. At that point you cross the line, loving your desire and/or truth more than God's desire and/or truth. 2 Thessalonians 2:9–11: ". . . the one whose coming is in accord with the activity of Satan, with all power and signs and false wonders, and with all the deception of wickedness for those who perish, *because they did not receive the love of the truth so as to be saved.* And for this reason God will send upon them a deluding influence so that they might believe what is false." You must love God and the truth above all else, even over your own desires and/or truth, or it will cause you to have a blind spot—blinding you from God's desire and/or truth.

That is why I tremble when I see "miracle crusades" filled to the rafters, with indeed a Scripture or two given, *but all the emphasis is placed on receiving your desire and/or miracle.* This becomes very dangerous when we reach a point in time when people gather to seek their miracle and/or desire more than they gather to just seek God. We already know Satan will use miracles and Scriptures to cause someone to believe a lie. Please don't get me wrong, I'm not saying every miracle crusade is of Satan, but I do see it as one possible way for Satan to get us to let our guard down if miracles become our focus. *I very much believe in miracles, but the Word of God and God's truth should be the focus for believers, not the miracles.* Jesus used miracles to attract the unbelievers and to help the helpless. But in the Holy Scriptures, when the people became more interested in the miracle than the truth, they were notably and severely rebuked by Jesus.

I have prayed for people and I have seen God do miracles (doctor confirmed). But as believers should we not be in love with God and His truth more than our wants and desires? Would it not disturb you if all your children wanted from you is to have their desires fulfilled? Yes! So why then in times of trouble does God's Word and prayer become very important to us, but in times of plenty we just can't seem to find the time? When God becomes as important to us as our own life, then we will begin to know the truth, and the truth will set us free.

Finally, if you truly want discernment in your life, you must be willing to act on what you already know. John 7:16–17: "Jesus therefore answered them, and said, 'My teaching is not Mine, but His who sent Me. *If any man is willing to do His will,* he shall know of the teaching, whether it is of God, or whether I speak from Myself.'"

If we are truly in the last days let us remember Jesus' warning to us in Matthew 24:24–25, "For false Christ's and false prophets will arise and will show great signs and wonders, so as to mislead, if possible, even the elect. Behold, I have told you in advance."

Deuteronomy 13:1–3: "If a prophet or a dreamer of dreams arises among you and gives you a sign or a wonder, *and the sign or the wonder comes true,* concerning which he spoke to you, saying, 'Let we go after other gods (whom you have not known) and let us serve them,' you shall not listen to the words of that prophet or that dreamer of dreams; *for the Lord your God is testing you to find out if you love the Lord your God with all your heart and with all your soul."* Anything other than the truth about God is indeed another "god," even if it goes by the name "Christian." Therefore, keep your love and passion for the truth fervent, *for only God's truth will set you free!*

Chapter Twenty-two

The Priceless Gift

This commentary was inspired by an Email I received from Alex who lives in Russia. I began to think about how Christianity is becoming just another religion, a social group promoting good morals, with Christianity's clear distinction from other religions becoming blurred. Have we, by preaching the prosperity gospel, emphasized the cares and worries of this world to the point where our eyes are so focused on "things" that we have blurred the true gospel, which is *Christ in you?* Have we bandied the phrase "born-again" around so much that it has become little more than a cliché, and lost its preciousness—*its pricelessness?* Sometimes we Christians will get so bold as to call Christianity a relationship with God, but in reality it is so much more. But I do digress—back to the Email. The following is a paraphrase of the Email that I received from Russia and my response.

The Email I received today from Alex in Russia told me that I was being naive to think that the Russian people wanted my religion or faith—they just want anything they can get for free. For example, he just wanted my tapes to study English. Since Alex was just trying to be helpful, I decided to write back to him with the following response:

Dear Alex, Thank you for your Email and your concern. However, I am not naive; I do realize many will take advantage of this ministry's goodwill, but when it concerns eternal life, or eternal death in hell, it's worth the price. Some will ask for my tapes with evil motives and some with good, but God's Word will not return void (Isaiah 55:10–11). You see, there is a God and He is in control even if you feel like He is not. It is not my faith, nor my religion I'm trying to give away—it is God Himself. Most rejected Jesus when He was here on earth, *yet, knowing this in advance,* He still left heaven for us. God's only Son paid with His life that we may be with God, and in Him, have eternal life. Therefore, it is a small price for me to pay, a few cassettes, when God gave so much for us. Yes, as long as I have the funds I will mail my tapes (sermons) to those who ask, even if all laugh at me, because they also laughed at my Lord, and killed Him—*and He was God.* I cannot make someone accept God's salvation; they can reject it to their own destruction, but if I tell them about Jesus—then their blood will not be on my hands.

Alex, Christianity is real; it is not just a faith, or a religion. God is alive and Jesus did rise from the grave. Jesus' rising from the grave is very real and written history proves it, if you are willing to look at it with a sincere heart. I know it to be true because now God's Holy Spirit lives within me as a witness of the reality of God's salvation through His Son Jesus—each and every day of my life. *I can now look anyone in the eye and say from my heart, "Once I was dead, but now I live."* The gift of eternal life instead of hell is so priceless, I will spend all I will ever have, even if it saves just one person from hell and death in my lifetime of work. That is the priceless gift I wish to give away and all for the price of a few cassettes—*that's a good deal indeed!* Yes, I will continue to give—until I can give no more. God bless, Raymond D. Sopp.

I must tell you from my heart that if Christianity was just a promoter of values, or just a kindly relationship with God, i.e., someone to tell your troubles to, I would not be sitting here in a basement alone, doing without—spending what little I have—working eighty hours a week; when all I would have to do is get you a pet. *After all, you could have a great relationship with a pet, could you not?* You can talk to your pet and your pet will always love you—yes, just as you are. Have you ever heard that said before pertaining to God? And if I wanted to promote values all I would have to do is get a group together and constrain you by peer-pressure, and maybe even make a little money while I'm at it.

However, the gospel is about so much more than a mere relationship with God or a promotion of values. If not, how then do you explain Peter, a fisherman who left everything, including his profession, to follow Jesus? And later he was so full of fear, he disavowed Jesus three times before Jesus' resurrection, but afterward, was also willing to be crucified for Christianity. How do you explain the change in this man?

How do you explain Paul, well educated, an upcoming leader in a very moral group called the Pharisees, who also walked away from everything to follow Jesus? The Apostle Paul never looked back even though his new life was full of trials: 2 Corinthians 11:23–27, ". . . in far more labors, in far more imprisonments, beaten times without number, often in danger of death. Five times I received from the Jews thirty-nine lashes. Three times I was beaten with rods, once I was stoned, three times I was shipwrecked, a night and a day I have spent in the deep. I have been on frequent journeys, in dangers from rivers, dangers from robbers, dangers from my countrymen, dangers from the Gentiles, dangers in the city, dangers in the wilderness, dangers on the sea, dangers among false brethren; I have been in labor and hardship, through many sleepless nights, in hunger and thirst, often without food, in cold and exposure."

And finally, why have I given up my life, my dreams, and my desires for someone I have never met before in Russia, on the other side of the world, knowing full well I will never be compensated for my trouble and most likely never even receive a "thank you" (well, not in this life anyway)? *If all Christianity was, was a religion or even just a simple relationship, would we not pity Paul, Peter, and yes, even me?* But thanks be to God, it is so much more than a mere relationship—it is an *adoption* into God's own family!

Ephesians 1:3–6: "Blessed be the God and Father of our Lord Jesus Christ, who has blessed us with every spiritual blessing in the heavenly places in Christ, just as He chose us in Him before the foundation of the world, that we should be holy and blameless before Him. In love He predestined us to adoption as sons through Jesus Christ to Himself, according to the kind intention of His will, to the praise of the glory of His grace, which He freely bestowed on us in the Beloved." Yes, we are now God's beloved children, supernaturally born-again, through His Son Jesus. We Christians, by the blood of God's only Son for the forgiveness of sin, have been born-again into God's very own family to the point we can cry out, "Abba, Father"—*My Father!*

So, what do I mean by the phrase, "born-again"? Describing to someone the true meaning of the phrase born-again would be akin to describing to a blind person the vivid colors in a sunset; especially if the blind person was born blind and did not have even the slightest concept of color. You must agree, taking on such an undertaking would be an exercise of futility because we realize with-out even the concept of color, our mere words would be so com-pletely inadequate that they would just fall to the ground. In truth, our mere words would be utter nonsense to the blind person's car-nal understanding.

Since this person was born blind, he remains ignorant of even the existence of color. However, we now have something we can tell the one who is blind, although we cannot explain the concept of color, we can tell him about the existence of color. However, in order to do this, the person who is blind would have to have a trust (faith) in the person who is telling him about the reality of color. Remember, he was blind at birth, and to him there is no such thing as color. And in his world that would be 100 percent correct; however, in reality, we who can see know that color does exist.

People who can see can easily testify of color existing in the world, but the one born blind just cannot accept it without seeing it—no pun intended. Therefore, he will never believe that color exists. However, we who can see know without a doubt that color not only exists, but it exists in a vivid display of great beauty, and it exists abundantly. But, if the blind person had a friend he could trust, then as this friend tells him about color, perhaps he would then make a leap of faith and say, "Yes, I believe in the existence of color." Yet, he would still remain blind to color's beauty inasmuch as he still lacks the actual experience of seeing color in its vivid display of beauty and abundance.

In the same way, we who are born-again know that being born-again is as real as color, and yet it is impossible to prove to those who are blind the concept of being born-again. We can tell the blind of its existence, but it will require the blind to make a leap of faith to believe it. If the blind wish to accept it, they do have a very trustworthy friend in the Word of God. The Word of God has been the only book on the face of the earth that has remained intact over the centuries. Its trustworthiness has been confirmed time and time again. Even when we think it to be wrong, the passage of time constantly proves the Word of God to be trustworthy.

Our trusted friend, the Word of God, speaks of being born-again in both the New and Old Testaments. Ezekiel 36:26–27: "Moreover, I will give you a new heart and put a new spirit within you; and I will remove the heart of stone from your flesh and give you a heart of flesh. And I will put My Spirit within you and cause you to walk in My statutes, and you will be careful to observe My ordinances." Again in John 3:7–12: "Do not marvel that I said to you, 'You must be born-again.' The wind blows where it wishes and you hear the sound of it, but do not know where it comes from and where it is going; so is everyone who is born of the Spirit. Nicodemus answered and said to Him, 'How can these things be?' Jesus answered and said to him, *'Are you the teacher of Israel, and do not understand these things?* Truly, truly, I say to you, we speak that which we know, and bear witness of that which we have seen; and you do not receive our witness. If I told you earthly things and you do not believe, how shall you believe if I tell you heavenly things?'"

If you do not believe in the trustworthiness of God's Word, then I challenge you to take the time to see if God's Word can be trusted. However, be sincere in the challenge, as if your very eternal life hangs in the balance, *because it does*—unto everlasting hell by doing nothing, or everlasting life with God. Now if the trustworthiness of your friend, the Word of God, causes you to take that leap of faith, and you agree that there is such a thing as a real born-again experience—the replacing of your dead spirit with God's Holy Spirit (which truly is abundant life)—then you can go on to step two and experience it. Unlike the blind person who may accept the fact of the existence of color, but can never experience it, you can experience being born-again. Actually becoming one of the ones that can see—seeing all the beauty, the stark reality, and abundance of life in being born-again.

Step two consists of acknowledging the need of a Savior, unless, of course, you happen to be perfect. Since no one is, this becomes a very easy step to take. Just look in the mirror one morning and say to yourself, "I am perfect in all my ways." Then after you pick yourself up off the floor laughing at yourself, you will find yourself in need of a Savior. (*Now remember I said perfect, not better than someone else.*) You will then begin to realize that your old dead spirit within you likes being a little nasty, and does not want to give it up, because your old dead spirit likes the darkness of sin. Hopefully, at that point you will begin to realize the need to be born-again from above with God's very own Holy Spirit, because your old dead spirit will never be able to please God—in this life, nor in the afterlife.

You may ask, *"So what do I do?"* It's easy! All you have to say is, "God I know I am a sinner (not perfect), and I am in need of a Savior. I also realize that my old dead spirit within me does not have the ability to please You; therefore, in the name of Your salvation for me (Jesus), I accept His blood for the forgiveness of my sins, and I want to be born-again with Your Holy Spirit that I may not be blind any longer." At that point, it will not be long before you begin to notice a difference in your life. You will begin to realize the reality of being born-again. Like those before you, you will also find yourself unable to explain the concept of being born-again to the blind, but can only hope that God will touch their hearts with His love, and trustworthiness; so that they, like you, would be able to take the leap of faith unto everlasting life.

Why do I consider God's gift literally priceless? Because once I was also very blind, but now I can see. Once I was dead and condemned to everlasting hell, but now I'm alive unto everlasting life. Who could ever put a price on such a gift? It would be impossible—it's *priceless!* This is not a religion of peer-pressured good works, or some kind of a "friendly God" relationship. Christianity is about a supernatural work of God unto salvation and everlasting life by the replacing of our fallen spirit with His Holy Spirit. And through God's Holy Spirit within us, we begin to produce good works, not through the Law, but from within our born-again heart.

As the blind man cannot understand the concept of color, how can I explain to the spiritually blind why I'm willing to give up all, and spend my lifetime proclaiming the gospel, even if just one person is saved? The answer is I cannot, because using mere words to describe color (born-again) to a blind man cannot even come close to the actual experience of seeing color.

1 Corinthians 2:6–16: "Yet we do speak wisdom among those who are mature; a wisdom, however, not of this age, nor of the rulers of this age, who are passing away; but we speak God's wisdom in a mystery, the hidden wisdom, which God predestined before the ages to our glory; the wisdom which none of the rulers of this age has understood; for if they had understood it, they would not have crucified the Lord of glory; but just as it is written *'Things which eye has not seen and ear has not heard, And which have not entered the heart of man, All that God has prepared for those who love Him.'* For to us God revealed them through the Spirit; for the Spirit searches all things, even the depths of God. For who among men knows the thoughts of a man except the spirit of the man, which is in him? Even so the thoughts of God no one knows except the Spirit of God. Now we have received, not the spirit of the world, but the Spirit who is from God, that we might know the things

freely given to us by God, which things we also speak, not in words taught by human wisdom, but in those taught by the Spirit, combining spiritual thoughts with spiritual words. *But a natural man does not accept the things of the Spirit of God; for they are foolishness to him, and he cannot understand them, because they are spiritually appraised.* But he who is spiritual appraises all things, yet he himself is appraised by no man. For who has known the mind of the Lord, that he should instruct Him? But we have the mind of Christ."

I thank God every day for the privilege of conveying His gospel (good news) to whosoever will listen. I thank God every day for those of you, who by your financial help and/or prayers, help me to fulfill my passion; which is also God's passion, as He said, "I wish none to perish, but all to have life, and have it abundantly." My passion for God's gospel is so great for two reasons: I know the time is short, and I know the pricelessness of His gift to us. But regardless of the reason, I just know I have to do this, because for some people there may be no tomorrow. Just like the lady I sent my tapes to and then discovered that she passed away about a week after my tapes arrived. *Therefore, Lord, my prayer is, "As long as I live Lord, use me to touch one more soul—to help one more weary one to reach the finish line, which is eternal life—and have life abundantly."*

CHAPTER TWENTY-THREE

When God Says *No*

Ephesians 6:1–3: "Children, obey your parents in the Lord, for this is right. Honor your father and mother (which is the first commandment with a promise), that it may be well with you, and that you may live long on the earth."

Why is teaching our children to obey their parents so important? This should be obvious; we as parents have lived much longer, and know much more about the dangers of this world than our children. Accordingly, we try to guide our children with our accumulated wisdom for their own good, which means we often find ourselves having to say *"no"* to our children's desires and requests.

Any parent who fulfills their child's every desire (afraid to say no) is simply not being a good parent by trying to become their child's friend. All too often we see parents trying to become friends to their children in order to gain their children's approval instead of being a parent, a guiding force in their children's lives. The times you have to say no to your children for their own good may indeed cause your children to become angry for a season; but that comes with the job of being a good parent. The child becomes angry because he or she, in their limited knowledge and foresight, only understand that they cannot have their own way.

Why does this commandment come with a promise of a long life for our children? For the same reason you teach your dog to obey your commands. Is it not to save your dog's life someday if your dog decides to suddenly run into the street? *Do we love our children any less?* When children have parents who are excessively concerned with their child liking them, those parents are also more likely to give their children anything they ask. Therefore, it is self-evident that any parent who allows their child to fulfill the desires of their flesh simply does not have the best interest of their child as a priority. How can parents who truly love their children allow their children every wish and desire without the loving direction of their accumulated wisdom and knowledge filtering their child's requests?

We as God's children (no matter how old or smart we think we are) must realize God has much more wisdom and foresight than we do. If we realize this, then why are we so amazed that God would actually say *"no"* sometimes to our requests made to Him in prayer. If you would like a father who says *"yes"* to your every demand and/or desire, there is one who is ready to say yes—Satan! Satan doesn't care if we run into the street to meet our death. *God is a good God!* This is true, but somehow we have lost the perspective of what makes God such a good Father to us—*He knows how to tell us* "no."

In Deuteronomy 8:3, God allowed His people Israel to go hungry. Now, if that was all we read and knew, would we not question God's love for Israel? However, as we read on we discover that God allowed them to go hungry so the people of Israel would learn, "Man does not live by bread alone, but by everything that proceeds out of the mouth of the Lord." Sound familiar? It should! That was the Scripture Jesus used when Satan tempted Him in the wilderness when He was exceedingly hungry. *In other words, Israel had to learn to obey God and not the desires of their flesh in order that they may have life, and have it abundantly.* Yes, Israel was led into the wilderness by God to learn this very important lesson, or in Jesus' case, Satan just tried to get Jesus to stumble.

When some of the spies came back from the promised land and had reported seeing giants, God had to say "no" to their desire to enter into the promised land, a land flowing with milk and honey. Was God being a bad Father to withhold this from Israel, or did God know because of their lack of faith and obedience that Israel would have been destroyed if they had gone in? Therefore, God (being a good God) had to say "no" to their request in order to save their lives, even though saying "no" did not make God very popular with His children Israel. Because of God's love for Israel, *He was more concerned for His children's lives than His own popularity.*

The story of Jesus' friend Lazarus is a good example for us to look at to understand this concept. In John chapter 11, we find that Jesus purposely delayed His coming and allowed His friend Lazarus to literally die. Then Jesus had the audacity to say it was good that Lazarus died. Don't you think that statement—that *"no"* from Jesus—was extremely hard to understand? You know it was! *Jesus' popularity was definitely not at its peak.* However, later on we discovered God had a better plan. Through the experience of Lazarus' death and resurrection it would help the faith of many to believe, and therefore, be saved.

This brings us to yet another reason God will say "no" to our requests. And once again this is based on God's goodness, wisdom, and foresight. God's will and plans for us are not always centered on our immediate happiness, or fulfillment, but rather on His desire to serve others through us. Matthew 20:25–28: "But Jesus called them to Himself, and said, 'You know that the rulers of the Gentiles lord it over them, and their great men exercise authority over them. It is not so among you, but whoever wishes to become great among you shall be your servant, and whoever wishes to be first among you shall be your slave; just as the Son of Man did not come to be served, but to serve, *and to give His life a ransom for many.*'" Are we not supposed to follow Jesus' example?

Are you saying it may be in God's plan to say "no" to our desires in order that we may serve others? Yes, and amen! This may be hard for us to believe at times, but our selfish plans just may not be God's plans. As with Lazarus' death and resurrection, our pain just may be used to bring life to many. Maybe now we can begin to understand what the Apostle Paul was trying to say in Colossians 1:24, "Now I rejoice in my sufferings for your sake, and in my flesh I do my share on behalf of His body (which is the church) in filling up that which is lacking in Christ's afflictions."

God said "no" to Jesus when he wanted to avoid the cross. Why? To serve us—to save us! When in the garden Jesus prayed to take this cup of suffering from him (Mark 14:36). *Jesus prayed knowing that all things were possible for God.* However, Jesus also prayed, "Let your will (plan) be done, not mine." God did answer Jesus' prayer; not as Jesus wanted as He peered deep into His cup of sufferings, but God answered Jesus' prayer filtered through His love, wisdom, and foresight. God's answer to Jesus' prayer is found in Luke 22:43, "Now an angel from heaven appeared to Him, strengthening Him."

We see the same kind of answer to prayer in Acts 4:24–31 when the disciples were threatened. Instead of removing the threat, God's answer to their prayer was, ". . . they were all filled with the Holy Spirit and began to speak the word of God with boldness." Although God did not deliver them from their sufferings, God did give them the strength, not only to endure, but gave them the courage to speak the word with boldness in the face of threats. 1 Corinthians 10:13: "No temptation has overtaken you but such as is common to man; and *God is faithful,* who will not allow you to be tempted beyond what you are able, but with the temptation will provide the way of escape also, that you may be able to *endure* it."

Ask yourself, what would have happened if Jesus refused God's plan for Him to suffer an agonizing death on the cross? Jesus could have refused to take God's *"no"* for an answer and deliver Himself from the pain of the cross (Matthew 26: 53–54). And again, what would have happened if the disciples turned away from God's provision to their prayer, *boldness,* and taken the easy way out by staying silent in order to avoid their cup of suffering? The answer to both questions is the same. *You and I would still be dead in our sins and looking at an eternity in hell!*

Remember Satan's temptation to Jesus in Matthew 16:22, "And Peter took Him aside and began to rebuke Him, saying, 'God forbid it, Lord! This shall never happen to You.'" Satan was tempting Jesus by saying through Peter, and I paraphrase, "Have it your way Jesus; God forbid that you should suffer. How could God love you and allow you to suffer?" Jesus' answer was Matthew 16:23, "Get behind Me, Satan! You are a stumbling block to Me; *for you are not setting your mind on God's interests but man's.*" God's ways will always be higher than our ways, and His thoughts will always be higher than our thoughts.

All too often we present our prayers based solely on our desires with no consideration of God's love, wisdom, or foresight. At times we act just as rebellious children would act, who have no respect for their parent's love, wisdom, or foresight. We kick our feet, scream, and storm off (move away from God) in a huff if we don't get our own way. The rebellious children (we) may even accuse their parents (God) of not being loving toward them.

In the pride of our childish, rebellious heart do we refuse to take *"no"* for an answer, saying, "I do not want your way, Lord. My way is right in my eyes, and best for me"? We must always remember God resists the proud, but loves the humble. Jesus said in John 5:30, "I can do nothing on My own initiative. As I hear, I judge; and My judgment is just, because I do not seek My own will, but the will of Him who sent Me." You mean Jesus spent His time in prayer seeking God's will and not His own? *Yes! What a novel idea!* Ask yourself this question: "Do I pray for God to follow me and my desires, my wants, or do I pray to hear God's voice, and desire His ways, His will, and His plans?"

Sometimes during our prayer times do we feel like the heavens are like brass and God is not listening? *On the contrary, it is written that God's ears are always attentive to His children's prayers.* Perhaps the times we think God isn't listening to our prayers are the times we may not be getting the answer we think we should, or times when the answer is not as quick as we think it should be. Or perhaps, we think God is not listening because we're being taught nowadays that a good God cannot say *"no"* to our precocious prayer requests.

We must always remember, "Every good thing bestowed and every perfect gift is from above, coming down from the Father of lights, *with whom there is no variation, or shifting shadow"* (James

1:17). Remember also that a God who loves us enough to send His only Son to suffer on the cross to save us, even when we were yet sinners, can be trusted when He gives us a *"no"* as an answer to our prayers. We should know that a God who loves us enough to give us His only Son has only good in mind for us, even if we cannot understand it in our limited wisdom and foresight. Yes, even in the death of a loved one, God's love is perfect. Isaiah 57:1–2: "The righteous man perishes, and no man takes it to heart; and devout men are taken away, while no one understands. For the righteous man is taken away from evil, he enters into peace; they rest in their beds, each one who walked in his upright way"

As Jesus did, we also must resist Satan, the accuser, when he tries to divide us from God by falsely accusing God of being unloving, uncaring, or powerless to help us. Ephesians 6:11–17: "Put on the full armor of God, that you may be able to stand firm against the schemes of the devil. For our struggle is not against flesh and blood, but against the rulers, against the powers, against the world forces of this darkness, against the spiritual forces of wickedness in the heavenly places. Therefore, take up the full armor of God, *that you may be able to resist in the evil day,* and having done everything, to stand firm. Stand firm therefore, having girded your loins with truth, and having put on the breastplate of righteousness, and having shod your feet with the preparation of the gospel of peace; in addition to all, taking up the shield of faith with which you will be able to extinguish all the flaming missiles of the evil one. And take the helmet of salvation, and the sword of the Spirit, which is the word of God."

Do not ever be afraid to quote, and believe in your heart, Romans 8:28–31, "God works all things together for good to those who love Him, . . . *according to His purpose.* And if God be for us who can be against us?" It is written that God loves us and will answer our prayers. But do we love, respect, and trust God enough to submit to His will when His answer is *"no"* to our wants and desires? *Can we be like Jesus when He prayed, ". . . nevertheless not as I will, but as You will"?*

Chapter Twenty-four

Do You Fear God for Nothing?

Job 1:8–9: "And the Lord said to Satan, 'Have you considered My servant Job? For there is no one like him on the earth, a blameless and upright man, fearing God—turning away from evil.' Then Satan answered the Lord, *'Does Job fear God for nothing?'*"

What a statement Satan made, "Does Job fear God for nothing?" *What did Satan mean by this?* The definition of the word "fear" used in this Scripture is reverence, respect, or honor. Satan was accusing Job of having a reverence toward God based solely on the fact that God had placed a hedge around him, i.e., Job had a good life. Satan went on accusing Job before God saying, "If You take Your hedge away—Job will turn against You! If You would allow me to take Job's happiness and well-being away, You will see Job's fear and respect for You evaporate into thin air." According to Satan, Job's reverence and love for God was directly related to his happiness and well-being.

I may surprise you here, but Satan had good cause to suspect Job's reverence toward God. No, Job had no history of betrayal toward God, but mankind in general does; and Satan was depending on that history of weakness and betrayal. Job was just a man, and history is full of men and women betraying God when circumstances in their life would turn bad. For example, in the Book of Exodus, when Israel was in the wilderness, time and time again they would betray God. Every time their "needs" were not fulfilled, it was God's fault. The people would turn against God saying all kinds of evil about Him. Numbers 21:5: "And the people spoke against God and Moses, 'Why have you brought us up out of Egypt—to die in the wilderness? For there is no food, no water, and we loathe this miserable food.'"

Having permission from God, Satan went on to destroy Job's wealth, family, and health; yet in all of this Job would not curse, or denounce God. Yes, Job questioned what was going on in his life, but Job did not relinquish his fear of God—his respect for God. In the end Job very humbly said, "Therefore I retract and repent in the dust and ashes" (Job 42:6). If you read the chapters just before that verse, you will find that God did not explain Himself at all to Job, nor did God promise Job anything in return for his respect. Nevertheless, Job did repent in fear and respect for God without understanding what had happened to him. Job did not receive anything back until he accepted God's dealings without question. Therefore, Job's fear (respect) for God was proven to be genuine and Satan's accusation against Job—that Job's fear (respect) of God was for nothing—was proven false.

I would like to tell you a very personal story that allowed me to understand this a little better. I knew all the Scriptures about the fear of God and how angry God would be at us when our fear and respect toward Him would be like the morning dew, i.e., as soon as the heat of the sun would come up, the morning dew would quickly disappear. Again, like a plant on stony ground without depth of root that would spring up quickly; but when the heat came, it quickly withered because it had no root.

The personal story I would like to tell you about is the story of a failed marriage in my distant past. You may ask, "What does your marriage have to do with our relationship toward God?" In Ephesians 5:32, the relationship between Christ (the Husband) and the Church (His Bride), was compared directly to our relationship as husband and wife here on earth. Wives were to be subject (fear) to their husbands and husbands were to love their wives as Christ loved the Church. In the Book of Hosea, the picture of God was that of a loving husband who yearns desperately to have a faithful wife. However, Israel (the wife) will have none of it. Throughout the Holy Scriptures everyday personal experiences were used to help explain the spiritual.

Hosea was never portrayed as the perfect husband because that was not the point of the story. The story was used to paint a picture from everyday life with the hope of bringing spiritual understanding. Never—and I mean never—was the Book of Hosea meant to disparage Gomer and exalt Hosea, nor do I wish for my story to disparage or exalt anyone. The Scriptures are clear: no one is perfect—not Hosea nor I.

I fell in love with a beautiful young lady and she loved me. We just could not get enough of each other. Her mother would tell me how much her daughter loved me and of the way she would light up as soon as I would walk into the room. Soon thereafter we got married.

Not long after we were married, she began to get very upset with me. I was no longer fulfilling all of her wants and desires. I would come home exhausted from work and she could not understand why she was no longer the center of attention. She exclaimed, "If you loved me, you would be concerned about fulfilling my needs!" Day after day I would try to tell her how much I loved her, but she could not understand. All she could understand was that I was not fulfilling her wants and desires, therefore, I did not love her. Within six months of our marriage, she was in the arms of another lover.

Never had I ever felt so rejected. Not only could I not convince her that I loved her; I could not hold her love and respect (fear) for more than six months. I thought to myself, *"What a wretched husband I must be!"* Then God began to show me that I should not take it so personally by showing me again in the Scriptures, that although He was perfect, the same thing happened to Him all the time.

Whenever His Bride (the Church) was fulfilled and everything was going well, God's Bride (the Church) would praise Him, fear (respect) Him, and say wonderful things about Him. Jesus would have very large crowds when the people were being fed; but when Jesus had hard things to say, the crowds would disappear like the morning dew. Jesus' bride only wanted to hear what He could do for her. "Take up my cross and deny myself"—*never!* The Bride (the Church) would think to herself, *"It's time for me to find another lover, one who will tell me what I want to hear—a lover who will fulfill my desires."*

God then showed me His mercy. When Jesus was no longer perceived as being desirable to His Bride (the Church), even His twelve close disciples left Him. Jesus was now completely rejected, yet He still laid down His life for His Bride—His Church. At that moment Jesus looked down from the cross at His beautiful Bride and prayed, "Father forgive them for they know not what they do." I could no longer hold on to my pain; I also had to pray for God to forgive my Bride. To this day, I have no regrets.

Although my bride never came back, I rejoice that through my sorrow, my understanding of God was now a little clearer. My reverence and love for God would now never be based on my circumstances or well-being. My God will always be worthy of my reverence, praise, and love—in the darkest valley, as well as when I'm on the mountain top. I would never again measure God's love for me by my circumstances. Instead of cursing God when things do not go the way I think they should, or questioning God's love for me if He does not fulfill my every desire, *I'll use it as an opportunity to prove my reverence (fear) for God is genuine by fulfilling His desire instead*—"By doing justly, loving mercy, and walking humbly before my God" (Micah 6:8).

I have a real concern today when I see churches that preach, "God will fulfill your desires" filled to capacity and churches preaching self-denial are empty (2 Timothy 4:3). I'm concerned when people say they feel like a hypocrite if they give God praise when everything is going wrong, instead of realizing it as an opportunity to prove your reverence (fear) and love for God to be genuine. I'm concerned when marriages breakup in the Church, because he or she doesn't "feel" fulfilled or loved any more, instead of seeing it as an opportunity to prove their love genuine for the other. *Did God send His Son to suffer the cross to show us how to become a sponge, always taking in—never giving?* No! Jesus gave us an example of how we are to empty ourselves and take the form of a bond servant (Philippians 2:1–8).

It is written that in the last days there will be a great falling away (apostasy) from the faith just before our Lord returns (2 Thessalonians 2:3). Are we being setup for this falling away today by the preaching and teaching of self-gratification instead of self-denial, and to have a faith in God that costs us nothing? *Are we being taught to have shallow roots, to be like the morning dew, because preachers are afraid of losing their congregation?* Matthew 13:20–21: "And the one on whom seed was sown on the rocky places, this is the man who hears the word, and immediately receives it with joy; yet he has no firm root in himself, but is only temporary, and when affliction or persecution arises because of the word, immediately he falls away."

Luke 22:31–34: "'Simon, Simon, behold, Satan has demanded permission to sift you like wheat; but I have prayed for you, that your faith may not fail; and you, when once you have turned again, strengthen your brothers.' And he said to Him, 'Lord, with You I am ready to go both to prison and to death!' And He said, 'I say to you, Peter, the cock will not crow today until you have denied three times that you know Me.'" Let us pray that our faith will not fail when we find that we must take up our cross and deny ourselves—*that our fear (respect) and love of God would not just evaporate in the heat of our trials.*

Luke 14:26–35: "If anyone comes to Me, and does not hate his own father and mother and wife and children and brothers and sisters, *yes, and even his own life,* he cannot be My disciple. Whoever does not carry his own cross and come after Me cannot be My disciple. For which one of you, when he wants to build a tower, does not first sit down and calculate the cost, to see if he has enough to complete it? Otherwise, when he has laid a foundation, and is not able to finish, all who observe it begin to ridicule him, saying, 'This man began to build and was not able to finish.' Or what king, when he sets out to meet another king in battle, will not first sit down and take counsel whether he is strong enough with ten thousand men to encounter the one coming against him with twenty thousand? Or else, while the other is still far away, he sends a delegation and asks terms of peace. So therefore, no one of you can be My disciple who does not give up all his own possessions. Therefore, salt is good; but if even salt has become tasteless, with what will it be seasoned? *It is useless either for the soil or for the manure pile; it is thrown out.* He who has ears to hear, let him hear."

Even King David knew that to give to God something that cost us nothing was worth nothing. 2 Samuel 24:23–24: "'Everything, O king, Araunah gives to the king.' And Araunah said to the king, 'May the LORD your God accept you.' However, the king said to Araunah, 'No, but I will surely buy it from you for a price, for I will not offer burnt offerings to the LORD my God which cost me nothing.'"

Do you fear God for nothing? Now is the time to count the cost before you find yourself in the arms of another lover, who in reality is no lover at all (Proverbs 7:1–27)!

Chapter Twenty-five

The Work and Evidence of the Holy Spirit

I have two major concerns in regards to the general understanding in the Church today of the work and evidence of the Holy Spirit in our lives. The first being that the work of the Holy Spirit has been trivialized by some by placing the emphasis on speaking in tongues. Some Christians say *"the"* evidence of the Holy Spirit is speaking in tongues. My second concern is what I perceive to be the ignoring of the Holy Spirit by some Christians in their lives and/or ministries. This is a subject that has concerned me for nearly as long as I have been a Christian.

Let us first take a look at the statement, "The evidence of the Holy Spirit is speaking in tongues." In John 16:5–15, Jesus describes the work and evidence of the Holy Spirit in very descriptive language, but conspicuously leaves out the term "speaking in tongues." If *"the"* evidence of the Holy Spirit was speaking in tongues, would this not be the place for Jesus to mention it, if it was as important as we seem to make it today? Yet, not only does Jesus not place any emphasis on speaking in tongues; He is silent altogether on the subject. However, Jesus did have much to say about the work and evidence of the Holy Spirit, which we will come back to later.

In contrast, the Apostle Paul had much to say about speaking in tongues in 1 Corinthians 14:1–40. Paul begins in verses 1–3, how we are to earnestly desire spiritual gifts for the purpose of edification, exhortation, and consolation of others. But in verse 4 Paul makes it crystal clear that speaking in tongues is for the edification of the speaker (self). Nevertheless, in verse 5, Paul also makes it clear that speaking in tongues has a role to play in our lives by saying, "I wish that you all spoke in tongues." Then Paul ties it all together as he places it in the right perspective when he says in verses 18–19, "I thank God I speak in tongues more than you all; however, in the church I desire to speak five words with my mind, that I may instruct others, rather than ten thousand words in a tongue."

So why then speak in tongues at all? Speaking in tongues speaks not to men, but to God; and the one who speaks in tongues edifies himself (1 Corinthians 14:2&4). And again in Romans 8:26, "And in the same way the Spirit also helps our weakness; for we do not know how to pray as we should, but the Spirit Himself intercedes for us with groanings too deep for words." There are times in my life I am so down that the only words I have are my groans, yet to know that God not only hears my groans, but understands—brings me great comfort. Was there ever a time in your life when you did not have the words that would adequately express your gratitude toward God? How wonderful it is for me to be able to praise God in tongues—knowing I am giving God a level of praise that mere words could not attain. At other times, I would find myself disturbed within my spirit about something, but I did not know what it was, yet by praying in tongues I found my relief.

Speaking in tongues is a real manifestation of the Holy Spirit, but it is not *"the"* evidence of the Holy Spirit in your life. The emphasis should never be placed on speaking in tongues. As a matter of fact, as you read 1 Corinthians 14, you cannot help but come away with the feeling that speaking in tongues is, at best, the *least* of all God's gifts. Nonetheless, I along with the Apostle Paul wish that all would speak in tongues. When it comes to my weakness, and when words begin to fail me—I thank God for tongues.

Now to address my second concern of ignoring the Holy Spirit in our lives and/or ministry. Let me take you to Acts 1:4–5, "And gathering them together, He *commanded* them not to leave Jerusalem, but to wait for what the Father had promised, 'Which,' He said, 'you heard of from Me; for John baptized with water, but you shall be baptized with the Holy Spirit not many days from now.'" In these verses, Jesus *commands* His disciples not to leave Jerusalem, but wait for the Holy Spirit.

Why did the disciples have to wait for the Holy Spirit? We find the answer in Acts 1:8, ". . . to receive *power* . . . to be My witnesses both in Jerusalem . . . and even to the remotest part of the earth." Notice that Jesus did not *"ask"* His disciples to wait, but *"commanded"* them to wait. Since Jesus commanded His disciples to wait, He must have had a very good reason for it. Yet, how many of us wait on the Holy Spirit today in our lives and/or ministries?

When we seek to be God's witness to someone, and/or seek to make disciples, we gather all kinds of books and other paraphernalia unto ourselves for help; but do we wait on the Holy Spirit? Have we gotten so wrapped up in the techniques of witnessing, and discipleship, that we do not even think about asking the Holy Spirit to empower us anymore? When we go out to witness to others, do we concentrate on the witnessing handbook, or the Holy

Spirit? Is your church lacking? Do you look for a book on church growth, or do you look for the Holy Spirit? It is important that we ask ourselves these questions or, as we will see, without the Holy Spirit all of our efforts will be in vain.

In John 16:7, Jesus said, "I tell you the truth, it is to your advantage that I go away, for if I do not go away, the Helper shall not come to you." *Did you hear what Jesus said?* It was good for Emmanuel (God with us) to go away so the Father could send us another Helper. Jesus placed such importance on the Holy Spirit, He actually said it was good that He was going away so we could have another helper—the Holy Spirit—in our lives. When Jesus, our physical Emmanuel (God with us) died on the cross, another Emmanuel took His place: the Holy Spirit. Now our Helper, the Holy Spirit, was no longer confined in one place as was the person of Jesus. Emmanuel, the Holy Spirit, was now omnipresent—ever present with us—wherever we may be. Our helper Emmanuel is now spirit, but no less real; and no less God than Jesus (God in flesh). Ignoring, or trivializing the Holy Spirit in our lives would be akin to the disciples ignoring, or trivializing Jesus in their lives.

Now let's look to the words of Jesus that we may begin to understand what the *major* work of the Holy Spirit is, which then must also be the *major* evidence of the Holy Spirit through the performance of said work. What is the work of the Holy Spirit that was so important that Jesus called it "an advantage?" John 16:8–13: "And He (the Holy Spirit), when He comes, will convict the world concerning sin, and righteousness, and judgment; concerning sin, because they do not believe in Me; and concerning righteousness, because I go to the Father, and you no longer behold Me; and concerning judgment, because the ruler of this world has been judged. I have many more things to say to you, but you cannot bear them now. But when He, the Spirit of truth, comes, He will guide you into all the truth; for He will not speak on His own initiative, but whatever He hears, He will speak; and He will disclose to you what is to come." Why were (are) these works of the Holy Spirit so important? Let's take a look at them one by one.

To convict the world of sin: Before you can have repentance, before you can seek forgiveness, you must first be convicted of sin. Therefore, God sent the Holy Spirit to convict the world of sin in order to save us. The role of the Holy Spirit is to place us in a position to seek out God's forgiveness. That is why it is written, "No one can come to Me (Jesus) unless it has been granted him from the Father" (John 6:65). This is why without the Holy Spirit all of our efforts to witness are in vain as we, by ourselves, cannot even get someone to step one—the conviction of sin. Although, through our eloquence and ability to persuade, we may be able to make someone feel "sorry" for sin, only the Holy Spirit can "convict" someone of sin. Human sorrow can bring mankind to a point of remorse and shame, but only *true* conviction can bring mankind to a place of repentance. Therefore, even John the Baptist had to be filled with the Holy Spirit in order to prepare the way for the Lord through the baptism of repentance. The road to Jesus can only be paved with repentance. *There is* no *other way to God!*

Did you ever get around some people, and for no reason at all, they hated you; and even just your presence made them uncomfortable? Well, that's evidence of the Holy Spirit being with you, and on you, because it's the Holy Spirit's job to make them uncomfortable—to convict them of sin, hopefully unto salvation. In Acts 6:15 & 7:1–60, Stephen with a face of an angel, and filled with the Holy Spirit, caused the council to be cut to the quick, and they began gnashing their teeth. In this case, the evidence of Stephen being filled with the Holy Spirit was their hatred of Stephen unto his death. *Yet in reality the council were not gnashing their teeth at Stephen, but at the Holy Spirit.*

To convict the world of righteousness: After we are convicted of sin, the next step on the road to our salvation begins with the Holy Spirit convicting us of our righteousness through our acceptance of Jesus as our Lord and Savior. God would never convict us of sin unless He was also willing to convict us of righteousness. Therefore, God had a plan to give us His righteousness through the death, and resurrection, of His Son Jesus.

In my journey on the Calvary road to the cross, I was so convicted of sin, that for about two years I could not go to sleep at night without taking a drink. There was no amount of consoling that could lift the weight of sin from me. There was nothing I could do to make up for my sins. There was nothing anyone could say to me to make me feel better. Until one day, I went to a church and I became convicted of righteousness by the supernatural work of the Holy Spirit, and I never looked back. It had nothing to do with what the pastor said—I had heard it all before. *There was nothing in this world that could lift the weight of sin off me—nothing!* The evidence of the Holy Spirit that night in that little church was not someone speaking in tongues; it was I, being convicted of righteousness, and having the weight of my sins lifted from me.

To convict the world of judgment: Before I could be convicted of righteousness, sin had to be judged. Our God is a Holy God, and therefore, He cannot just wink at sin and say all is forgiven. There had to be a judgment brought upon my sin, and in my case, that judgment was totally laid on Jesus when He cried out, *"My God— My God—Why have You forsaken me?"* At that moment all of my (our) sins were judged and paid in full. We now have a choice: for our sins to be judged along with Satan's and go where he is going—or our sins can be judged and paid in full at the cross with Jesus and go to heaven where He is; the choice is ours to make.

The world and Satan hate judgment—only two ways to choose—how dreadful! This world does not want to judge between right and wrong; whatever feels good should be our guide. I remember several years ago when I was at work, there came in the store a homeless beggar, looking for a handout. He went to each person in the store asking for a handout. He then came to me. I was just smiling at him, when out of nowhere, fear filled his face and he said to me, "I know who you are, leave me alone." I never said a word to him, nor had I ever seen him before that day; but as his fear gave way to panic, he almost went through the glass door trying to get away from me. Was he trying to get away from me or the Holy Spirit? The world is judged; the demons know it. Why does mankind kick against the prompting of the Holy Spirit?

Finally the Holy Spirit's work is to lead us into all truth: It is the truth that will set us free. Not part truth and part error, but the whole truth. If we did not have the Holy Spirit to lead us, who would fill the void? If you guessed Satan, you would be right. *We cannot be so foolish and prideful to think that on our own we could find the truth—could we?* Yes, at times we can be so foolish, and history proves that to be true. What seems right to man will bring death, but with the Holy Spirit's leading, the truth will set men free.

"Wait in Jerusalem for the power of the Holy Spirit!" What sound advice Jesus gave us that day. The Holy Spirit came upon them as tongues of fire, and the same men who turned their backs on Jesus, suddenly became bold as lions! Yes, they came out talking in other languages, which the spectators miraculously all heard in their own native tongue. However, that's not the miracle we should be

emphasizing as *"the"* evidence of the Holy Spirit. We need to read a little farther to find the awesome miracle we should be emphasizing. Acts 2:37–41: *"Now when they heard this, they were pierced to the heart . . . and there were added that day about three thousand souls."* You see, only the Holy Spirit could have saved three thousand souls that day. That's the evidence of the Holy Spirit I want to see, and emphasize, in my life and ministry.

Is saying *"the"* evidence of the Holy Spirit is speaking in tongues, trivializing His work? I think so, and now I hope you will agree with me. And for those who wish to leave the Holy Spirit out of their plans—their lives—my advice would be: wait in Jerusalem (or wherever you may be) until you receive the power from above, or all of your work will be in vain. Yes, you may still have a large church, but the work you are called to do, the salvation of souls, will be in vain without the Holy Spirit.

Chapter Twenty-six

The Shepherd Boy

Today, as well as in the days of the Bible, a shepherd is looked upon as nothing special in society; just a common laborer with nothing of "real" value to offer to the world. He had no great wisdom to offer to the masses—no great inventions to change the world—no diplomas to hang on the wall. Yes, a shepherd was just a very ordinary person who usually smelled as bad as the sheep he watched over. Therefore, I chose the title "The Shepherd Boy" specifically to show how God always uses the foolish things of this world to confound the wise.

Let us start with Moses as described in Acts 7:20–34: A man of greatness, well educated, powerful in both word and deed. Hearing the call of God within his heart at the age of forty, Moses went off to visit his brethren, the sons of Israel. When Moses killed the Egyptian, he assumed the people of Israel would realize that God was going to deliver them from Egypt through him. Yes, Moses, the mighty Prince of Egypt—powerful in word and deed—educated for forty years in the finest the world had to offer, would deliver Israel from Egypt. Yes, God had found a way to place Moses next to the throne of Egypt so he could deliver God's people from Egypt. What a great plan God had! Yes, what an awesome God we serve! However, there was just one problem: it may have seemed like a good plan to us, *but it wasn't God's plan.*

Moses found himself rejected by his people and had to flee into the desert, where God began to reeducate Moses for another forty years by making him a shepherd. God humbled Moses until he could honestly say from his heart, "Who am I, Lord?" Exodus 3:10–11: "Therefore, come now, and I will send you to Pharaoh, so that you may bring My people, the sons of Israel, out of Egypt. But Moses said to God, 'Who am I, that I should go to Pharaoh, and that I should bring the sons of Israel out of Egypt?'" Could God use (in the eye's of the world) such a worthless shepherd to deliver His people from Egypt, when he (Moses) failed to deliver Israel as a Prince of Egypt? *Before God could use Moses as the Deliverer of Israel, God had to take Egypt out of Moses by bringing Moses to a place where he was no longer powerful in both word and deed.*

In the same vein the story of Saul and David is also an interesting one. Although both Saul and David were chosen by God, God used this opportunity to teach all of us a very good lesson. Saul was a very large man, taller than anyone else. The prophet Samuel said in 1 Samuel 10:23–24, "Do you see whom the Lord has chosen? Surely there is no one like him among all the people." *Surely, a man of this stature could lead Israel to great victory over their enemies!* Yes, just what the people wanted—a man to lead them—a man of great strength and stature. Although God chose Saul, we must also remember that God never wanted His people to have a king in the first place (1 Samuel 8:1–22). Choosing a man to rule over them instead of God: what a foolish, and disastrous decision.

Well, King Saul did not turn out to be a very good king. So after King Saul angered the Lord, God decided to appoint another king over His people Israel. God sent Samuel to the house of Jesse. When Samuel saw Eliab, Samuel thought he had found the new king. However, once again, man's choice was not God's, and we begin to understand the lesson that God was trying to teach us. God told Samuel that He did not look at what man looks at—the outward appearance—but He looks at the heart (1 Samuel 16:6–7). Once again, God chose the lowly "shepherd boy" David, who in the eyes of the world, was a boy of no apparent significance.

I find it very interesting that we today still fall into the same trap of relying on outward appearances to make our judgments. For example, the pictures we see of Jesus are pictures of a very tall and handsome man. A man that if He walked by, heads would turn. We paint Jesus in this way, because He was the Son of God. Surely the Son of God would be a very handsome man, would He not? However, the Scriptures describe a very different Jesus. *Isaiah 53:2: "For He grew up before Him like a tender shoot, and like a root out of parched ground; He has no stately form or majesty that we should look upon Him, nor appearance that we should be attracted to Him."* That's right, Jesus' appearance, or stature, turned no heads at all. Can you imagine what would happen if someone would paint an unattractive Jesus? Why, that would be close to blasphemy—close to the unpardonable sin! I'm sure glad it was the prophet Isaiah who described Jesus as neither being attractive, nor stately, so I would not be accused of blaspheming.

Don't you find it interesting that even today we associate someone's stature and beauty with both his virtue and worth? In reality those attributes really have nothing whatsoever in common with one another. Thank God that He looks at the heart and not the outward appearance. Don't you think we should apply God's wisdom in our own lives when it comes to picking our friends, our church, and our spouses? *Should we not take the time to see into their heart?* You may ask, "How do I do that?" You look at the *fruit* (Matthew 12:33). Don't misunderstand, I'm *not* talking about perfection; for only One is perfect, and that One is God. However, we can look at the general lifestyle as being godly or ungodly, forgiving or unforgiving, arrogant or humble, hating evil and loving good, and so on. When I chose a church, it was not for the pastor's charismatic appeal, but for his love of God and the truth, at any cost; i.e., I looked at his heart. But I digress—let's continue with Jesus.

Now here comes Jesus, not a diploma to be found, a son of a lowly carpenter, one who works with his own hands. He had no stately form or majesty that we should look upon Him, nor an appearance that we should be attracted to Him. To make matters worse, Jesus was from Nazareth, which at that time, was what we now would call a ghetto. John 1:46: "And Nathanael said to him, 'Can any good thing come out of Nazareth?'" People took offense at Jesus: Mark 6:3: "'Is not this the carpenter, the son of Mary, and brother of James, and Joses, and Judas, and Simon? Are not His sisters here with us?' And they took offense at Him." *If only Jesus had a PhD, was good looking, and had lots of charisma, then just maybe the people would have listened?* Could such an ordinary looking man, with no "formal" training, really be *God in the flesh?*

Now let's take a brief look at the disciples. Out of all the people that Jesus could have chosen from, look at who He picked: the lowly fishermen, a tax-collector (in that day the worst of the worst), the uneducated, and so on. Jesus chose no one of great statue or importance. Yes, God will always choose the foolish things in this world to confound the wise. 1 Corinthians 1:26–29: "For consider your calling, brethren, that there were not many wise according to the flesh, not many mighty, not many noble; but God has chosen the foolish things of the world to shame the wise, and God has chosen the weak things of the world to shame the things which are strong, and the base things of the world and the despised, God has chosen, the things that are not, that He might nullify the things that are, that no man should boast before God."

I see people every day falling into this trap of judging by outward appearances: people just accepting what someone says without checking out for themselves if what was said was true or not; accepting what they were taught just because that person may be charismatic, has a doctorate, or some other attractive attribute. On the other hand, I see people rejecting what someone had to say, because he was somewhat ordinary. *If this is the case, then who today would listen to Jesus?* And what about John the Baptist who was so poor he ate locusts, wore clothes made from camel hair, and just maybe smelled a little like a camel? Who today would listen to him? *People every day are getting into trouble, because they are attracted by the external and disregard the heart inside.*

So we discover from these stories in Scripture that God is not impressed at all by our charisma, education, or attractiveness, as God looks only at the heart. What am I trying to say by all of this? First, if someone comes into your life, do not accept, or dismiss them by their outward appearance, but take your time to know their heart. Do not believe anyone, even with a doctorate, without checking the Scripture first to see if what he had to say was true or not. Anyone who teaches should just facilitate your growth in God and not be your sole source of wisdom. Do not be duped into a state of passivity by outward appearances, which have the resemblance of wisdom, but in reality are not wisdom at all.

Second, if you have an advanced academic degree, do not rely on your degree for your wisdom. In the eyes of God, a degree means absolutely nothing if your heart is not right. 1 Corinthians 13:2: "And if I have the gift of prophecy, and know all mysteries and all knowledge; and if I have all faith, so as to remove mountains, but do not have love, *I am nothing.*" In contrast, the Apostle Paul, well educated—a Hebrew of Hebrews—a Pharisee of Pharisees, counted it all as *dung* to know Christ (Philippians 3:4–12). The Apostle Paul was even embarrassed to talk about his "qualifications;" instead he wanted to boast about his weaknesses (2 Corinthians 11:22–12:9). Therefore, my advice to those who are more learned than I is: do not lay hold of (rely) on your education, but treat it as dung, in order that you may lay hold of Christ.

Third, for those of us less educated: put away the thoughts of inadequacy as you read 1 John 2:27, "And as for you, the anointing which you received from Him abides in you, and you have no need for anyone to teach you; but as His anointing teaches you about all things, and is true and is not a lie, and just as it has taught you, you abide in Him." And again in Acts 4:13: "Now as they observed the confidence of Peter and John, *and understood that they were uneducated and untrained men,* they were marveling, *and began to recognize them as having been with Jesus.*" Spending time with Jesus is the beginning of wisdom.

Therefore, do not say as Moses said before the burning bush, "Who am I," and invite the anger of our Lord (Exodus 4:10–14), but just lay hold of Jesus. Remember, it has always been, and always will be, God who gives the power to change lives—the Holy Spirit—to both the great and the weak in the eyes of the world. Zechariah 4:6: "Then he answered and said to me, This is the word of the Lord to Zerubbabel saying, *'Not by might nor by power, but by My Spirit,'* says the Lord of hosts." In other words, let the wise become as fools that they may lay hold of Christ, and let the foolish say, "I am wise because I laid hold of Christ."

May I invite whosoever to go to God's seminary? Psalm 51:10–13: "Create in me a clean heart, O God, and renew a steadfast spirit within me. Do not cast me away from Thy presence, and do not take Thy Holy Spirit from me. Restore to me the joy of Thy salvation, and sustain me with a willing spirit. *Then* I will teach transgressors Thy ways, and sinners will be converted to Thee." It matters not if you are well educated in this world, nor if you are eloquent in speech, nor if you have a lot of charisma. But if you can appropriate Psalms 51:10–13 in your life—in your heart, you will have a very effective and successful ministry. Maybe not as the world defines success, but nevertheless in the eyes of God, your ministry will be successful indeed. Then just maybe you will hear the words, *"Well done, good and faithful servant."* After all is said and done, that is all that truly matters.

Isaiah 66:1–2: "Thus says the Lord, 'Heaven is My throne, and the earth is My footstool. Where then is a house you could build for Me? And where is a place that I may rest? For My hand made all these things, thus all these things came into being,' declares the Lord. 'But to this one I will look, *to him who is humble and contrite of spirit, and who trembles at My word.'"

Chapter Twenty-seven

A Parable of Two Fathers

A small child was playing in his yard with a large ball. The little one was quite content and happy bouncing his ball on the grass in the confinement of his play yard. The yard was small, but the child knew nothing other than his yard, until one day the gate to his play yard was left open. Walking outside the confinement of his play yard for the first time, the child became very excited. His eyes became enlarged, and a feeling of jubilation coursed through his body.

"What is this?" the child said to himself. "I have never seen a play yard this large before; its boundaries are limitless, and look how high my ball bounces on this hard surface!" The child began to play. He never had so much fun! The ball bounced so high on the hard surface, and he could run forever without the confinement of his yard. The child exclaimed, *"I have found a piece of heaven!"* Yes, complete freedom from any boundaries at all. As far as he could see, there was the freedom to run and play. He thought, "I have never had so much fun bouncing the ball so high in the air, jumping, running, and skipping." Overwhelmed by this freedom, he thought there would be no end to his joy.

Suddenly, he heard his father's voice: *"Son, get in the confinement of this yard right now!"* The son thought to himself, "Why did my father sound so upset? Surely when I tell him how much fun I was having he will be happy for me and allow me to stay and play in this wonderful place. Truly my father would want me to be happy and have fun!" However, his father forbade his son to ever leave the confines of his play yard again.

Confused, the son exclaimed, "Why does my father hate me so? Father just does not understand how much fun I was having. This new limitless play yard felt so good. Surely, anything that felt so good cannot be bad, can it? Surely if my father really loved me, he would want me to be happy!" However, the father was unrelenting.

A neighbor passing by saw how unhappy the small child was and asked him what was wrong. The son explained: "It's my father! He does not want me to be happy, or have any fun at all!" The neighbor exclaimed, "How terrible!" Quickly the neighbor confronted the child's father. "How could you take away this child's fun, his limitless freedom, and still look me in the eye and say you love him?" But, the father paid no attention to the neighbor's criticism and remained unrelenting. The father soon became the scorn of the neighborhood and was hated by all.

On the other side of town there was another small child having the same experience as the first. However, when his father saw him having so much fun, it made him very happy. He called to his neighbor and said, "Look at my son playing. He is having so much fun, and is so happy. My son is bouncing his ball so high, jumping, running, and skipping with freedom as far as his eyes can see." The neighbor thought to himself: "Oh! Look how much he loves his son—allowing him to be so happy—allowing his son the freedom to follow his feelings, and do whatever makes him happy.

Truly this father is *"enlightened"* and knows how to be loving toward his son."

Suddenly, a crowd began to gather where the father last saw his son playing. When the father went to see what was going on, to his horror, he found his son dead. *The new limitless play yard the small child thought to be so wonderful was in reality a very busy street!*

You see, the first father knew of the danger to his son, while the child knew only of the fun and nothing of the danger. The child thought his father hated him and didn't want him to have any freedom, or any fun. However, the truth was he loved his son more than himself and faced both the anger of his son, and the scorn of his neighbors in order to save his son from death. The father knew that his son, in his naivete, did not perceive the danger. Therefore, he was not angry with his son, nor did he hate his son; the father simply wanted to save his life. However, the neighbors, as naive as the child was to the dangers, perceived the father as evil and thought he actually hated his son.

The father of the second child was taken to court over the death of his son. The judge, knowing that the child's father was also ignorant of the danger, found him guilty only of reckless endangerment and child neglect. You see, to the judge, ignorance of the law or danger was no excuse. However, the father did receive a lesser penalty than if he had knowingly exposed his child to the dangers. If the father had known of the dangers to his son and said nothing, then the child's blood would be on his hands, and the penalty would have been much more severe.

You have probably guessed by now the first father represents God. *Although God's discipline may seem unfair and unloving at times, we must never forget He truly loves us.* When we do not understand

God's dealings with us, we must remember He has a much better vantage point to see the danger which lies before us. So even if it "feels" really good, and we perceive no danger, we must trust God and allow Him to guide us. We already know by the death of His Son that God loves us, and wants us to live. When He disciplines us, He only wants us to share in His holiness and have abundant life—eternal life (Hebrews 12:5–10).

The second father represents Satan himself. With one exception: Satan does know of the danger and he is more than happy to give us all the freedom we want. He'll even allow us to become like little gods, following our feelings, lust, and short sightedness to the point of death. Therefore, Satan's punishment will be of the severest kind. Yes, Satan loves to let you do anything that makes you "feel good," because then you are fulfilling his ideology, "*do what thou will,*" unto death and hell.

We as Christians must be like our Father in heaven: loving people enough to tell them the truth, even if it means we will be hated by both them and this world. We will be looked upon as evil, unloving, against freedom of choice, and just no fun. The world may be encouraging people to sin, have abortions, or to be a homosexual, but we know they are playing in the street, about to face eternal hell and death. If we keep silent, knowing of the dangers, their blood will be on our hands (Ezekiel 33:6).

Jesus, being our example of true love, faced the hatred and scorn of this world, even unto death, in order to save both you and me. We can no longer hide our heads in sand—staying silent for fear of man—staying silent by having the desire to be liked by man. That would be loving ourselves more than others, the exact opposite of what Jesus taught us to do. Even the world finds it contemptible, and will hold us accountable, when we have knowledge of a worldly danger but then do nothing to warn people of that danger.

The world believes the definition of love is allowing you to do as you wish. Therefore, we should not be surprised that the world is following Satan's ideology: *"Do what thou will!"* However, it is not so with God. Those whom He loves, He disciplines (Hebrews 12:6). Remember that God disciplines us to save, not to hurt. And Jesus, following the Father's instructions, came to earth to save, not to judge (John 12:47). Therefore, if we judge, we are no longer doers of the law (James 4:11–12). Nevertheless, as a Christian, if you speak out in order to warn and to save, you are fulfilling the law of God. Jesus would leave all ninety-nine sheep just to save the one that is lost (Luke 15:1–7).

Therefore, if you are filled with God's love, go into the highways and byways exposing sin as sin, not as a judge, but as one who loves—as one who wishes none to perish, warning of the danger of eternal hell and death. Pray that God would give them eyes to see, and ears to hear. But if we know of the dangers, and do nothing and/or keep silent, *we will be held accountable.* If the time is truly as short as we think it to be, stop whatever you are doing! Pray for God to send His Holy Spirit upon each of us in order to touch the lives of those around us, and ask God where you can support a ministry that is doing so.

Today, I'm ashamed to say, a large number of Christians in the U.S.A. seem to be more interested in what God can do for *"me,"* than the true cause of Christ (2 Corinthians 5:18–21). This is confirmed by the fact that most of the largest churches, and successful preachers today, teach health, wealth, and prosperity: a teaching which engages the hearts and minds of God's Church with the worries, cares, and riches of this world to the utter fruitlessness of the Church (Luke 8:14). These are the things the world seeks after (Luke 12:29–34). We should have more important matters to attend to. Jesus, when tempted by Satan, turned down all the riches of this world to suffer the cross for our salvation, thereby, worshiping God (Matthew 4:8–11).

Let us never lose sight of the reason God gave His only Son. It was not so we can live in palaces nor so we can meet in palatial cathedrals while the world goes to hell. It was to save lives (yes, even just one) from an eternity in hell, through the gospel of our Lord and Savior Jesus. As His Body, should we not begin to follow our Lord's example?

In John 17:15 Jesus prayed, "I do not ask to take them out of the world." Did Jesus want us to stay in this world to become rich, or to be the salt and light in this world? Being the salt and light in this world has always brought with it tribulation. *So be prepared to count the cost and be prepared for this world to hate you (John 15:18–21).* We, as God's Church—as Christ's Body—must become aware of the times we are living in or we will become as complacent as the people were in the days of Lot (Luke 17:28–30). As I look around at this world, and all its wickedness, I don't get angry; I weep because I know they are in danger of eternal hell and death.

Chapter Twenty-eight

A Love Story

When I started my walk with God I wanted to get inside of Him; I really wanted to know His heart. When I first picked up the Scriptures, I prayed, "God I do not want to just memorize the words, but I want to know the heart that produced the words." *That prayer request started me on a journey, which, at best, I would describe as an adventure.* I'm reminded of the Scripture in Matthew 20:22, "You do not know what you are asking for. Are you able to drink the cup that I am about to drink?" God has been granting me my prayer request by giving me insight into His heart, not through the goose bumps of jubilation, but through His cleansing holy fire. Relentlessly, God is burning up the chaff in my life by the testing of my faith through the refining fire of tribulations. The following is a love story in my past which my Lord used to help me know His heart, and change my heart forever; but first I had to learn to surrender to God's Word, God's will.

It all started with a woman who came into my life whom I did not pay much attention to at first. She was just another Christian sister who needed help and to be encouraged in both God's Word and His faithfulness. However, as time passed by, I found myself falling in love with her, but there was a huge problem: from the beginning, I knew she was not attracted to me. *I found my peaceful life suddenly disrupted and suffering a despondent heart just for trying to do something good—trying to help someone!*

I began to pray about this situation. I prayed: "God how could you allow me to fall in love with a woman who is not attracted to me? What did I do wrong? I was just trying to help." Oh, I was so mad at God! *This just wasn't fair!* God's reply to my prayer was very simple, but also very blunt. 1 Corinthians 13:5: "Love does not seek its own" and Luke 6:32–33: "And if you love those who love you, what credit is that to you? For even sinners love those who love them. And if you do good to those who do good to you, what credit is that to you? For even sinners do the same."

Being stubborn, I again prayed: "Yes, I know Lord, but why did you allow this to happen?" This battle with my Lord continued on for about a week, and God continued to give me the same answer. Finally, I realized (thank God for His patience) that God's kind of love has nothing to do with a quid pro quo (one thing in return for another). In other words, I will love you as long as you love me back, and/or look at all I've done for you, and since I see nothing in return, I'll never do anything for you again.

A "quid pro quo" kind of love is abhorrent to the symbolism of the cross, and to everything it teaches us. Do you believe for one minute if Jesus' love for us was based on a "quid pro quo" attitude that He would have gone to the cross? Just imagine for a moment what your response would be if on the way to the cross, the same humanity you were going to save by suffering the excruciating death of the cross, spit in your face. Matthew 27:28–31: "And they stripped Him, and put a scarlet robe on Him. And after weaving a crown of thorns, they put it on His head, and a reed in His right hand; and they kneeled down before Him and mocked Him, saying, 'Hail, King of the Jews!' And they spat on Him, and took the reed and began to beat Him on the head. And after they had mocked Him, they took His robe off and put His garments on Him, and led Him away to crucify Him."

You may say, "That's Jesus; what does that have to do with me?" Romans 5:6–8 tells us: "God *demonstrates* His own love for us in that while we were yet sinners Christ died for us." Notice the word used there was not "Jesus," but "Christ," which means the Anointed One. *As God puts His Holy Spirit within us, are we not to be the "anointed one" so we can also demonstrate God's love to a lost and dying world through the laying down of our lives—our wants and desires?* So, could this Scripture not only be talking about Jesus, but also perhaps His Church—His body—you and I? In John 10:17–18, Jesus said something very beautiful: "For this reason the Father loves Me, because I lay down My life that I may take it again." *Could it be?* As I lay my life down voluntary, I will actually be raised to life? Luke 9:23–24: "And He was saying to them all, 'If anyone wishes to come after Me, let him deny himself, and take up his cross daily, and follow Me. For whoever wishes to save his life shall lose it, but whoever loses his life for My sake, he is the one who will save it.'" *Could it be?*

No, I was not being punished by God for helping someone; I was the one who actually benefited the most from this relationship. God, through this experience, was answering my prayer to know His heart. Immediately, as I surrendered to God's Word, my heart came to rest. Truly, for the first time in my life, I was now free to give that which I freely received: *God's love*—and do it without regret. Without regret because I was now free to give without looking for any kind of repayment. *Finally, I was free to unconditionally serve my Lord—I was free to voluntary lay down my life for another!* And to my surprise, what first sounded like a contradiction (I found my life by losing it)—I found a peace and rest which went beyond carnal reasoning—I found His yoke to be easy.

When we get into a situation that we do not understand, we have a decision to make: Do we choose to get mad at God and say, "Look at all I'm doing for you, Lord, and You let this happen to me? (That sounds like a 'quid pro quo' kind of love affair to me)." Or do we just trust God through it, and believe Romans 8:28, "And we know that God causes all things to work together for good to those who love God, to those who are called according to His purpose"? I think I'll choose to believe God's Word, even if I do not understand what is happening to me. It is written that His ways will always be higher than our ways. *So who can ever say, I understand?* Yet, we do understand that God's love for us is not a "quid pro quo" kind of love. Hence, God's love cannot be influenced by outside forces, and therefore, His love for us cannot change even as it is impossible for God's nature to change. We can always trust God in the flames of our trials because we know He loves us. *Yes, in spite of all, we can know God loves us!*

You may ask, "If God loves us in this way, how can there be a hell?" Hell is simply a place where there is *no* God. For example, as we began to take God out of the U.S.A., we began to see "hell" take shape. Our carnal nature began to manifest itself into unbridled passion—always taking; never being satisfied—burning within with a lust which nothing can quench. We quickly degenerated unto children killing children without any remorse. 2 Timothy 3:1–4: "But realize this, that in the last days difficult times will come. For men will be lovers of self, lovers of money, boastful, arrogant, revilers, disobedient to parents, ungrateful, unholy, unloving, irreconcilable, malicious gossips, without self-control, brutal, haters of good, treacherous, reckless, conceited, lovers of pleasure rather than lovers of God."

Thankfully, God remains in control here on earth, or no flesh would be left alive (Matthew 24:22). But in the literal hell, there will be *no* God to help; no peace, no love, always driven, and never satisfied; flames of fire that are never quenched with your cries for help falling to the ground, because there is no one who cares. Yes, it's just as you wanted it: *no* God at all in your life. Not for a day or two, but for eternity. An eternity of the complete absence of God's love, as it is completely replaced by a "quid pro quo" kind of love. Inasmuch as a "quid pro quo" love, loves only itself, there will never be any rest, just the burning flames of discontentment. In the same way, I had encountered briefly no rest or contentment with the woman I was trying to help, until I let God into the relationship and accepted His ways. *Yes, hell on earth, or the literal hell of eternity is a place we choose to go by rebelling against, and/or eliminating God and His ways from our lives;* ergo, both the reality of God's unconditional love—and hell—can coexist.

The question about hell has *never* been "if God loves you;" *He does!* The question is, will you accept God's love, and embrace a loving relationship with Him? As with my past relationship, I could love her expecting nothing in return, but a loving relationship between us could only begin by her accepting my love and returning it. You may ask, "Is this not a 'quid pro quo' kind of love by her needing to return the love?" No, because the word "relationship" presupposes the involvement of *more than one*. God wants that love relationship with us so much, He sent His only Son Jesus to die for our sins, which opened the door for that relationship. But will anyone receive the expression of God's love, Jesus, and return it in a relationship? The sad reality is, only a few will accept God's love, and begin a relationship with Him. Matthew 7:13–14: "Enter by the narrow gate; for the gate is wide, and the way is broad that leads to destruction, and many are those who enter by it. For the gate is small, and the way is narrow that leads to life, and *few* are those who find it."

You may ask, "How can anyone return such a love?" It is written, "to know the love of God is to be filled with it." In Ephesians 3:18–19 the Apostle Paul prays that we, ". . . may be able to comprehend with all the saints what is the breadth and length and height and depth, and to know the love of Christ which surpasses knowledge, that you may be filled up to all the fullness of God." Let me ask you, "if knowing God's love is being filled with the fullness of God, how can you not return it?" Now that God has allowed me to taste His love through knowing within my heart what it means "love seeks not its own," I can't wait to be in His presence and become perfect in His love! Through obedience, I've gained a taste, and now more than ever—*I want it all!*

In Exodus 33:13 Moses prays, "If I have found favor in Your sight, let me know Your ways." In my lack of understanding, I only saw the situation with this woman as an opportunity to both get hurt, and to get mad at God. *However, God meant it for good!* Without this experience, I would have never come to know in my heart this facet of the multifaceted jewel called God's love. No, I was not betrayed nor mistreated by God, but I had found favor in His sight because He allowed me to know His ways.

We must never forget that whatever trials we find ourselves in, *God is in control!* Yes, Satan himself needed permission from God before he could afflict Job, but then God not only used the affliction to refine Job, but also used Job's story to help a myriad of people through this life as they read his story in the Bible. Have you been through some hard times? Then use what you have learned from it to help others get through their flames of adversity (2 Corinthians 1:3–7). Remember, all of us at one time or another will go through testing (Hebrews 12:26–29). So let us exult in our tribulations for they give to us proven character, and a hope, which does not disappoint (Romans 5:3–5), *and allow ourselves to be changed by God from glory to glory, for the praise and glory of our God who loves us!*

Now is a good time to ask yourself the question, "When I say I love God, with what kind of love do I love God?" Is it a "quid pro quo" kind of love, or is it a God kind of love, expecting nothing in return? When you are obedient to His Word are you expecting something back, or are you doing it just because you love Him? Can you say from your heart, my reward is in the doing, because I love God (Luke 17:7–10)?

John 13:34–35, "A new commandment I give to you, that you love one another, even as I have loved you, that you also love one another. By this all men will know that you are My disciples, if you have love for one another." *Be a disciple of God today: give His love to someone, and expect nothing in return!*

Chapter Twenty-nine

In the Pursuit of Holiness

I saiah 64:6: *"All of our righteous deeds are as filthy rags."* I wanted to start with this verse of Scripture so we can begin to understand what really defines holiness. As we can see, this Scripture does not say our *evil* deeds are as filthy rags, but our *righteous* deeds are as filthy rags. We must come to an understanding that our righteous deeds as compared to another man's righteous deeds may indeed have an allusion of being righteous; yet those same "righteous" deeds when compared to the deeds of a Holy God are as filthy rags. *Hence, it is reasonable to come to the conclusion that our deeds of "righteousness" will never allow us to be, or cause us to be, holy.* Now you may ask, "If our deeds of 'righteousness' cannot make us holy, why then do we have the Law of Moses? Inasmuch as, the Law of Moses, or any law for that matter, is based solely on our deeds, or works." This question is a good one, and it is answered in Romans 7:13: The Law was given to make sin utterly sinful.

Jesus, knowing the Law's purpose, used the Law to demonstrate our hopelessness in regards to holiness through the Law.

Jesus pointed this out to us in Matthew 5:21–22, "You have heard that the ancients were told, 'You shall not commit murder' and 'Whoever commits murder shall be liable to the court.' But I say to you that everyone who is angry with his brother shall be guilty before the court; and whoever shall say to his brother, 'Raca,' shall be guilty before the supreme court; and whoever shall say, 'You fool,' shall be guilty enough to go into the fiery hell." *And verses 27–28:* "You have heard that it was said, 'You shall not commit adultery'; but I say to you, that everyone who looks on a woman to lust for her has committed adultery with her already in his heart." Again we read in James 2:10, "For whoever keeps the whole law and yet stumbles in one point, he has become guilty of all." *Indeed, the Law was given to us to dramatically prove to all that none is righteous, no, not one!*

For those who would misuse the Law to gain an appearance of holiness for themselves, Jesus had this to say in Matthew 23:25–28, "Woe to you, scribes and Pharisees, hypocrites! For you clean the outside of the cup and of the dish, but inside they are full of robbery and self-indulgence. You blind Pharisee, first clean the inside of the cup and of the dish, so that the outside of it may become clean also. Woe to you, scribes and Pharisees, hypocrites! For you are like whitewashed tombs which on the outside appear beautiful, but inside they are full of dead men's bones and all uncleanness. Even so you too outwardly appear righteous to men, but inwardly you are full of hypocrisy and lawlessness." *Wow!* That sure does not leave much room for debate.

In essence, the Law became an immense stumbling block to those who wish to misuse the Law as an instrument to become holy in the eyes of man and/or God. Instead they should have allowed the Law to expose their own hopelessness, and their great need of mercy and grace, just as the Law was designed to do. The greatest problem Jesus had (and still has) is convincing mankind that we cannot reach heaven by our works. I pray you can begin to see that it is impossible for any of us to achieve holiness, which is essential for entering into heaven, by our works. That being the case, how can we sit in judgment of our brothers and sisters concerning salvation when we see only their works? I know a lot of people which "appear" on the outside more righteous than I, but does that alone make them holy, and assure them a place in heaven? *Definitely* not!

Now, since we cannot achieve holiness through our works of righteousness, how then can we achieve it? First, we must define the word holiness as the Bible defines it. Holiness is defined as something that is set apart for a particular use. *When something is holy, it can never be used for common everyday use, or for more than one purpose.* Let me give you an example. The temple utensils were not holy because they were made of pure gold (works), but they became holy only when set aside for God's use by the sprinkling of blood. *This is so essential to understand, please allow me to say it again!* The temple utensils were not holy because of their outward pureness (works), but became holy by the setting apart for God's use by the sprinkling of blood. Can you see the awesome symbolism in this? It was not the level of "worldly" purity that accomplished the holiness, it was the act of being set aside for God's use by the sprinkling of blood.

Another area in which we must have an understanding is that God is Spirit, and being Spirit, He looks past our works and looks directly into our hearts (spirit) for holiness. *Or you can say it this way: God looks into our hearts for that setting aside unto Himself.* Let me give you an example of what I'm talking about with the story of King Saul and King David. In 1 Samuel 15:10–33, we see Saul bringing back the best of the Amalekites after God had told him to utterly destroy everything. When confronted, Saul said he did obey, but it seemed "right" to him to bring back the best for the Lord. Samuel's response was, *"It is better to obey than to sacrifice, and rebellion is as witchcraft."*

Saul, fearing punishment said, "I sinned, because I feared the people and listened to them." *Saul was after man's heart, not God's!* Samuel's response was, "Because you have rejected the Word of the Lord, He has also rejected you." You see, Saul's heart was not broken because he disobeyed, nor did he seek forgiveness through repentance, i.e., have a change of direction. If Saul had desired in his heart to truly do God's will (repented), he would have carried out God's command and killed King Agag instead of allowing Samuel to do it. We can see by Saul's actions that his heart was not after God's. We find Saul being double minded as he wanted to please both man and God, whereas, God's holy temple utensils had only one purpose, i.e., to serve God.

In contrast, the Scriptures describe King David as a man after God's own heart. Although, David actually committed "greater" sins than Saul, inasmuch as, he committed adultery and then murdered to cover it up, yet King David still found grace in God's eyes. Yes, there were grievous consequences to David's lawless actions, but David never lost his throne, nor God's favor. King David severely missed the mark (sinned) many times, yet he always repented from his heart, because in his heart, he truly wanted to do God's will. *Once again, we find that God does not look at the outward appearance, but He looks at the heart.* 1 Samuel 16:7: "But the Lord said to Samuel, 'Do not look at his appearance or at the height of his stature, because I have rejected him; for God sees not as man sees, for man looks at the outward appearance, but the Lord looks at the heart.'"

What does this all mean for us? First, we cannot win God's favor by our works, as our works of righteousness are as filthy rags. Second, God is Spirit, therefore, He looks at our spirit (heart) to see if it has been set aside for His use, i.e., a heart after His own. Third, if our heart is after God's, how can we habitually sin without being convicted within our heart, and then ultimately repent as King David? Finally, no matter how pure you appear to be on the outside, you still must be sprinkled with blood in order to be set aside for God's use. In other words, as we, through the Law, realize that our heart misses the mark for holiness, God who is great in mercy and grace sprinkled us with His Son's blood and created within us a new heart (spirit), set aside for just Him, i.e., we are literally born-again—*if we accept God's gift of eternal life, by accepting Jesus' sacrifice.*

We all must come to terms with the fact that our fallen nature (spirit) is simply incapable of being set aside for His use, i.e., made holy. But we do not lose heart, because now through the sprinkling of the blood of Jesus upon our heart through the acceptance of God's plan of salvation, our spirit is reborn unto God, set aside for His use—a holy spirit—a heart which naturally seeks after God's own heart. Why? *Because He replaced our heart of stone with His holy heart—His Holy Spirit!*

Although, God only looks at the heart, we now also realize that a holy (set apart) heart will only produce good fruit. *Although, works of righteousness cannot produce holiness, holiness will always produce righteous works.* First, we must clean the inside; then and only then is the outside considered clean or holy (Matthew 23:26). We are now doing works of righteousness not because of the Law, but because we have a *desire* to do so from within our heart—from within our born-again spirit. The times we do fall short of the mark (sin), as we all do, we simply cannot continue to sin, because God's seed (spirit) is now within us (1 John 3:9). As with King David, if we happen to miss the mark (sin), we will also remain in God's love as He looks at our heart—His own heart reborn within us through the blood of Jesus our Lord and Savior. An innocent holy blood, which continually atones for our sins, past, present, and future. *If, and only if, we accept the works of God, which is Jesus!*

Being reborn with God's Holy Spirit is a supernatural work of the most majestic kind. *How can we turn away from such a magnificent gift and work of God?* You may ask, "How do I know if I'm born again?" Let me ask you, "How do you know when you are in love?" The answer is the same for both: *When you have it, you'll just know!* Furthermore, we have God's word on it: Acts 2:21, "And it shall be, that everyone who calls on the name of the Lord shall be saved." It's real, supernatural, and free to whosoever will come. Be honest with yourself and see that by the Law everyone falls short of the mark; and then accept the blood of Jesus for the forgiveness of your sin, and receive it as sprinkling upon your heart to set your heart (spirit) apart unto God—a new born-again heart, in essence, making you holy.

Ask God to give you His heart, and become born-again. *Then watch your life change from glory to glory, as you are now no longer in pursuit of holiness, but you are holy through the rebirth.* Yes, reborn holy in God's sight, not by looking at our works, but by looking at His own heart (Holy Spirit) reborn within us, ready to do His will. No, we Christians have nothing to boast in, nor can we look down on anyone, because at one time we were also sinners. Yet now we're saved by grace—born again in holiness through the blood of Jesus, producing the fruit of holiness as described in Galatians 5:22–25; not by our own will or effort, but by His Spirit which now resides within us. *Our pursuit of holiness is finally over, for in Christ Jesus—it is finished!*

Galatians 5:22–25: "But the fruit of the Spirit is love, joy, peace, patience, kindness, goodness, faithfulness, gentleness, self-control; against such things there is *no* law. *Now those who belong to Christ Jesus have crucified the flesh with its passions and desires.* If we live by the Spirit, let us also walk by the Spirit."

Chapter Thirty

The Gospel of John Chapter Six

This morning as I opened my Bible and began to read the Gospel of John chapter six, I found it to be so alive and pregnant with inspiration that my heart leaped within me. To say that I felt inspired would be an understatement. Therefore, I will be departing from my usual topical format for a mini-Bible study of John chapter six. I pray that whoever reads this mini-Bible study will come away as inspired and as blessed as I was after writing it. *And if I may make a suggestion, you may want to read the portion of John chapter six that is noted, before you read my comments about it.*

John 6:1–14:

We start this passage of Scripture with Jesus using the situation around Him at the time to teach an important lesson. Jesus begins the lesson by testing (refining) Philip with this question: "Where are we to buy bread that these may eat?" In other words, "to whom can we go to, Philip, to supply our present need?" Philip, being overwhelmed by this situation of feeding so many people, responded in such a way that it was abundantly clear that he was at a loss for what to do. The problem was just too great for Philip to handle.

Then Andrew, after frantically looking around, found a lad with two fishes and five loaves. All of which told me that the disciples were looking to humanity for an answer to a problem, which was larger than themselves. That's right, they looked to humanity, who is in all practicality *no* greater than they were, to solve their problem. *Would you not say, that was really dumb?* But then why do we also find ourselves doing the same thing by looking to humanity for a solution to a problem which is too large for us to handle? *Why isn't God always the first one we look to for help?*

In the Church today, we find our brothers and sisters more than willing to help, but why do so few mention that God is the one we really need to go to for our help? Perhaps it makes us feel important if we can keep someone dependent on us rather than on God. However, the problem with looking to humanity for help, if the truth be known, is that we cannot help anyone out of a wet paper sack, let alone help someone with a real problem. *If we in the Church today want to be truly helpful, let's do what Jesus was trying to do with His disciples; teach them that God, and only God, has the answer.* Are we not just giving God lip service when we first look to humanity for our help? God may indeed use humanity to fill a particular need in our lives, but we *must* learn to go to God first. Otherwise, the *solution* we seek may cause us much more harm than our *need* initially caused us.

John 6:15–25:

Here we find our Lord sending His disciples on a mission: go to the other side of the sea. As soon as they were out three or four miles into the middle of the sea, a contrary (violent) storm came up. How strange! This should not be happening? Should not Jesus have known this was going to happen. Did the disciples misunderstand Jesus' directions? Maybe Jesus was not the person they thought Him to be, or maybe there was no God at all? Suddenly, in the midst of the storm, they see a figure of a man. No! It must be a ghost! There cannot be anything good in this storm—can there? Jesus then cries out, *"Do not be afraid, it is I."*

This same type of bewildering situation happened to Israel in Numbers 21:5, "Did God bring us out here in this wilderness to die?" And what about Paul when God sent him to Macedonia, where he ended up beaten and thrown into jail (Acts chapter 16). Do you find this sort of thing happening to you when you try to follow God's direction for your life? Yes! Then allow me to lead you to Romans 8:31–39, ". . . nothing will separate you from God's love!" *In other words, "Do not be afraid—it is I."*

John 6: 26–29:

Oh, how we all can relate to this situation. Isn't our devotion to God usually limited to the fulfillment of our appetites and/or desires? *Instead, should we not be focusing on the greatest gift of all, eternal life?* Here is a good question to ask ourselves: Am I coming to God because of His gift of eternal life, or to have my appetites and/or desires fulfilled? A good way to find out is to examine what we murmur and/or complain about.

Another wrong motivation to come to God is for the power. Verse 28: "What shall we do, that we may work the works of God?" You know as well as I do they meant the *power* of God! To which, Jesus just lovingly pointed them back to the issue of eternal life: *"The work of God is to believe in Him whom He has sent."* You see, the kingdom of God is not found in the abundance of things, nor in the power, but it is found in Jesus; who gives eternal life to all who seek forgiveness (repentance), and accept His death on the cross for the payment of their sins!

John 6: 30–58:

How do we usually react when we hear a hard word, or a difficult statement to understand? Do we do what mankind has always done? Do we begin to grumble at and attack the messenger? Verse 42: "Is this not Jesus, the son of Joseph?" In other words, who does this Jesus think He is! Throughout the Bible, God's people are always killing, ignoring, or making fun of the prophets/pastors of God so they can have an excuse not to listen. *It has always been much easier to have an excuse not to listen than to live godly, and/or to live by faith.*

John 6: 59–65:

This passage of Scripture is very important for us to understand! This hard saying of Jesus' could not be understood unless our Father in heaven gave us the understanding. Therefore, we can deduce from this passage the following: We cannot be schooled unto understanding the spiritual issues of the Bible. And we cannot set out with our own abilities to understand the things of God, i.e., we cannot boast in our knowledge. Nevertheless, at the same time, God is *very* willing to give us the Holy Spirit to help us to understand, if we are willing to ask (Luke 11:13).

This fact also reveals to us an obvious conclusion: we come to know Jesus only because God loved us first. Verse 65: "For no one can come to Jesus unless it has been granted him from the Father." So once again our boasting is excluded! *And if God loved us first, who then can bring a charge against us?* Therefore, when Satan would have us to look toward our circumstances, (i.e., a contrary storm) to get us to question God's love for us, once again we just need to go to God's Word, Romans 8:31–39.

Now would be a good time to read Romans 8:31–39, "What then shall we say to these things? If God is for us, who is against us? He who did not spare His own Son, but delivered Him up for us all, how will He not also with Him freely give us all things? Who will bring a charge against God's elect? God is the one who justifies; who is the one who condemns? Christ Jesus is He who died, yes, rather who was raised, who is at the right hand of God, who also intercedes for us. Who shall separate us from the love of Christ? Shall tribulation, or distress, or persecution, or famine, or nakedness, or peril, or sword? Just as it is written, 'For Thy sake we are being put to death all day long; We were considered as sheep to be slaughtered.' But in all these things we overwhelmingly conquer through Him who loved us. For I am convinced that neither death, nor life, nor angels, nor principalities, nor things present, nor things to come, nor powers, nor height, nor depth, nor any other created thing, shall be able to separate us from the love of God, which is in Christ Jesus our Lord."

John 6: 66–71:

Finally, Peter gets it right: *"To whom shall we go? You have the words of eternal life."* First, we must realize that God is the *only* one we can go to for help, e.g., prayer. God may then direct us to a brother or sister for help, but we *must* go to God first! Second, if we have eternal life, we already have everything we will ever need—God's eternal love.

In conclusion, let us always be willing to ask ourselves these two questions. Where do I look first for help in my time of need? And have I come to Jesus to just fulfill my desires and/or appetites, or for the greatest gift of all—*eternal life?*

Chapter Thirty-one

A Lost Love

Iwould like to dedicate this commentary to the two people who have influenced me the most in my life. First, my Mom, who started me on the road to understand God's *agapao* love by defining this unconditional love to me by simply lavishing it upon me. Second, my pastor and friend Justin Alfred, who showed me what it meant to love the truth more than yourself, by loving people enough to speak God's truth no matter the personal cost. *Mom and Justin, your labor of love was not in vain!* 1 Corinthians 15:58: "Therefore, my beloved brethren, be steadfast, immovable, always abounding in the work of the Lord, knowing that your toil is not in vain in the Lord."

I titled this commentary *"A Lost Love,"* because I have had trouble finding God's agapao love within God's Church. And as I look toward the horizon of the future, I do not receive very much encouragement of it getting any better. *Perhaps if we the Church can begin to see within our hearts that there is a problem, maybe we'll begin to cry out to God and capture once again within our hearts this most elusive lost love, which God's Word calls agapao.* My intention with writing this commentary was not to judge but to simply define this "lost love" according to Holy Scripture. Hopefully, this will place before all of us a much higher aspiration to race toward in our lives.

This *"lost love"* is revealed to us in John 21:15–22, "So when they had finished breakfast, Jesus said to Simon Peter, 'Simon, son of John, do you love (*agapao*) Me more than these?' He said to Him, 'Yes, Lord; You know that I love (*phileo*) You.' He said to him, 'Tend My lambs.' He said to him again a second time, 'Simon, son of John, do you love Me?' He said to Him, 'Yes, Lord; You know that I love You.' He said to him, 'Shepherd My sheep.' *Verse 17:* He said to him the third time, 'Simon, son of John, do you love (*phileo*) Me?' Peter was grieved because He said to him the third time, 'Do you love Me?' And he said to Him, 'Lord, You know all things; You know that I love You.' Jesus said to him, 'Tend My sheep.' Truly, truly, I say to you, when you were younger, you used to gird yourself, and walk wherever you wished; but when you grow old, you will stretch out your hands, and someone else will gird you, and bring you where you do not wish to go. *Now this He said, signifying by what kind of death he would glorify God.* And when He had spoken this, He said to him, 'Follow Me!' Peter, turning around, saw the disciple whom Jesus loved following them; the one who also had leaned back on His breast at the supper, and said, 'Lord, who is the one who betrays You?' Peter therefore seeing him said to Jesus, 'Lord, and what about this man?' Jesus said to him, 'If I want him to remain until I come, what is that to you? You follow Me!'"

In the above portion of Scripture we see a side-by-side comparison of two very unique and different kinds of love, and in the original Greek it is known as *agapao* and *phileo*. Throughout this passage of Scripture, except at verse 17, Jesus uses *agapao* and Peter uses *phileo* for the word we translate in English as love. In verse 17, Jesus finally used *phileo* also as it appeared that Peter was just unable to comprehend what Jesus was trying to tell him. In spite of this, Jesus attempts yet another approach and says to Peter, "A time will come when you will stretch out your hands and go where you do not want to go." Peter still thinking *phileo* within his heart said, "But what about this other disciple?" Peter just could not understand within his heart the point Jesus was trying to make.

Although Peter could not understand at that time the point Jesus was trying to make, he did come to a full understanding later on in his life when he was crucified upside down for his testimony and belief in Jesus as the Messiah—Immanuel—God's Son. Now in hindsight, let's see if we can come to an understanding, with the Holy Spirit's help, as to what was in Jesus' heart when He asked Peter: "Do you love (*agapao*) Me?" Let's start by defining these two *very* unique and different kinds of love. *Phileo is mankind's love, a love that depends solely on common interests.* For example, as long as you do things that are in my interest, benefit me, and/or bring me joy, then I will love you. *On the other hand, there is agapao love, which can come only from God.* It is a love that *never* wavers, even if the circumstances to love become contrary to our carnal reasoning.

When we fall short of the mark (sin), as we all will, God's love for us never wavers. He covers us, forgives us, and/or helps us in our weakness. Even when God gave us the law, His objective was to save, not to hurt us. God gave us the law so we could see our need to be saved. *By the Law, sin became utterly sinful for the sole purpose of driving us to Jesus—our salvation.* On the other hand, I see much too often in the Church today faultfinding, not for the purpose of helping someone, but merely to satisfy our own pettiness, and exalt ourselves in our own eyes. In contrast, Jesus knowing our faults set out to save us, even unto the laying down of His own life. Jesus gave His life not only to the people who claimed to love Him, but even to the people who openly hated Him, if they would acknowledge both Him, and their need to be cleansed— their need to be born-again.

I've seen much too often members of a church criticize their pastor, not concerning doctrinal issues, but just because he wasn't speaking enough on what Jesus would do for them, and how he "seemed" not to be concerned enough about their needs. *Does not such criticism expose their love as a "phileo" kind of love?* A worldly kind of love that is based solely on common interests. In essence, they were saying to their pastor, "If you would do these things for me, then I will love you." In their criticism of him, God's *"agapao"* kind of love that covers, forgives, and/or helps was completely absent—the God kind of love which drove Jesus to the cross. And if that is the case, then by default we (the Church) are imitating this world's kind of love instead of God's. I thought we were to influence this world by becoming as salt and light to a *"phileo"* loving world, not imitate it.

To my horror, I see that many of our largest churches today are built upon a foundation of sermons, which proclaim how Jesus will give to you all your desires and make you happy. In essence, this kind of teaching can only reinforce our natural fleshly (worldly) *phileo* love. Jesus tried to get Peter to understand that this *phileo* kind of love would not be sufficient if Peter wanted to follow and obey Him.

What would happen to a *"phileo"* love-centered church if Jesus, like with Peter, gave them a direction in life that they did not want to follow? Would they turn their back on Jesus as quickly as some have done to their pastors? Is it not true that whatever you do to His body, you do to Jesus? *When our petty, common (worldly) inter-*

ests are no longer coddled, will that cause God's Church to fall away and their fleshly (worldly) phileo love to grow cold? Don't be too quick to say: "My love would never grow cold; I would die for Jesus!" Mark 14:29–31: "But Peter said to Him, 'Even though all may fall away, yet I will not.' And Jesus said to him, 'Truly I say to you, that you yourself this very night, before a cock crows twice, shall three times deny Me.' But Peter kept saying insistently, 'Even if I have to die with You, I will not deny You!' And they all were saying the same thing, too." *Having a phileo kind of love is simply not enough to follow Jesus.*

A tragic sign that this fleshly *phileo* love is beginning to permeate God's Church is seen in the fact that divorce is as high in the Church as it is in the world. And what are the reasons for most divorces today in the church? You don't make me happy anymore! Our interests are no longer in common! You really hurt me, so I will not forgive you! *These reasons are all centered around a fleshly phileo love, i.e., what's in it for me.* Which is the exact opposite of God's *agapao* love. We seem to easily run at the first sign of any personal discomfort. Yes, before a cock crows twice, we quickly say goodbye to our vows of eternal love that we professed to have in our marriage ceremony.

Nowadays, even God's truths seem to take second place when it comes to our personal comfort. Sorry Jesus, I cannot forgive him/her, because they just hurt me too much. Sorry Jesus, it is no longer in my interest to speak the truth, it may hold me back, or keep my church from growing. Sorry Jesus, I will be unpopular if I speak out about sin. Sorry Jesus, this church does not entertain me any more. All of these excuses are motivated from self-interests, or fleshly (worldly) *phileo* love. *You can almost hear Jesus ask, "My bride, do you love (agapao) Me?"*

We seem to have in the Church today a mentality that only judges the evidence of God's Holy Spirit by talking in tongues and/ or the performing of miracles. For some reason we have lost sight of the only true evidence of God's Holy Spirit, which is: *God's agapao love!* Have we lost sight of this love because it is so much easier to speak in tongues than to lay down our lives? Is it because our main focus is on impressing people with miracles and/or with our great knowledge by speaking on the great mysteries of God for hours? If that is the case, we have a *huge* problem according to 1 Corinthians 13:1–13, when there is no evidence of *agapao* love. That church may be making a lot of noise, but at the same time, it is not exhibiting any distinction from the world. *Agapao* love is the only thing that cannot be counterfeited by Satan.

It is written, that if Jesus is lifted up, speaking of the cross, that He would draw men unto Himself. *Can the Church draw mankind to Jesus by becoming like the world?* Or should we draw mankind to Jesus by taking up our cross daily? Inasmuch as the cross is the essence of *agapao* love, are our lives motivated by *agapao* love unto the laying down of our lives even as Jesus did; thereby, drawing men to Him and not to ourselves? May both you and I take heed of the warning before Jesus returns and tells us, "Get away from Me, I never knew you" (Matthew 7:13–23). *Oh, that we, His bride, would know the breadth, length, depth, and height of His love so that we would be filled with the fullness of God (Ephesians 3:14–19).*

Now that we have a better understanding of the two Greek words *agapao* and *phileo*, we should be able to gain insight on what Jesus was trying to get Peter to understand. Jesus was trying to reveal to Peter that there was coming a time when just *phileo* love would be proven to be totally inadequate when it came time to go where he did not want to go. Hence, Jesus asked Peter, do you love (*agapao*) Me? Isn't Jesus asking the same question today of His bride (the Church)? *My bride, do you love (agapao) Me? Yet the bride's response seems to be the same as Peter's before the Holy Spirit was given! Yes Jesus, you know I love (phileo) You!*

Let us in the Church today build our house on the solid foundation of Jesus Christ with the precious gold that comes down from heaven, *agapao love*, and not with the hay, wood, and stubble of fleshly *phileo* love. Then, just maybe, we will hear God say, *"Well-done good and faithful servant."*

The Author Raymond D. Sopp is the Founder and President of:

Raymond D. Sopp International Ministries
P.O. Box 25352
Colorado Springs, CO 80936
(USA)

Website: www.SoppMinistries.org

Email: RDSopp@SoppMinistries.org

To order additional copies of this book,
please visit www.redemption-press.com
Also available on Amazon.com and BarnesandNoble.com
Or by calling toll free 1+ (888) 305-2967

CPSIA information can be obtained at www.ICGtesting.com
Printed in the USA
LVOW11s1410091014

407264LV00001BA/35/P